The Office Industry:

Patterns of Growth and Location

The MIT Press
Cambridge, Massachusetts
and London, England

The Office Industry:

Patterns of Growth and Location

A Report of
the Regional Plan Association

Prepared by
Regina Belz Armstrong

Edited by
Boris Pushkarev

Copyright © 1972 by
Regional Plan Association

This book was designed by The MIT Press Design Department.
It was set in Linotype Baskerville
by the Colonial Press Inc.
printed on Warren's Filmkote II
by The Colonial Press Inc.
and bound by The Colonial Press Inc.
in the United States of America.

Library of Congress Cataloging in Publication Data

Armstrong, Regina Belz, 1938–
  The office industry.

  "A report of the Regional Plan Association."
  1. Offices. 2. Industries, Location of—U S. 3. Industries, Location
of—New York metropolitan area. I. Regional Plan Association,
New York. II. Title.
HC110.D5A8   338'.0973   70–169013
ISBN 0–262–18052–9

Contents

Foreword

Offices, their number and their location, are emerging as a key, strategic element in the planning of major metropolitan areas. Urgent issues—such as the integration of the urban ghettos into a white-collar economy, the provision of viable public transit, the attraction of the middle class to the central city—are all related to office growth and location. Yet, the impact of offices on urban form has been so little understood in the United States that they are barely noticed in government statistics. Laboriously piecing together the data, this study fills in many of the missing facts; against the background of broad national trends, it focuses on the New York Region.

The Office Industry represents the eighth in a series of research reports for the *Second Regional Plan,* which was released in a "draft for discussion" in 1968. It is also a sequel to the 1967 Second Plan report, *The Region's Growth.* That work dealt with economic and demographic projections for the New York urban region as a whole and did not go into the allocation of the projected growth within the Region; this subject was reserved for a proposed companion report on Regional Activities. Subsequently, the topic of office location was singled out for the more detailed treatment given in the present monograph.

The reason is that early in our work on the Second Plan it became all too clear that the fast pace of office growth might make offices the hinge on which any plan for the New York Region might swing, that neither forecasts of a probable shape of the future Region nor proposals for change could be made without an understanding of the potential scale and locational requirements of the office industry. A number of conclusions of national importance have been drawn from this study by Regional Plan Association: (1) The nation is becoming white collar at a faster rate than commonly believed; (2) large metropolitan areas are and seem likely to remain its dominant office centers; (3) despite heavy odds in favor of dispersal, the central business districts of the nation's largest twenty-one metropolitan areas have been, on the whole, holding their own in the past decade; while population decentralized, offices did not; (4) because office jobs are suited to city centers, they offer the nation a chance to harness private enterprise to renew older cities and keep them attractive to all income and ethnic groups. The alternative—for the new economy to turn its back on the older cities—can only aggravate the urban crisis and unnecessarily despoil the natural environment.

Some conclusions for the New York Region also pose a challenge to present conceptions of public and private policy makers: (1) Despite recent overbuilding of office space in Manhattan, which will dampen the volume of new construction for several years, there is long-term market demand for office space requiring the equivalent of at least 17 more World Trade Centers in Manhattan until the end of this century. The opportunity of a respite should be seized to improve conditions for the next cycle of office development, in terms of both physical design and its social setting. (2) If both the out-migration of the skilled labor force from New York City and the slow upgrading of skills of the City's resident population continue at their past pace, the City will be left with a surplus of unskilled labor, while twice the present number of office workers will have to be imported to Manhattan from the suburbs. Manpower development, through education and retraining must concentrate on the preparation of white-collar skills, or the already apparent deficits will deter future office growth from taking place. Lacking this source of new employment, the Region's economy will not generate enough jobs for the natural increase of its population. (3) While current transportation programs are adequate to cope with the projected increase in Manhattan office employment in the near term, in the long term, alternatives to long-distance commuting must be sought in new transportation technology, and in attractive redevelopment at high densities of residential areas close to Manhattan. (4) In the Region outside Manhattan, there will be market demand for the equivalent of 30 World Trade Centers over the next thirty years. Scattered around the countryside at suburban campus-type densities, these offices would consume close to 25,000 acres of land and require about 400 miles of six-lane expressways. If current trends continue, only 20 percent of this office space will locate at higher densities in existing older centers, such as Downtown Brooklyn, Newark, Jamaica, White Plains, Paterson, Trenton, New Haven or Stamford. (5) It is realistic to expect that at least 45 percent of this decentralized office space, including many corporate headquarters, could be attracted to the older cities and other centers outside Manhattan, if rules of land development—notably zoning and taxation—were changed, and public policies geared to making these centers attractive. The benefits of such a policy would include reduced reliance on the automobile, less intrusion into the suburban landscape, viable public transit, an environment of richer interaction for the offices, and economic opportunities for the older cities.

The findings of this study were discussed with leaders of several industries, including major office builders, in a series of meetings. While the business leaders agreed that the projections of the report would come about if social conditions allowed, they were concerned about the *if:* the deteriorating housing conditions in the Region's older cities, the inadequacy of their school systems, the difficulties of public transportation, and the general drabness of the old urban environment. Cor-recting some of these distortions of the Region is what the Second Plan is all about, however, and this volume can only be read as supportive of it and, in a sense, dependent upon it. While selected costs of different locational patterns are indicated here, a fuller documentation of the costs and benefits, both public and private, of alternative office locations remains on the agenda for future work.

Acknowledgments
The initial work during 1966–1967 leading to this book was funded by the Avalon, Ford, Rockefeller Brothers, and Taconic foundations as part of their support of the Second Regional Plan. The manuscript was completed during 1969–1971 by the Association with its general funds. Max Abramovitz and Morris D. Crawford, Jr., have led the Association as Chairmen during these years, and their contributions have added significantly to this report.

The original direction of this study was provided by the late Stanley B. Tankel, Planning Director of the Association from 1960 to 1968. The basic content of this report is in full measure the work of Regina Belz Armstrong, Chief Economist. Boris Pushkarev, Vice President, Research and Planning, edited the final version of the manuscript and contributed sections to it. Earlier versions of the draft were reworked by Alan Donheiser and Philip Israel; research assistance was provided at various stages by Susan Stevens, Arthur Letter, and Noelle Melhado. Illustrations were designed by Caroline Jewett, Senior Graphic Designer, and Jerome Pilchman, Cartographer. Secretarial assistance was provided by Rosalyn Ader and Diane Trevor. The index was compiled by Ellen B. Jeronimo.

We are further indebted to individuals and agencies too numerous to mention for assistance in the collection and interpretation of data. Foremost among them have been the Tri-State Regional Planning Commission and Mr. John Stern, Planning Analyst II; Mr. Carl Franzman of the Port of New York Authority; and the Economic Development Section of the New York City Planning Commission. To those who have reviewed the manuscript, and from whose comments we have benefited, special thanks are in order: Dean Dick Netzer, New York University; Dr. Edgar Hoover, University of Pittsburgh; Dr. Benjamin Chinitz, Brown University; Mr. Peter Pattison, Uris Buildings Corporation; Mr. Seymour Durst, The Durst Organization.

John P. Keith, President
Regional Plan Association

September 1971

The Office Industry:

Patterns of Growth and Location

Introduction

Office Jobs in the Urban Economy

Before 1980, the majority of all jobs in the United States will pass to workers in white-collar occupations. In the New York Region, the balance was tipped from blue- to white-collar work about 1955, and by the end of this century nearly two-thirds of all jobs will be white collar. Since the end of the past century, the white-collar revolution has been quietly gathering momentum. Today, the trend shows no sign of abatement. Our urban areas, creatures of the boisterous Industrial Revolution some two hundred years old, must face the challenge of a new world by reshaping their institutions both to facilitate the flow of ideas rather than goods and to adapt to the needs of personal contact more than physical production. To be sure, aspects of the former industrial economy will remain a viable part of the future urban region just as remnants of an agrarian world are still with us today. But the places of physical production will be more evenly distributed throughout the nation, their functioning will be less obvious in the transport of raw materials and finished goods, and their requirements for the labor of man will be less stringent per unit of physical output. Small- and medium-sized cities, including isolated "new towns" of a hundred thousand people or so, will be even less viable in a white-collar economy and unlikely to prosper unless they become part of an agglomeration growing toward the 1-million mark.

Moreover, the shift of the economy toward activities requiring more interpersonal links both within and outside the firm suggests that the urban skyline will peak higher, in a sharper contrast with the surrounding residential and industrial plains. White-collar activity traditionally has necessitated vertical, high-density development; this pattern sharply contrasts with the less-dense, horizontal assembly-line layouts that have characterized goods production. While new transportation and communications technology will undoubtedly affect future development patterns, their impact may be in both of two diametrically opposed directions. New technology will permit greater concentration of activities seeking the socioeconomic benefits of being within walking distance of each other. Simultaneously, technology will allow a greater degree of locational freedom to those operations relatively indifferent to the special qualities of an urban center.

White-collar occupations are associated with a variety of activities located in urban areas, including elementary schools and universities, hospitals and research laboratories, factories, warehouses, retail stores, and private homes. However, the largest single component are jobs in office buildings. Jobs in detached office buildings account for about 25 percent of all white-collar jobs in the nation and 40 percent in the New York Region. These proportions have been rising in recent years, both here and abroad.

As the pace of the white-collar revolution has quickened during the past two decades, it has triggered a worldwide boom in office buildings.[1] The office skyscraper, once a trademark of New York and Chicago, is now changing the skylines of cities all the world over and overshadowing the medieval temples of religion and the smokestacks of early industry. The downtowns of one hundred major cities outside the United States and the Soviet bloc are currently adding some 40 million square feet of office space to their building stock each year. Foremost among them are Paris and Tokyo-Yokohama, each adding 4 million square feet a year; others, such as London, São Paulo, Sydney, Montreal, Toronto, Lima, Brussels, and Johannesburg follow, each with more than 1 million square feet of new office space per year.[2]

In the United States, office construction in cities and suburbs reached a record 191 million gross square feet a year in 1969; over one-fifth of that, or 42 million square feet, were placed under construction in the New York Region, 30 million in Manhattan. During the last decade, the Manhattan central business district has been building about 9 million square feet of new office space each year, or about 8 percent of the national total, while the entire New York Region captured about 15 percent. Expressed as net additions to office stock, Manhattan and 20 other major downtowns in the nation have been gaining 20 million square feet of office space each year over the past decade. Office construction in the United States now accounts for nearly one-fifth of all nonresidential private construction, in dollar volume. In 1969, investment in new private office construction nationwide totaled $5.3 billion, a figure comparable to such items in the federal budget as the space program or agriculture.

Of course, the importance of offices to the urban economy goes far beyond these indicators. Offices are the places where information, the key product of the new economy, is processed, and where decisions shaping the economic and political climate are made—a factor that should make office planning and location a matter of strong public concern. There are other, more specific considerations. Office concentrations require convenient access to a large, skilled, and diverse pool of white-collar workers within an urban region and reliable communications to other regions. Activities in office buildings attract people from longer than average distances and thus place the greatest relative burden on the transportation network. However, offices are built at densities higher than those for other building types, and have thereby the best chance of being served by public transportation. Office employees generally prefer to work in an urbane environment, in the proximity of shopping and eating places, as well as cultural and entertainment opportunities. All this makes offices a prime force in the revitalization of old urban centers, in the creation of new ones, and in the structuring of regional form.

Vital urban centers, with universities and hospitals, libraries and museums, department stores, theaters, and places of public assembly, attached to clusters of office buildings, are important for many segments of society— not merely the affluent. Traditional downtowns have become typically embedded in the ghettos of the disadvantaged. Thus, downtowns, if they have enough economic vitality, and if they have access to or possess programs and community institutions which invest in human resources, can become important escalators out of the ghetto for the disadvantaged. It now appears excessively costly to try to attract to the ghetto blue-collar jobs that, due to economic or technological necessity, are migrating elsewhere. Unfortunately, these blue-collar jobs match best the limited skills possessed by the disadvantaged. In the long run, the most fruitful alternative thus seems to be the raising of occupational sights to jobs with a future—such as office jobs. The location of office activity in an urban area ceases to be an isolated concern of the real estate agent, and becomes an important matter of social policy.[3]

The ability of most downtowns of the nation's metropolitan areas with populations over 1 million to attract a sizable share of the nation's new office construction during the past decade and to retain their share of the nation's office stock belies earlier prophecies of the inevitable demise of the downtown, of its eventual dissolution in an amorphous "spread city" with "community without propinquity." Yet the fact still remains that most new office construction is located in a dispersed manner in the suburban belts of metropolitan areas, where virtually all of the nation's population growth takes place. Whether and how this force can be harnessed to create a more structured, socially and visually richer pattern of subcenters on the growing urban periphery is another worthwhile policy issue.[4]

The Purposes of This Study
Despite the obvious importance of office jobs and office

1. For a largely pictorial review of recent office building architecture, see Reinhold Hohl, *Office Buildings; an international survey* (New York: Frederick D. Praeger, 1968).
2. *100 International Cities* (New York: René Frank Associates, Ltd., 1969).

3. *Jamaica Center*. A Report of the Second Regional Plan (New York: Regional Plan Association, April 1968). *The Potential of Paterson*. Regional Plan News Number 92 (New York: Regional Plan Association, February 1972).
4. *The Second Regional Plan: a draft for discussion* (New York: Regional Plan Association, November 1968).

buildings for the urban economy, the saying can be repeated that more research has been done on the planting of peanuts and the marketing of toothbrushes than on the location of and the market for office buildings. The pioneering work by Robert Murray Haig, *Major Economic Factors in Metropolitan Growth and Arrangement,* published in 1927 under the auspices of the then Committee on Regional Plan of New York and Its Environs, did touch on office location but was not followed up for three decades.

The *New York Metropolitan Region Study,* conducted between 1956 and 1960 for Regional Plan Association by Raymond Vernon and other distinguished scholars at Harvard University, was primarily responsible for alerting the public to a growing white-collar orientation of the nation's economy; many of the concepts and methods in this report are derived from the Harvard study. However, the study's projections of white-collar activity have proved too modest. The rate of increase in white-collar jobs between 1956 and 1965 was twice as high as predicted, while the manufacturing sector, which had been slated for a 20 percent increase, actually rose a scant 3 percent. Contributing heavily to the shortfall was an unforeseen decline in manufacturing jobs within New York City. Simultaneously, the rise in white-collar industries far outstripped expectations; nearly a quarter-million jobs were added, compared to the 75,000 forecast. Manhattan captured the bulk of this New York City growth, thereby confirming the Harvard study's presumption that the central business district will continue to attract substantial amounts of office employment. A separate volume on office activity, in addition to the nine published volumes and appendix, was initially planned by the Harvard study under the title, *America's Front Office.* But a manuscript, prepared by Krooss, never reached publication because of severe limitations in available data. The manuscript has been available for this study, and some of the historical elements in this book are derived from it.

The "region-shaping" nature of office jobs was emphasized on the basis of new analytical material and revised projections in *The Region's Growth* (A Report of the Second Regional Plan, New York, May 1967). The report estimated that, between 1965 and 2000, white-collar jobs in office buildings in the New York Region will double, whereas production jobs in manufacturing will remain virtually at a stable level. However, a more detailed locational analysis of office jobs was reserved for this study, which is a direct descendant of *The Region's Growth.*

Since publication of *The Region's Growth,* the first monograph on the office industry appeared: *The Office: A Facet of Urban Growth,* by Peter Cowan and others (New York: American Elsevier Publishing Co., 1969).

It was written abroad and deals with various aspects of office use in London which, in 1962, had in its central area 125 million square feet of office floor space, an increase of some 9 million since 1957. The three-page bibliography does not list a single work dealing with the office industry as such, a fact that the authors lament in their introduction.

The present study is then the first American monograph on the subject, and its limited purposes should be pointed out at the outset. While it does engage in analysis and interpretation, part of its purpose is simply to pull together and present hard-to-obtain data tabularized and in one place for convenient reference. The study was begun in 1966, and, while some material is up-to-date as of the spring of 1971, no systematic effort was made to update all tables. The tables pertaining to the early sixties retain their usefulness for analyzing relationships at one point in time, for historical reference, and for an indication of the type of material that is obtainable on the subject.

Severe data limitations lamented by both Vernon and Cowan have so far been a major roadblock to a study of the office industry. The Standard Industrial Classification Code (SIC) classifies economic activity by its principal product or service, not by the characteristics of its labor force or its buildings. For example, Manhattan is listed as having 700 employees in agriculture and 2,700 in mining; one is in no way led to suspect that there is no farm or extractive employment in Manhattan. An editor in a publishing house is listed as a "manufacturing" employee, a draftsman in a contractor's office as a "construction" worker, yet a municipal garbage collector is a "government" employee. A detailed tabulation of occupations was, until 1970, reported by the U.S. Census only by place of residence; there is still no tabulation of building types in which these occupations occur, nor is there, apart from the real estate inventories of the Depression period, a national census of buildings.

Thus, a major purpose of this study was to synthesize data on office employment in office buildings, by small area, for the New York Region, a process that is more closely described in the beginning of Chapter 4. Of major help in this respect were the 1963 Tri-State Regional Planning Commission *Land Use Inventory* and the *Home Interview Survey,* which first became available in 1967. The former was the Region's first census of buildings; the latter made it possible to cross-tabulate "industries" and "occupations" by small area, leading to the kind of analysis presented in Chapter 4. In the absence of similar data for the nation as a whole, various indirect or reconstructed measures of office employment are presented in this report. As a guide to public policy, we have presented some projections in Chapter 5. We

Unfamiliar new skylines of world cities, framed by office buildings. Debates on how to insert the new building bulk into a traditional city fabric keep raging on. In its Paternoster Development (*facing page, top*) London opted for excessively low building density (note deserted plaza space) which nevertheless encroaches upon St. Paul's Cathedral. In the Quartier de la Défense (*facing page, bottom*), located 5 miles west of the historic center, Paris opted for high density in a tight cluster supported by new rail, rapid transit, and bus stations, as well as an underground expressway interchange and a 20,000 car parking garage. The platform above provides for 11 million square feet of office floor space. The medium density office redevelopment schemes of Moscow (*above*) and Stockholm (*left*) are built into the old city core.

consider them essential, even though the exact shape of the future is always unpredictable.

The "hottest" policy issue in office location pertains to the costs and benefits, both public and private, of locating different types of offices in very large centers, such as Manhattan, central London, or central Paris; in medium-size subcenters, such as Jamaica in New York, Croydon in London, or Défense in Paris; in small, suburban clusters; or in dispersed, suburban development. New York and London stand at opposite poles on this issue, the former trying to encourage, the latter using strong government tools to discourage office growth in the major center.[5] The entire structure of this report is geared to shed some light on this issue. However, more precise answers will have to await future work.

5. A good source on the current status of the British policy are the Annual Reports of *Location of Offices Bureau,* a government commission established in 1963 to encourage the decentralization of office employment from central London. Since its inception, it has facilitated the moves of about 50,000 office jobs.

Chapter 1

The Office Industry in the United States

Impact of Technology on the Office Function

Offices, or places where written information is processed and the basis for decisions is prepared, have existed since the invention of writing which, not coincidentally at all, coincided with the emergence of cities. For more than five thousand years, however, offices were rather inconspicuous places, tucked away in buildings that were primarily ceremonial, commercial, or residential in purpose. An identifiable office "industry," which employed a substantial number of specialized workers, occupied buildings of its own, and had its own managers, did not emerge in the United States until after 1880, in response to the increasing complexity and specialization of a rapidly expanding economy.

The 1880s and 1890s were a period synonymous with the rise of the American city and the emergence of the large business corporation. The cumulative effects of the advancing industrial revolution spurred office activity as had those of no previous era. Changes in production technology, the scope of markets, communications, business size and organizational complexity, and the extent of capital commitments associated with technological progress created the modern office industry. Simultaneously, this process also created an urban environment which hastened further rounds of industrialization.

In the period preceding the Civil War, businesses tended to be small and oriented toward local markets. The owners of the era's essentially uncomplicated enterprises were at once salesmen, managers, and financiers. Detailed needs for planning and record-keeping were minimal not only because the proprietors themselves had modest needs for written information but also because there was no extensive government pressure to employ standardized bookkeeping and reporting practices. The early nineteenth-century businessman was interested in physical production and often viewed the office as a parasitic activity.

But in the decades of rapid industrial growth that followed the Civil War, when large-scale production and mass distribution became feasible and when "vertically integrated" operations combining several stages of production and marketing within one enterprise became desirable, business operations took on unprecedented complexity. Andrew Carnegie, John D. Rockefeller, and others created organizations so massive and diverse that it became necessary for their managers to attempt to control markets as well as production, essentially difficult tasks to accomplish with small office staffs. Large-scale enterprises also raised the stakes of investors in business operations; hence, *control* of both production and distribution became a prerequisite for corporate survival. On the production side, efforts to control the business environment included "Taylorism" or scientific management. "Pooling" to encourage price stability and maintain market shares was an example on the distribution end of corporate activity. The complexity of business problems intensified as technological advances became commonplace, thereby paving the way for the creation of an assortment of specialized office occupations including, among others, organization and management experts, financial analysts, advertising specialists, cost accountants, and engineers. In short, corporate managements were established which separated ownership from control and preempted influence in business decision-making. They had to be supported by junior personnel—typists, stenographers, clerks, draftsmen. As had happened in manufacturing during the early phase of the industrial revolution, one person no longer concerned himself with all phases of the production process; rather each step became distinct, and appropriate jobs were created in response.

This was an early advantage for cities such as New York because finance and foreign trade, already located here, had begun creating specialized office forces to carry out their own activities. The existence of a large, capable labor pool helped attract other offices and contributed to the snowballing pattern that created the large, office-oriented central business district (CBD).

The new generation of office-oriented, manager-controlled businesses not only multiplied rapidly but persistently increased in importance at the same time that small proprietor-run establishments began to decline in importance. Further, the office-bound manager-technician's role was destined to be progressively enhanced since he, along with his fellow administrators, was capable of making the types of decisions which could guarantee the growth of the firm in a world of rapid, technologically induced change. Thus, office activity, because it is intimately connected to the nation's economic mainsprings and processes of economic goal formation, has come to represent a subject whose importance is greater than its apparent impact on land use, the labor market, or any other single facet of the urban economy.

The growth of the office industry was made possible, both directly and indirectly, by a series of specific inventions. Stenography constituted a major innovation in the communications process; telephones, typewriters, and other business machines presented the occasion for quantum leaps in the transmission of information within and between offices. The advent of the steel-framed skyscraper office building with its vertical mass transportation system, the elevator, encouraged office concentrations sufficiently intense to produce "agglomeration effects"—the economies attendant upon dense office concentrations. Similarly, the electrified trolley car brought workers from both the city and growing suburbs

Table 1.1. Some Inventions Affecting Development of the Office Industry

Energy supply and application

1834	Electric motor (M. H. von Jacobi)
1854	Hydraulic passenger elevator (E. G. Otis)
1879	Electric lamp (T. A. Edison)
1881	First commercial electric power plant (Pearl Street, New York)
1887	First successful electric street railway (F. J. Sprague, Richmond)
1887	First electric elevator

Information transmission

1833	Electromagnetic telegraph (F. Gauss and W. Weber)
1866	First successful transatlantic telegraph cable
1876	Telephone (A. G. Bell)
1878	First commercial telephone switchboard (New Haven)

Information handling

1837	Stenography (Pitman)
1874	Commercial adaptation of the typewriter (Remington)
1888	Stenography (Gregg)
1894	Commercial adaptation of the mechanical calculator (W. S. Burroughs)

Building construction

1884	Steel frame (Home Insurance Co. Building in Chicago, ten floors, by William Le Baron Jenney)
1889	First steel frame high-rise building in New York (Tower Building at 50 Broadway, eleven floors, by Bradford L. Gilbert)

Source: Regional Plan Association, based on selected reference sources.

to central office clusters. Early recognition of the need for central office concentrations led to real estate development and transportation policies which reinforced office trends and guaranteed a later industry maturation in the Wall, LaSalle, and Montgomery streets of New York, Chicago, and San Francisco. A chronology of the major inventions that enabled the development of the office industry is given in Table 1.1.

Historical Growth Patterns
The wavelike growth of the office industry since 1880 has reflected the impact of wars and business cycles. Underneath the peaks and troughs of the cycles has been a dramatic secular trend. Office-type occupations in the United States increased from 7 percent of all jobs in 1870 and 8 percent in 1880 to 23 percent in 1930 and almost 40 percent in 1970 (office-type occupations here denote all white-collar jobs except salesmen; less than half of all office-type occupations presently occur in detached office buildings). This shift reflects long-term tendencies toward the mechanization and automation of manual labor, and the drain of the labor force from primary or extractive industries (such as agriculture and mining) toward secondary industries (manufacturing and construction) and, finally, toward tertiary industries (trade, finance, services, transportation, and government). In the progress of the American economy away from handling goods and toward performing services and handling information five dates stand out:
1. Soon after 1880, tertiary and secondary employment together exceeded primary employment, and income from tertiary activities exceeded that from any one of the other groups;
2. About 1935, tertiary activities began to account for more than half of total employment (they account for two-thirds now);
3. Soon after 1900, blue-collar employment exceeded farm employment;
4. About 1955, white-collar employment exceeded blue-collar employment;
5. Before 1980, white-collar employment will account for more than half of total employment.

The first impetus to office development came as the economy emerged from the depression of 1873–1879. The latter year also marks the consolidation of the Standard Oil empire, and the beginnings of mass distribution—the first Woolworth Store. Office employment registered steep and impressive gains by 1910. Nearly 3 million of the nation's 37 million workers were engaged in office pursuits at that time, most of which still occurred in locations adjacent to production. In addition, between 1890 and 1910, the number of women employed in office occupations rose from one-fifth to one-third of total office jobs, no doubt providing an impetus to the

women's suffrage movement. In the decade between 1900 and 1910, the number of stenographers and typists trebled to one-third of a million, or one-tenth of total office workers. Though miscellaneous clerical jobs remained the most numerous activity in the office, specialized bookkeeping and accounting positions ranked second. Engineers and other technical professionals increased their number fifteenfold to 150,000 in the four decades preceding 1910.

This first cycle of office growth received its most visible expression in the financial district around Wall Street in Manhattan, whose famed skyline took shape during that period. Building height shot up from 11 stories for the first steel-framed building in 1889 to 30 stories in 1899 (Park Row Building) to 50 stories in 1909 (Metropolitan Life Insurance Building) to 58 stories in 1913 (Woolworth Building). By the latter year, there were 61 buildings 20 stories or more in height in Manhattan, all but 10 of them office buildings.

A second cycle of office development began with the vigorous economic expansion which followed World War I. An enormous stock of central city office space was built in the nation during the period, which peaked in the late 1920s and recorded a level of expenditure for office construction (measured in constant dollars) which was not equaled until recently. By 1929, the number of buildings over 20 stories high in Manhattan tripled to 188—exactly half of the nation's total at that time. It was at this time that the development of midtown Manhattan as an office center took shape. This northward push was encouraged by the new subway network and the electrified suburban rail lines into Grand Central Terminal and Pennsylvania Station, while developers capitalized on the lower land costs to be found in midtown compared to downtown.

The depression did not arrest office construction immediately—in Manhattan work continued on a number of large projects conceived or initiated in the prosperous 1920s, among them such landmarks as the Chrysler Building, the Empire State Building, and Rockefeller Center. In toto, during the 15 years from 1920 to 1935, office space in Manhattan almost doubled: 58 million square feet were added to the roughly 68 million built during the first cycle of office growth.

New office space planning, however, was drastically curtailed in the mid-1930s, and during the following fifteen years, office construction was virtually at a standstill: little more than 2 million square feet were added by 1950. Initially, there were three reasons: first, there was a shortage of funds for investment; second, the payoffs did not look very attractive to investors, a problem exacerbated by an office market that was still trying to absorb a space backlog that had been either created or planned during the twenties; and third, the economy during the thirties temporarily reoriented itself to the production of essential goods. The first two points were part of the general problem facing investors of the period; the third point presents a problem unique to the office industry and warrants elaboration.

During the thirties, white-collar employment remained practically stable in its share of the total job market. This was partly a reflection of declining income earned by goods production. Companies had to concentrate their reduced resources on the production end of the economy and therefore could not sustain the more elite "nonproductive" office function. It also reflected the fact that households were unable to spend their reduced incomes for the intangible services of a white-collar corps.

Later, the war effort of the forties further sustained this deflection of the long-range trend toward office jobs. The wartime economy was geared for the output of war goods. Though administrative personnel were needed for wartime production, the pressure to detach and bring office workers to physically separate, downtown locations was reduced from what it had been in peacetime. Thus, during World War II vacancies in office buildings averaged over 10 percent nationally, space allocations drifted down from previously more liberal levels to 110 square feet per employee, and average rentals dropped.

The period following World War II and extending through to the present may be viewed as a third cycle of office development. It did not begin immediately. Recovery from World War II was arrested by a return to a war-based economy during the Korean War. The production of both producers and consumers goods and services dropped sharply. When the war ended, industry, though it had both the need for additional office space and financial resources to construct facilities, simply did not have the time to make the appropriate investment. Instead, industry chose to increase output by hiring more blue-collar labor until market pressures abated and improved technology could be introduced with less short-run sacrifice. Not until the mid-1950s did industry begin to rapidly assimilate new technology. Manpower was then released for the tertiary activities which, by this time, were commanding increasing shares of consumer and industry budgets.

The fifties period also was marked by the infusion of capital investment into the office industry in the form of versatile business machines. It began with widespread employment of tabulating, billing, and addressing machinery and advanced to the use of high-speed electronic data processing equipment. The programmed electronic computer, developed toward the end of World War II by Howard Aiken and others in the United States, and by Konrad Zuse in Germany, first appeared on the commercial market in 1954. In 1958, solid-state devices

Table 1.2. Number of Electronic Computers in Use in the United States, 1955–1971

1955	214
1956	746
1957	1,290
1958	2,150
1959	3,100
1960	4,100
1961	6,700
1962	10,400
1963	13,900
1964	19,600
1965	25,000
1966	32,900
1967	44,100
1968	56,500
1969	70,600
1970 (estimated)	83,200
1971 (estimated)	107,100

Source: International Data Corporation.

Lower Manhattan at the end of the second cycle of office development in 1935, with 60 million square feet of office floor space, some 0.8 million under construction. Note elevated rapid transit line forming a belt around the skyscraper cluster and entering the ferry terminal (*lower right*).

Lower Manhattan at the height of the third cycle of office development in 1970, with 100 million square feet of office floor space, of which some 18 million are seen under construction, including the 10-million square foot World Trade Center in the upper left.

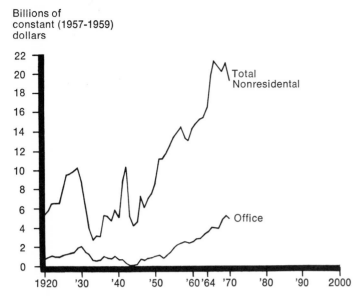

Billions of
constant (1957-1959)
dollars

Figure 1.1 Value of office and nonresidential building construction
in the nation, 1920–1970

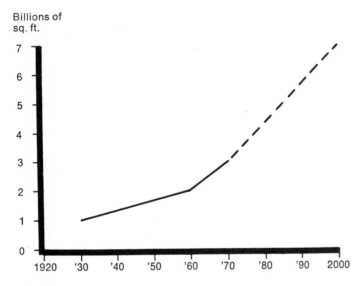

Billions of
sq. ft.

Figure 1.2 Estimated national inventory of office floor space,
1930–2000

began to replace the bulky electron tube. The subsequent triumphant march of the most powerful office machine is portrayed in Table 1.2.

The progress of the office industry thus paralleled the development phases of manufacturing. The initial phase was ushered in with a relatively undifferentiated labor force; later it became a separate, distinct entity characterized by a high degree of occupational specialization. This metamorphosis was similar to the way the manufacturing work force had evolved from the agricultural economy. Thus, the second phase could be termed a period of maturation and elaboration for both industry groups. This was followed, in both cases, by a third phase which brought heavy capitalization and advanced technology to the office industry.

However, the impact of increased capitalization on the white-collar industries appears to be the opposite from that on the production sector. While manpower requirements in the production sector shrank as capital was substituted for labor, the infusion of capital into the white-collar sector did not stop it from expanding its manpower requirements. Office-type occupations as previously defined increased from 30 to almost 40 percent of all jobs in the United States between 1950 and 1970.

The effect of increased capitalization, increasing manpower requirements, and an increased concentration of office workers in detached office buildings is reflected in an accelerated pace of new office building construction. Construction expenditures in constant dollars have risen higher than during the boom of the 1920s. Over the post-World War II period from 1946 to 1964, $30 billion in office and warehouse construction was authorized nationally. This is twice the value, in constant 1957–1959 dollars, of all comparable construction that occurred over the preceding twenty-six-year period (1920–1945). Public construction of administrative and service buildings in that period totalled $8.8 billion for 1920–1945 and $7.3 billion for 1946–1964 (Figure 1.1). Paradoxically, the boom has also been accompanied by a radical decline in vacancy rates of office buildings. This has been caused not only by increases in the size of the white-collar labor force but also by gradually increasing demands for floor space per employee, which have absorbed available footage and helped push rentals to new heights.

The following figures indicate the total amount of office space (including alterations and conversions) placed under construction in the United States during three successive four-year periods:
1957–1960: 294,000,000 square feet
1961–1964: 365,000,000 square feet
1965–1968: 490,000,000 square feet
Thus, not counting the unknown but minor effect of demolitions, it appears that the rate of growth of the nation's office building stock has increased from about 4

percent annually to about 5 percent annually over a recent 12-year period, which means that offices are growing three times as fast as population. In the nation as a whole, the total amount of office floor space can be estimated to have increased from about 1 billion gross square feet in 1930 and 1.3 billion in 1950, to 2 billion in 1960 and 3 billion in 1970. Barring a national disaster, there is no reason to expect a major or early downturn in this growth (Figure 1.2).

Functionally, the growth of the office industry has become essential to the continued growth of the cities themselves. At one time, cities could "export" nearby raw materials or locally manufactured products and earn the income needed to sustain the local economy. When the city lost its location advantage for these primary and secondary industries over other less urbanized places, the office industry emerged as a superior way in which the city could export services instead of goods and thereby earn the dollars needed for economic survival (many offices, for example local-market oriented offices, do not export services; the export function is closely tied into head offices). The superiority of office over predecessor industries stems from an incomparable growth in demand for office jobs that are generally relatively high paying and that provide the labor force with working conditions and fringe benefits considerably above many of the "sweat shop" and other low-paying types of operations which have mostly departed from the city. Then, too, office activity fills important "holes" in both the city landscape and in the city economy as space-intensive manufacturing operations move outward into the urban fringe.

Table 1.3 portrays the growth in private office space, 1900–1970, in the Manhattan CBD and in the CBD of Dallas, Texas. The latter is representative of a number of smaller, but strongly office-oriented cities, and is included because a consistent data series, not available nationally, was available for it. The upswing in office activity between 1950 and 1970 is apparent in both places—an 80 percent increase in Manhattan and more than a 200 percent increase in Dallas. Finally, Tables 1.4 and 1.5 (Figures 1.3 and 1.4) present a broad background of national trends in employment over the period of a century—1870 to 1970, which was discussed previously, and against which the growth in office demand ought to be viewed.

The tables and figures portray changes in the nation's economy in two ways. First, they show employment by type of industry, that is, primary or extractive (agriculture, forestry, fisheries, mining) versus secondary (manufacturing and construction) versus tertiary (finance, trade, transportation, government, etc.). Second, they show employment by type of occupation, that is, white-collar versus blue-collar versus service and farm workers.

Table 1.3. Gross Floor Space in Private Office Buildings in the Manhattan and Dallas, Texas, Central Business Districts, 1900–1970 (in millions of square feet)

	Manhattan CBD	Dallas CBD
1900	30	0.1
1920	68	1.8
1930	113	4.2
1936	126	4.7
1950	128	6.0
1960	160	15.6
1963	184 (+18.8 in public buildings)	17.3
1970	226 (+20.8 in public buildings)	22.5

Sources: Manhattan figures from Tri-State Transportation Commission, *The Manhattan CBD* (Revisions, 1971). Dallas figures from Central Business District Association, Dallas, Texas; City of Dallas, Department of Planning and Urban Development, Dallas, Texas.

Table 1.4. United States Work Force by Industry Characteristics, 1870–1970 (in millions)

	1870	1880	1890	1900	1910	1920	1930	1940	1950	1960	1970
Tertiary (trade, finance, service, transportation, government)	3.2	4.5	7.3	10.1	13.9	16.7	23.0	29.5	30.4	38.3	49.1
Secondary (manufacturing, construction)	2.6	3.9	5.5	7.2	10.7	12.9	14.1	14.5	18.1	21.3	24.1
Primary (agriculture, forestry, mining)	7.1	9.0	10.5	11.8	12.8	12.8	11.7	11.1	7.9	5.0	3.0
Total	12.9	17.4	23.3	29.1	37.4	42.4	48.8	55.1	56.4	64.6	76.2
Tertiary as percentage of total employment	24.8%	25.9%	31.3%	34.7%	37.2%	39.4%	47.1%	53.5%	53.9%	59.3%	64.4%

Table 1.5. United States Labor Force by Major Occupation Groups, 1870–1970 (in millions)

	1870	1880	1890	1900	1910	1920	1930	1940	1950	1960	1970
White collar	1.2	1.9	3.3	5.1	8.0	10.5	14.3	16.1	21.6	28.7	35.8
Professional	.4	.6	.9	1.2	1.7	2.3	3.3	3.9	5.1	7.4	
Managerial	.4	.6	.9	1.7	2.5	2.8	3.6	3.8	5.2	6.7	
Clerical	.1	.2	.6	.9	2.0	3.4	4.3	5.0	7.2	9.7	
Sales	.3	.5	.8	1.3	1.8	2.0	3.1	3.4	4.1	4.8	
Blue collar (craftsmen, operatives, laborers)	3.7	5.4	8.0	10.4	14.2	17.0	19.3	20.6	24.3	25.6	28.8
Service (household and other)	1.2	1.5	2.1	2.6	3.6	3.3	4.8	6.1	6.2	8.3	9.8
Farm	6.8	8.6	9.9	10.9	11.5	11.4	10.3	9.0	6.9	5.4	2.2
Total	12.9	17.4	23.3	29.0	37.3	42.2	48.7	51.7	59.0	68.0	76.6
White collar as percentage of total	9.3%	10.9%	14.2%	17.6%	21.4%	24.9%	29.4%	30.9%	36.6%	42.2%	46.7%

Sources for Tables 1.4 and 1.5: U.S. Census, *Comparative Occupation Statistics for the United States, 1870–1940*; U.S. Census, *Historical Statistics of the United States, Colonial Times to 1957*; U.S. Census, *Census of Population: 1960, General Social and Economic Characteristics*; 1970 estimates by Regional Plan Association.

Notes: Prior to 1940, data are for civilian gainful workers 10 years old and over; for 1940 through 1970, data are for persons 14 years old and over in the experienced civilian labor force, which consists of all gainfully employed and unemployed workers with previous work experience. Major occupational groups for 1870 through 1890 are based on reportings of detailed, though not historically consistent, occupational characteristics. Detail may not add to totals because of rounding.

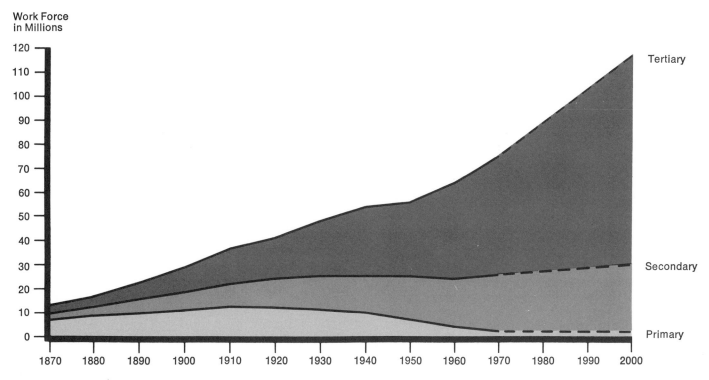

Figure 1.3 United States work force by industry characteristics, 1870–2000

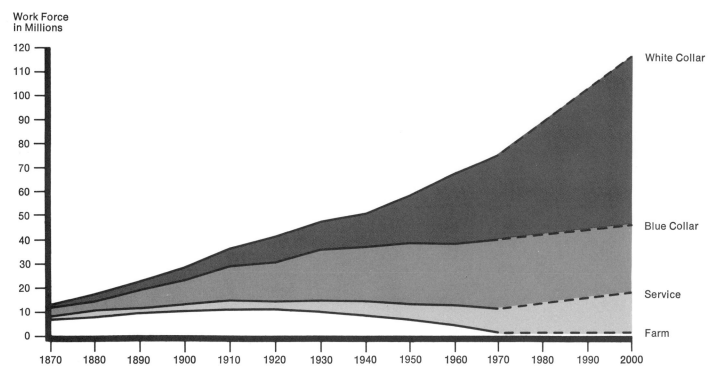

Figure 1.4 United States labor force by major occupation groups, 1870–2000

The two types of classification are by no means congruent (white-collar workers such as agronomists work in agriculture and engineers mostly in manufacturing and construction), but their trends are somewhat parallel. It is the strength of these parallel trends that is feeding the present unprecedented (and clearly long-term) expansion of the office industry.

The Central Location Tendency
If the office industry was the inevitable handmaiden of advancing urban and industrial revolutions, what factors led to its unique pattern of location in space? Why didn't offices tend to remain at the point of production? Clearly, some did and some still do remain attached to the plant. However, the majority did not. As mentioned previously, control of markets and production became increasingly essential to corporate success when business grew and intensified its capital requirements. But where production problems could be resolved some distance from the plant, sales problems could not be dealt with far from the market place. Moreover, direct communications with financial institutions became necessary because of the firm's need to quickly adopt cost-reducing innovations. In the jargon of the economist, office and production functions physically separated when the economic benefits of obtaining and comparing information within the market became greater for the detached office than the cost-savings of directing production from a plant-attached site.

At about the same time that industry's managers and office staffs were gravitating to downtown locations, production-line operations were beginning to move outward or even to other regions. Such centrifugal factors as cheap land, efficient single-story plants, and the availability of electrically transmitted energy, which tended to disperse production sites further and further, hastened the process of separation between office and plant and encouraged offices to congregate. Scale economies and the advantages of specialization also encouraged the separation of the place of decision-making from the place of production.

Nonetheless, changes brought about during the post-Civil War period were not solely responsible for detached headquarters operations and centralization of office activity. The urban economy traditionally housed disproportionate numbers of banks, law firms, foreign trade houses, wholesalers, and other assorted financial intermediaries. These firms were linked to the cities' traditional entrepôt and market functions. As a result, the new headquarters operations not only found the urban climate highly supportive but reciprocally contributed to the attractiveness of downtown locations for succeeding waves of middle- and local-market oriented

office activity—commerce begot commerce. The degree to which these cumulative processes drew office industry to highly urbanized areas is illustrated by Table 1.6 and Figure 1.5. It tells us that in 1960 the 100 largest standard metropolitan statistical areas (SMSAs) in the United States contained 54 percent of national population and 64 percent of office occupations. Metropolitan areas of over 1 million population, however, captured 43 percent of the office-type occupations with only 34 percent of the nation's population. This big-city attractiveness to office jobs is underscored by the distribution of manufacturing production jobs and related offices among metropolitan areas of 1 million or more. While 38 percent of the nation's production employment is located in the larger metropolitan areas, 49 percent of its nonproduction supervisory activity is in those areas. These data indicate that administration and control tend to be separated with the former function gravitating to the large metropolitan areas and the latter function settling in smaller urbanized areas. However, not all parts of the office industry are subject to the same centralizing forces.

The office market itself may be divided three ways: *headquarters, middle market,* and *local market.* Almost all headquarters jobs are jobs that export their services, from the viewpoint of any one metropolitan area. The market area of headquarters activity is often national or international in scope; the degree of complexity in this type of operation is at its greatest. Included here are the headquarters of the giants of industry, major business concerns in manufacturing, trade, service, financing, and transportation. The need for external economies and the benefits of concentration increase so rapidly at this level that only the highest order of urban centers are capable of supporting the ancillary services, specialized labor pools, and interfirm communication that are required by most national market functions. Moreover, only the largest urban centers are capable of conferring the "prestige" desired by these "image" conscious firms. National- and international-scale government functions must also be included in the category of headquarters jobs.

Middle-market activity includes regional, subregional, and national back office operations as well as utilities, and headquarters-serving functions such as advertising and public relations. These jobs are found in almost every region for the purpose of serving that region. The category includes few export office-type jobs, although occasionally a branch office may serve more than one region and considerable exporting may occur in indirect ways. The location of middle-market offices is strongly influenced by both the national population distribution and the location of headquarters operations. Middle-market jobs may serve a large region, say one as large as

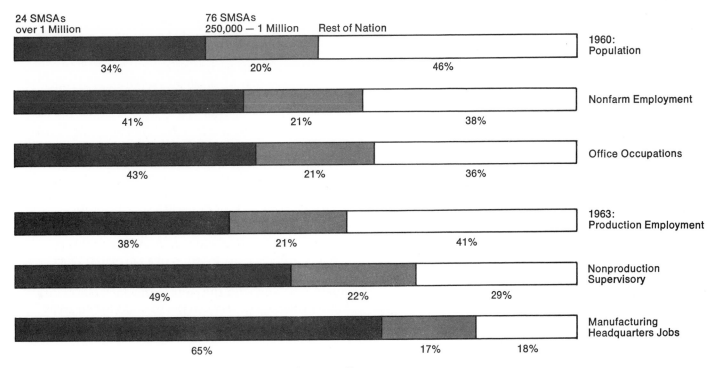

24 SMSAs over 1 Million 76 SMSAs 250,000 — 1 Million Rest of Nation

1960: Population
34% 20% 46%

Nonfarm Employment
41% 21% 38%

Office Occupations
43% 21% 36%

1963: Production Employment
38% 21% 41%

Nonproduction Supervisory
49% 22% 29%

Manufacturing Headquarters Jobs
65% 17% 18%

Figure 1.5 Distribution of selected activities by size of metropolitan area, 1960 and 1963

Table 1.6. The Nationwide Distribution of Selected Activities, 1960–1963

| | Top 100 SMSAs | | | | |
	24 SMSAs over 1 million	76 SMSAs 250,000– 1 million	Total	Rest of nation	Nation total
Population	34.3%	19.4%	53.7%	46.3%	100.0%
Nonagricultural employment	41.0	21.0	62.0	38.0	100.0
Office occupations	42.5	21.1	63.6	36.4	100.0
Production employment	38.5	20.8	59.3	40.7	100.0
Nonproduction supervisory	49.1	22.0	71.1	28.9	100.0
Manufacturing central administrative and auxiliary (CAO & A)	65.5	16.7	82.2	17.8	100.0

Sources: U.S. Census, *Journey to Work: 1960*; National Planning Association, *Regional Economic Projection Series*; U.S. Census, *Census of Manufactures: 1963*; U.S. Census, *Enterprise Statistics: 1963*, Part 2.

Table 1.7. Major Categories of Office Employment in the Nation and the New York Region (millions of jobs)

	Nation			New York Region		
	1959	1965	2000	1959	1965	2000
Total employment	65.9	73.4	118.19	7.23	7.80	12.30
Office-type occupations	23.6	28.2	58.64	3.20	3.60	6.88
Office jobs	13.5	16.4	36.60	1.94	2.34	4.50
Jobs in office buildings				1.42	1.56	3.26
Headquarters jobs				.39	.46	1.24
CAO&A	1.05	1.32	4.50	.21	.25	.67

Office employment as a percentage of total

	Nation			New York Region		
Total employment	100.0%	100.0%	100.0%	100.0%	100.0%	100.0%
Office-type occupations	35.8	38.4	49.6	44.3	46.2	55.9
Office jobs	20.5	22.3	31.0	26.8	30.0	36.6
Jobs in office buildings				19.6	20.0	26.5
Headquarters jobs				5.4	5.9	10.1
CAO&A	1.6	1.8	3.8	2.9	3.2	5.4

Sources: U.S. Census, *Census of Population: 1960, Detailed Characteristics*; National Planning Association, *Regional Economic Projection Series*. RPA estimates, utilizing data from both sources.
Note: Office projections exclude sales jobs in offices.

the New York Region, or smaller areas down to about the 150,000 population level. Their need for a sizable white-collar labor pool is a constraint on their freedom to move away from central cities.

Finally, local-market office jobs serve areas of roughly under 150,000 population and are located close by the populations being served. They are, therefore, the least likely to require the usual benefits of clustering. This category includes local government offices of small municipalities, branch banks, real estate offices, law firms in general practice, and similar establishments.

Thus, it is important to stress that the office industry is not homogeneous, but performs an array of different functions which have, geographically, quite different markets. The location and extent of these markets strongly influence the location of a particular office within a particular metropolitan area. They also have something to do with the pattern in which offices distribute themselves between the nation's urban areas, which is the subject of the next chapter.

Measures of Office Activity

As was pointed out in the Introduction, there is no generally recognized definition of the office industry, and the U.S. Census does not report office jobs as such. Therefore, several measures of varying detail had to be devised for this study, as shown in Table 1.7. With the exception of total employment, which represents the universe of jobs, the following major categories represent successively smaller components of a family of white-collar activity linked to the office.

Office-type occupations are here defined as all white-collar occupations minus the category of sales workers.[1] Included are the professional, managerial, and clerical categories, as defined by the U.S. Census classifications. However, many occupations included in these groups are not directly related to the performance of office work, or the use of office space, and must be deleted for a truer measure of office activity. Artists, musicians, pharmacists, and elementary school teachers are some of the more obvious examples. The complete or partial exclusion of other occupations, such as physicians and social workers, is based partly on judgment, partly on evidence from previous research.

Office jobs then represent all office-type occupations minus these deleted categories. Table 1.8 lists the selected occupations that contribute to the total of office

1. Nationwide, about 14 percent of sales workers are insurance and real estate agents and brokers, who generally do occupy offices, and some other categories of sales workers do likewise. However, for the sake of compatibility with earlier work on offices done as a part of the Harvard study on the New York Metropolitan Region, its definitions were adopted, except as noted.

jobs for the New York Region. However, not all office jobs are located in detached office buildings. Some are located in offices attached to factories, stores, institutional buildings, and so on. To obtain a pure measure of office jobs in detached office buildings, these categories have to be deleted.

Jobs in office buildings isolate that sector of office employment which has the most impact on the physical structure of an urban area. It has been derived for the New York Region by matching detailed geographical data on occupations against available inventories of floor space, as described later on in greater detail. The bulk of office building employment is not headquarters employment; however, nearly all headquarters jobs are located in detached office buildings.

Headquarters office jobs thus are a fourth index of office employment used. Locationally, they represent the most concentrated form of office activity, and their disproportionately high economic impact is obvious. Estimating these elite jobs on a nationwide basis was not feasible within the framework of this study. The data could only be constructed for the New York Region. For other metropolitan areas and for the nation as a whole, a proxy had to be used.

Central administrative office and auxiliary employment, or CAO&A, reported by the U.S. Census for several selected industry groups, is such a proxy for headquarters jobs. It has to be viewed as a subclass of headquarters activity which receives special treatment from federal statistical reportings and is the only available measure of changes in the composition and location of headquarters over a relatively recent time period.

The following chapter starts with the discussion of office-type occupations, nationwide and by major metropolitan area, and then proceeds to analyze headquarters location, as indicated by the CAO&A reportings. Some partial measures of office floor space are introduced, which are a good index of jobs in office buildings, for the nation and for selected metropolitan areas. However, in the absence of a national census of buildings, consistent floor-space data are available only for new construction. Finally, in Chapters 4 and 5, the measures that have been presented are employed to analyze the structure of the office industry in the New York Region.

Table 1.8. The Detailed Occupational Composition of Office Employment in the New York Region, 1960

Occupation	Total office employ.	As a % of the nation
Professional and technical workers	331,009	14.4%
Accountants and auditors	75,049	15.9
Architects	4,635	15.3
College faculty	15,738	8.9
Designers	19,389	29.4
Draftsmen	25,976	12.2
Editors and reporters	21,368	21.2
Engineers	103,093	12.0
Lawyers and judges	41,040	19.3
Personnel and labor relations	13,046	13.3
Public relations and publicity	6,758	22.3
Social Workers ($\frac{1}{3}$ of total)	4,917	15.3
Managers, officials, and proprietors	375,442	14.4
Buyers in stores	35,077	15.0
Credit men	5,686	12.2
Public administration officials	14,417	7.3
Purchasing agents and buyers	14,061	13.6
Society, lodge, and union officials	4,503	13.5
Selected salaried managers and officials	253,928	15.5
Selected self-employed managers and officials ($\frac{1}{2}$ of total)	47,770	14.0
Clerical and kindred workers	1,264,098	14.1
Agents	21,091	13.2
Attendants	11,181	10.9
Bank tellers	17,218	13.3
Bookkeepers	106,494	11.7
Cashiers	44,682	9.5
Collectors	2,683	8.8
File clerks	27,028	20.6
Insurance adjusters	9,329	16.9
Messengers and office boys	17,524	29.8
Office machine operators	49,275	16.0
Payroll clerks	12,515	11.7
Postal clerks	34,328	16.4
Receptionists	18,235	13.6
Secretaries	220,546	15.1
Shipping clerks	44,557	15.9
Stenographers	29,789	11.0
Stock clerks	39,047	12.0
Telegraph operators	1,510	7.5
Telephone operators	50,631	14.2
Typists	88,145	16.9
Other clerical workers	418,290	14.3
Total	1,970,549	14.2
Total including sales workers in offices	2,148,714	14.2

Source: Regional Plan Association, based on data from the U.S. Census, *Census of Population: 1960, Detailed Characteristics.*

Chapter 2

The National Pattern of Office Location

The Relation of Office Activity to Urban Size
At a time when the great bulk of manufacturing production is becoming more evenly distributed throughout the nation, office activity continues to gravitate toward large urban centers. A leveling out of transportation costs and the growth of regional markets has contributed to the diffusion in manufacturing, while in office activity, particularly central office activity, a more compact nationwide location pattern emerges. The dynamics of central office concentration reflect management demands for interaction between firms, highly skilled labor markets, and complementary ancillary business services. These locational benefits are available in an area only after a local economy has evolved through successive stages of development and has invested both in a range of basic employment opportunities and a physical infrastructure that upholds a viable office environment.

For an individual region, the process of growth thus bestows certain inevitable changes on the composition of its employment. Larger urban areas tend to contain disproportionately larger amounts of office activity—but, as we shall later see, size is hardly the sole determinant of office concentration. Statistically, one observes a pattern of office concentration emerging in urban areas larger than 1 million persons. In 1960, the top 100 metropolitan areas in the United States, which ranged in size from a quarter million to over 10 million persons, contained 64 percent of all office-type occupations but only 54 percent of the nation's population, as was shown in Table 1.6. Looking only at the top 24 of these 100 metropolitan areas, namely those with populations of over 1 million, reveals a strikingly greater disparity between office activity and residential base as a share of the nation. The areas over 1 million have 43 percent of the office occupations compared to 34 percent of the nation's population. This contrast is further underscored by the disposition of manufacturing employment in these largest areas. They have only 38.5 percent of the production jobs, but 49 percent of the nonproduction, supervisory activity and 65.5 percent of the manufacturing headquarters-type, central administrative and auxiliary jobs, as shown in Table 1.6.

The disproportionate share of office activity found to characterize the largest group of metropolitan areas may be best understood within the context of the traditional, but somewhat updated, economic base concept. Conventionally, the location of raw material deposits or the fashioning of industrial goods provided our urban areas with their major export. The success of exporting and the concomitant ability to import capital was an important stimulus to a region's overall growth and, more particularly, to the growth of its locally based service activities. With a sustained population increase and a viable export sector, local services flourished and diversified. In the largest areas, they achieved a scale sufficient to satisfy not only their own requirements, but also, to an extent, those of smaller urban areas, broad regions, and the nation.

Over the postwar years, many of our largest urban regions have experienced sluggish growth or even decline in their manufacturing sectors. Office jobs, however, are outpacing production jobs nationwide, and major office pursuits, which grew out of locally induced service needs or were attracted to certain areas for cluster advantages, are replacing conventional exports. Growth in a region's office component thus reflects national growth trends and the urban areas best equipped to house this specialty share to a greater degree in the wealth and productivity of the nation's economy.

However, not all of the largest metropolitan areas equally reflect the aggregate group's disproportionate share of office activity. Indeed, inspection of the data in Table 2.1 indicates that only selected metropolitan areas stand at the forefront, having achieved preeminence not merely in overall size but also in specialization. The differences in the employment base among the largest metropolitan areas may be summed up in the following classification:

1. Office Centers

All major metropolitan areas deviating markedly from their respective shares of population and employment in the direction of surplus office-type occupations, which correlates strongly with greater than average shares of nonproduction manufacturing employment and less than representative levels of production activity.

New York, Los Angeles, San Francisco, Boston, Washington, Minneapolis–St. Paul, Seattle, Dallas

2. Production Centers

With few exceptions, the inverse of the Case 1 relationship is true. For those areas underrepresented in office-type occupations, a greater share of production activity occurs than office activity and this industrial employment exceeds the share of total population and employment in the respective areas.

Chicago, Philadelphia, Detroit, Pittsburgh, St. Louis, Cleveland, Newark, Buffalo, Cincinnati, Milwaukee, Paterson

3. Balanced Centers

Only five regions approximate a balanced composition of office and production jobs, which may be attributed to their generally smaller size and to the greater geographic independence of most of them.

Baltimore, Houston, Kansas City, San Diego, Atlanta

Export of Office Services

Crucial to an understanding of office location is the distribution of the industry's most important export component. In Chapter 1, the office market was divided into three parts consisting of headquarters, middle, and local markets. The headquarters market can be viewed as equivalent to a region's export office function since its services usually extend beyond the limits of any one metropolitan area. Moreover, the existence of a headquarters or central office market creates economic opportunities for varied headquarters-related, middle-market activities. Generally speaking, one out of three office jobs in the largest metropolitan areas cannot be explained by the relationship of other middle-market and local-office requirements to the resident population.

Nationally, 12.2 office occupations service a population of 100 persons. However, major metropolitan areas over 1 million engage an average 15.2 persons per 100 residents, while the rest of the nation provides only 10.7 office occupations per 100 population.[1] We have indicated earlier that in metropolitan areas over 1 million, there appears no strict correlation between metropolitan size and the strength of the office activity. Rather, the "surplus" office activity of individual SMSAs (standard metropolitan statistical areas; see note, Table 2.1) more or less represents their specialization in office work, or their relative intensity as office centers.

Table 2.2 provides estimates of the degree to which the selected metropolitan areas specialize in export-oriented office jobs. Those areas of strongest export orientation, such as New York and Washington, correspond with the previous classification of office centers. Conversely, major metropolitan areas that are more specialized in production activities, such as Detroit and Pittsburgh, are weak exporters of office services. The results of both indicators, viewed in context with the respective inventories of downtown office space,[2] suggest that the re-

1. For purposes of estimating the extent of exogenously demanded office activity, we have used a convenient though simplistic ratio of per capita surplus in office occupations. Our assumptions have been that all office jobs, other than the ones attributable to export activities, are a function of population size and that the national average outside of the largest metropolitan areas reflects these local office demands which must be satisfied at a nearby location.

2. Figure 2.4 presents the estimated inventories of downtown office floor space by rank order of metropolitan area size.

Table 2.1. Population and Employment in Metropolitan Areas with Populations over 1 Million, 1960 and 1963

	1960						1963					
	Population		Employ. in office occupations*		Nonagr. employ.		Total		Mfg. employ. production		Nonproduction	
	Number (× 1,000)	Share of nation	Number (× 1,000)	Share of nation	Number (× 1,000)	Share of nation	Number (× 1,000)	Share of nation	Number (× 1,000)	Share of nation	Number (× 1,000)	Share of nation
United States	179,323.2	100.0%	21,948.8	100.0%	60,877.7	100.0%	16,961.0	100.0%	12,232.0	100.0%	4,729.0	100.0%
New York–N.E. N.J. SCA	14,759.4	8.2	2,391.6	10.9	6,383.1	10.5	1,779.3	10.5	1,191.0	9.7	588.3	12.4
New York SMSA	10,694.6	6.0	1,884.2	8.6	4,755.4	7.8	1,147.2	6.8	760.8	6.2	386.4	8.2
Newark SMSA	1,689.4	.9	254.7	1.2	733.4	1.2	250.2	1.5	160.3	1.3	89.9	1.9
Paterson SMSA†	1,186.9	.7	136.8	.6	406.0	.7	176.6	1.0	122.7	1.0	53.8	1.1
Chicago–N.W. Ind. SCA	6,794.5	3.8	999.6	4.6	2,980.5	4.9	958.6	5.7	669.6	5.5	289.0	6.1
Chicago SMSA	6,220.9	3.5	942.3	4.3	2,745.9	4.5	860.6	5.1	593.5	4.9	267.1	5.6
Los Angeles SMSA†	6,742.7	3.8	1,050.8	4.8	2,613.0	4.3	746.0	4.4	494.9	4.0	251.1	5.3
Philadelphia SMSA	4,342.9	2.4	579.5	2.6	1,697.6	2.8	535.8	3.2	374.8	3.1	161.0	3.4
Detroit SMSA	3,762.4	2.1	454.3	2.1	1,322.2	2.2	493.9	2.9	329.7	2.7	164.2	3.5
San Francisco SMSA†	2,783.4	1.6	452.2	2.1	1,100.7	1.8	196.2	1.2	126.0	1.0	70 2	1.5
Boston SMSA	2,589.3	1.4	430.4	2.0	1,140.5	1.9	293.2	1.7	192.6	1.6	100.6	2.1
Pittsburgh SMSA	2,405.4	1.3	282.2	1.3	852.6	1.4	272.2	1.6	181.1	1.5	91.1	1.9
St. Louis SMSA	2,060.1	1.1	270.2	1.2	805.6	1.3	259.7	1.5	179.4	1.5	80.3	1.7
Washington SMSA	2,001.9	1.1	408.7	1.9	832.1	1.4	50.1	.3	28.0	.2	22.1	.5
Cleveland SMSA	1,796.6	1.0	255.8	1.2	776.0	1.3	280.3	1.7	194.2	1.6	86.1	1.8
Baltimore SMSA	1,727.0	1.0	227.6	1.0	675.6	1.1	190.5	1.1	134.0	1.1	56.5	1.2
Minn.–St. Paul SMSA	1,482.0	.8	241.5	1.1	620.7	1.0	163.9	1.0	102.9	.8	61.0	1.3
Buffalo SMSA	1,307.0	.7	161.3	.7	469.9	.8	162.9	1.0	117.9	1.0	45.0	1.0
Houston SMSA	1,243.2	.7	176.7	.8	500.4	.8	108.6	.6	70.3	.6	38.3	.8
Milwaukee SMSA	1,194.3	.7	168.1	.8	499.2	.8	193.8	1.1	133.2	1.1	60.6	1.3
Seattle SMSA	1,107.2	.6	178.6	.8	409.7	.7	121.6	.7	70.2	.6	51.4	1.1
Dallas SMSA	1,083.6	.6	181.0	.8	436.1	.7	109.5	.6	73.0	.6	36.5	.8
Cincinnati SMSA	1,071.6	.6	151.3	.7	449.4	.7	153.9	.9	100.1	.8	53.8	1.1
Kansas City SMSA	1,039.5	.6	160.6	.7	418.4	.7	111.1	.7	75.4	.6	35.7	.8
San Diego SMSA	1,033.0	.6	127.1	.6	295.7	.5	60.3	.4	30.2	.2	30.1	.6
Atlanta SMSA	1,017.2	.6	155.8	.7	420.7	.7	95.7	.6	68.1	.6	27.6	.6
Total SMSAs	61,582.1	34.3	9,331.7	42.5	24,976.8	41.0	7,033.7	41.5	4,713.3	38.5	2,320.4	49.1

Sources: U.S. Census, *Journey to Work: 1960*; U.S. Census, *Census of Manufactures: 1963*; National Planning Association, *Regional Economic Projections Series*.

Notes: Detail may not add to totals because of rounding.

Standard Consolidated Areas (SCAs) and Standard Metropolitan Statistical Areas (SMSAs) are established by the Bureau of the Budget. Geographical boundaries are revised periodically to reflect changes in the land areas falling within the metropolitan classification. For the tables, figures, and overall analysis of the office activity, the year of data collection is taken to specify the geographical definition of the metropolitan areas.

Several of the major areas were redefined between 1960 and 1963, and, as a result, the reference areas for the separate years are not always comparable. For the information of the reader, the SMSAs affected by these changes are listed below: 1960 population according to the 1963 metropolitan area boundaries is presented for comparison. The data are in thousands of persons.

Los Angeles–Long Beach	6,038.8	Cleveland	1,909.5
San Francisco–Oakland	2,648.8	Milwaukee	1,232.7
Boston	2,595.5	Cincinnati	1,268.5
St. Louis	2,104.7	Kansas City	1,092.5

* Office-type occupations include professional, technical, managerial, and clerical workers. Farmers and farm managers working within the individual SMSAs are included because of the nature of published data, while the national total excludes them under the presumption that when the job location occurs outside large metropolitan areas the likelihood of occupying office space is minimal.

† Full titles for SMSAs are as follows: Los Angeles–Long Beach, San Francisco–Oakland, Paterson-Clifton-Passaic.

Table 2.2. Estimates of "Surplus" Office Activity in Metropolitan Areas with Populations over 1 Million, 1960

	Population rank	Jobs in office occupations per 100 population	Share of jobs in office occupations in export ("surplus") activities
SMSA			
Washington	10	20.4	over 35%
New York	1	17.6	over 35%
Dallas	20	16.7	over 35%
Boston	7	16.6	over 35%
Minn.–St. Paul	14	16.3	25%–35%
San Francisco	6	16.2	25%–35%
Seattle	19	16.1	25%–35%
Los Angeles	2	15.6	25%–35%
Kansas City	22	15.4	25%–35%
Atlanta	24	15.3	25%–35%
Chicago	3	15.1	25%–35%
Newark	13	15.1	25%–35%
Cleveland	11	14.2	15%–25%
Houston	16	14.2	15%–25%
Milwaukee	17	14.1	15%–25%
Cincinnati	21	14.1	15%–25%
Philadelphia	4	13.3	15%–25%
Baltimore	12	13.2	15%–25%
St. Louis	9	13.1	15%–25%
Buffalo	15	12.3	5%–15%
San Diego	23	12.3	5%–15%
Detroit	5	12.1	5%–15%
Pittsburgh	8	11.7	5%–15%
Paterson	18	11.5	5%–15%
SCA*			
New York–N.E. N.J.	1	16.2	25%–35%
Chicago–N.W. Ind.	2	14.7	25%–35%

Source: U.S. Census, *Journey to Work: 1960.*
* Standard Consolidated Area.

gions most specialized in office-type economies are six. Ordered by size of office work force, they are New York, Los Angeles, San Francisco, Boston, Washington, and Dallas. While other metropolitan areas, such as Chicago, have larger office sectors than several of those just listed, none evidence as high a degree of specialization. Both the absolute size of the office work force and its relative weight compared to the total population, as shown in Table 2.2, are represented graphically on Map 2.1. One should note that rank-ordering metropolitan areas by per capita jobs in office occupations, as done in Table 2.2 and Map 2.1, gives somewhat different results for the lower-order centers than the previous office center–production center classification.

Recognizing that export office activity is linked to national requirements and that alternative metropolitan areas are available to share in the future growth of this activity, an analysis of the major component of surplus office employment (that is, headquarters functions) is warranted at this stage. Indeed, it is operationally necessary to assess the potential for office growth in the New York Region vis-à-vis other metropolitan areas.

Headquarters Activity in Major Metropolitan Areas

As one progresses upwards on the hierarchy of office activity, market areas generally expand and operations become more complex. At the pinnacle of the hierarchy are the giants of the industry, headquarters operations of major business concerns in manufacturing, trade, services, financing, and transportation. Headquarters activity is primarily responsible for sharp interregional differences in export orientation as well as for the growth of secondary, branch office activity which is found to prosper in proximity to national market firms. The need for agglomeration effects or external economies of concentration appears to increase so rapidly at this level that only highest-order urban centers are capable of supporting the ancillary services, specialized labor pools, interfirm communication, and prestige required by most elite national market firms. For various institutional or historical reasons, some metropolitan areas of less than 1 million population have also come to house headquarters, or central administrative offices (CAO), in significant numbers. They are anticipated to maintain this role in the future, having established a viable ancillary sector that is out of proportion to the size of their economies. Other metropolitan areas, including some in the million and over size class, maintain office sectors that are either regionally oriented or exert lesser influence in competition for central office functions. Let us analyze in more detail the significance of major SMSAs as locations for headquarters employment and the magnitude of their involvement in this important activity.

A convenient, even if imperfect, index of headquarters

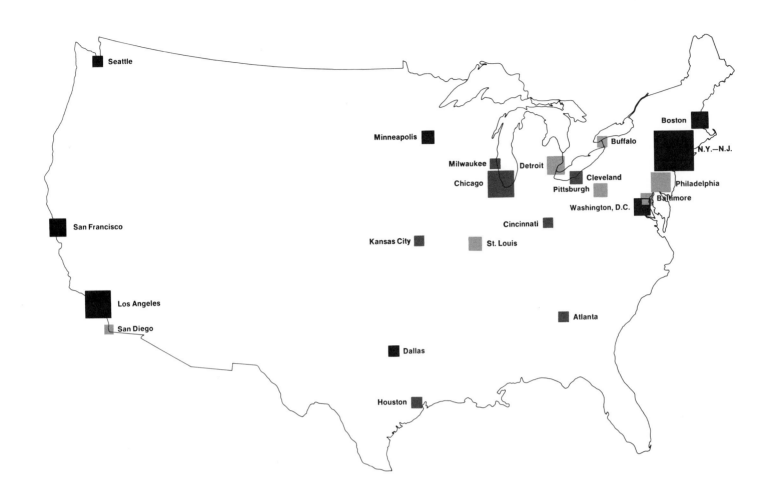

Workers Employed in Office Occupations

☐ 100,000

☐ 500,000

☐ 1,000,000

Office Occupations per 100 Population

▨ 11.5 — 13.3

▨ 14.1 — 15.4

■ 15.6 — 20.4

Map 2.1 National office centers

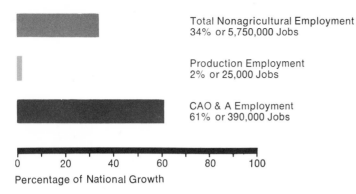

Total Nonagricultural Employment
34% or 5,750,000 Jobs

Production Employment
2% or 25,000 Jobs

CAO & A Employment
61% or 390,000 Jobs

0   20   40   60   80   100
Percentage of National Growth

Figure 2.1 Twenty-one major metropolitan areas' share of nationwide growth, 1954–1967

activity is U.S. Census reportings of central administrative and auxiliary employment (CAO&A) in the federal censuses of mining, manufacturing, construction, and business.[3] The relative weight of the CAO&A category in total employment was shown in Table 1.7. Although the study period of changes in CAO&A employment, 1954–1967, is short, it does reflect basic shifts that have been occurring within the economy for some time (Figure 2.1). Trends characterized by a de-emphasis on production employment, the increasing concentration of business power, and the invasion by automation and technology of back office operations, all contributed to a refinement of locational choice among major SMSAs on the part of headquarters functions. The data in Table 2.3 show that 21 large metropolitan areas,[4] with 40 percent of the nation's office-type occupations, contain roughly 65 percent of the central administrative employment. It is a rapidly expanding category which, nationwide, grew 84 percent between 1954 and 1967.

In view of this rapid growth, it is no wonder that there has been some decentralizing from the largest metropolitan areas. For example, Chicago's total CAO&A employment rose precipitously from 79,000 to 116,000 between 1954 and 1967, an increase of 47 percent. But, despite this gain, Chicago's relative share of all CAO&A employment slipped from 10 to 8 percent. By contrast, Cincinnati enlarged its CAO&A sector more than twice as rapidly as the nation.

Overall, the central administrative jobs in the top 21 metropolitan areas grew at a slightly slower pace than in the nation, while those in the New York SCA (standard consolidated area) grew at a still slower pace. Be-

3. Central administrative and auxiliary employment is an arbitrarily established employment grouping of the U.S. Department of Commerce which most nearly approximates the work force of detached headquarters locations. There are several deficiencies in the data from the perspective of this analysis; notably, the data are limited to the reportings of only selected industry groups by multiestablishment firms, and they combine enumerations of two distinct employment types, only one of which is truly central office activity. Between 1954 and 1963, CAO&A industry coverage consisted of mining, manufacturing, wholesale and retail trade, and selected services; in 1967 this base of five industries was expanded to include the construction industry. The major portion of data are gathered from central administrative office payrolls, and cover such positions as occur in general administrative, supervisory, purchasing, accounting, general engineering and systems planning, legal, financial, and other management functions performed centrally for other establishments of the same company. In the New York Region, where further research into the dimension of headquarters employment was feasible, the census reportings for central administrative office employment represented *less than half* of total headquarters employment as shown in Table 1.7.
4. This group of SMSAs is not strictly comparable to the earlier grouping of major urban areas. In total, four SMSAs have been excluded because of insignificant CAO&A reportings, and one SMSA under a million population has been included.

Table 2.3. Employment in Central Administrative Offices and Auxiliary Units in Major Metropolitan Areas, 1954–1967

	1954		1958		1963		1967		Growth rate, 1954–1967	
	Employ. (× 1,000)	Share of nation	Employ. (× 1,000)	Share of nation	Employ. (× 1,000)	Share of nation	Employ. (× 1,000)	Share of nation	CAO&A	Nonagr. total
United States	771.3	100.0%	986.9	100.0%	1,213.4	100.0%	1,416.1	100.0%	83.6%	34.7%
New York–N.E. N.J. SCA	160.7	20.8	200.5	20.3	231.1	19.0	265.3	18.7	65.1	19.3
New York SMSA	130.6	16.9	164.2	16.6	174.9	14.4	191.8	13.5	46.9	16.4
Newark SMSA	18.1	2.3	23.5	2.4	30.1	2.5	32.8	2.3	81.2	39.8
Paterson SMSA	4.3	.6	4.8	.5	9.9	.8	15.4	1.1	258.1	41.6
Chicago–N.W. Ind. SCA	78.5	10.2	83.0	8.4	99.9	8.2	115.5	8.2	47.1	24.2
Chicago SMSA	76.0	9.9	81.2	8.2	98.3	8.1	114.4	8.1	50.5	24.1
Los Angeles SMSA	(22.8)	3.0	33.0	3.3	45.4	3.7	52.7	3.7	131.1	50.9
Philadelphia SMSA	26.9	3.5	36.7	3.7	40.3	3.3	45.4	3.2	68.8	16.6
Detroit SMSA	63.5	8.2	75.9	7.7	89.6	7.4	102.0	7.2	60.6	12.4
San Francisco SMSA	(21.8)	2.8	23.2	2.3	30.5	2.5	34.8	2.5	59.6	38.6
Boston SMSA	(10.4)	1.4	27.8	2.8	35.5	2.9	36.5	2.6	251.0	23.4
Pittsburgh SMSA	34.6	4.5	42.8	4.3	42.8	3.5	48.3	3.4	39.6	6.0
St. Louis SMSA	(17.4)	2.3	21.2	2.1	25.5	2.1	27.4	1.9	57.5	28.5
Washington SMSA	4.9	.6	6.9	.7	13.1	1.1	15.5	1.1	216.3	63.3
Cleveland SMSA	16.3	2.1	21.0	2.1	25.0	2.1	25.6	1.8	57.1	24.2
Minn.–St. Paul SMSA	14.5	1.9	19.8	2.0	23.4	1.9	32.9	2.3	126.9	50.6
Houston SMSA	9.5	1.2	15.3	1.5	18.6	1.5	25.9	1.8	172.6	71.9
Milwaukee SMSA	(6.7)	.9	7.4	.7	9.5	.8	13.1	.9	95.5	40.7
Dallas SMSA	9.4	1.2	12.6	1.3	15.1	1.2	16.8	1.2	78.7	99.2
Cincinnati SMSA	(5.7)	.7	9.5	1.0	13.2	1.1	15.7	1.1	175.4	18.6
Kansas City SMSA	8.5	1.1	10.1	1.0	12.3	1.0	14.4	1.0	69.4	43.1
Atlanta SMSA	6.6	.9	8.5	.9	11.9	1.0	16.3	1.2	147.0	76.0
Wilmington SMSA	15.3	2.0	17.6	1.8	18.2	1.5	21.1	1.5	37.9	39.4
Total SCAs and SMSAs	533.9	69.2	672.7	68.2	800.7	66.0	925.3	65.3	73.3	29.3

Sources: U.S. Census, *Enterprise Statistics: 1963 and 1967*, Part 2; U.S. Bureau of Labor Statistics, *Employment and Earnings*, 1968.
Notes: Detail may not add to totals because of rounding. Bracketed () data are estimated. Data for 1967 are preliminary and contain, for the first time, CAO&A reportings of the construction industry in addition to the regularly reported minerals, manufacturing, and business groups. The two data series are not strictly comparable over the period because of areal redefinition of the selected metropolitan areas. Data for CAO&A are based upon areal definitions as of 1964. Nonagricultural employment estimates are based upon metropolitan area definitions as of date of estimation.

Table 2.4. Growth of CAO&A Employment as a Share of Total Nonagricultural Employment in Major Metropolitan Areas, 1954–1967

	CAO&A as % of nonagr. employ.			
	1954	1958	1963	1967
United States	1.6%	1.9%	2.1%	2.1%
New York–N.E. N.J. SCA	3.0	3.6	3.9	4.2
New York SMSA	3.3	4.0	4.0	4.1
Newark SMSA	3.3	3.8	4.4	4.3
Paterson SMSA	1.4	1.4	2.5	3.4
Chicago–N.W. Ind. SCA	3.1	3.2	3.7	3.7
Chicago SMSA	3.2	3.4	3.9	3.9
Los Angeles SMSA	1.3	1.6	1.9	2.0
Philadelphia SMSA	1.8	2.5	2.7	2.7
Detroit SMSA	5.1	6.7	7.4	7.2
San Francisco SMSA	2.6	2.6	3.0	3.0
Boston SMSA	1.1	2.7	3.2	3.0
Pittsburgh SMSA	4.4	5.5	5.8	5.8
St. Louis SMSA	2.6	3.0	3.4	3.1
Washington SMSA	.8	1.0	1.5	1.5
Cleveland SMSA	2.5	3.1	3.6	3.1
Minn.–St. Paul SMSA	3.0	3.8	3.9	4.6
Houston SMSA	2.5	3.5	3.5	4.0
Milwaukee SMSA	1.7	1.7	2.0	2.4
Dallas SMSA	3.4	3.6	3.4	3.0
Cincinnati SMSA	1.4	2.4	3.3	3.3
Kansas City SMSA	2.5	2.7	2.9	3.0
Atlanta SMSA	2.2	2.5	2.8	3.1
Wilmington SMSA	12.0	12.9	12.2	11.9
Total SCAs and SMSAs	2.7	3.3	3.6	3.6

Sources: U.S. Census, *Enterprise Statistics: 1963 and 1967*, Part 2; U.S. Bureau of Labor Statistics, *Employment and Earnings*, 1968.

tween 1954 and 1967, the former reduced their share of the nation's central administrative jobs from 69 to 65 percent, and the latter from 20.8 to 18.7 percent. However, about 3 million additional central administrative jobs can be expected in the nation by the year 2000. Even with continually declining shares, the top 21 areas could expect an increment of nearly 2 million, of which more than 400,000 would go to the New York SCA; this would imply more than a doubling of its present number of central administrative jobs. These jobs necessarily represent only a portion of front office activity as other industries, excluded from CAO&A census review, generate detached administrative offices of national market scope.

How does central administrative employment relate to total employment in each of the metropolitan areas? In the largest ones, such as New York, Chicago, and Los Angeles, a generally slow, but steady, increase in central administrative employment as a share of total employment can be observed, as Table 2.4 and Figure 2.2 show. Pretty much the same holds true for the next largest group in terms of central administrative employment—Pittsburgh, Minneapolis, Boston, San Francisco, and Philadelphia—even though in the recent decade, they seem to have maintained more of a stable share. Surprisingly, metropolitan areas in the next lower group, such as St. Louis, Cleveland, and Dallas, experienced declines in central administrative employment as a share of total employment. Lastly, the smallest concentrations of central administrative employment, such as Cincinnati, Atlanta, Kansas City, and Milwaukee, were also those where it grew, as a share of the total, at the most vigorous rate.[5]

While it is conventionally believed that a certain "critical mass" in central office employment must be achieved before a self-sustaining, or self-attracting, growth in headquarters firms takes hold, the size of a metropolitan area is only one variable among several contributing to this development. Office activity is a hybrid of many industries; it not only directs the production of the raw material and goods-handling sectors but also represents the production of many of the finance and service functions of the economy. Major industries experience differing rates of national and regional growth; further complicated by dissimilar propensities to generate office employment, the peculiar mix of industries in a region's economy may prove advantageous or limiting to the growth of office activity.

5. Some metropolitan areas, excluded from analysis by their present share in national CAO&A employment, will undergo the substantial growth in population and other activities which serves to attract a rapidly expanding base of CAO&A employment. It is unlikely, however, that they will surpass the selected grouping which will grow in absolute terms and continue to house the major share of national headquarters activity.

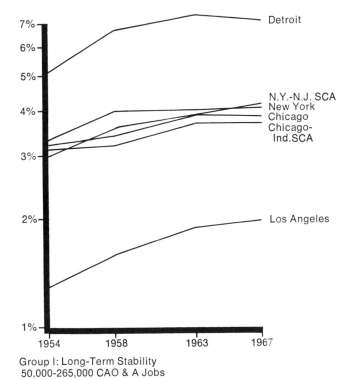

Group I: Long-Term Stability
50,000-265,000 CAO & A Jobs

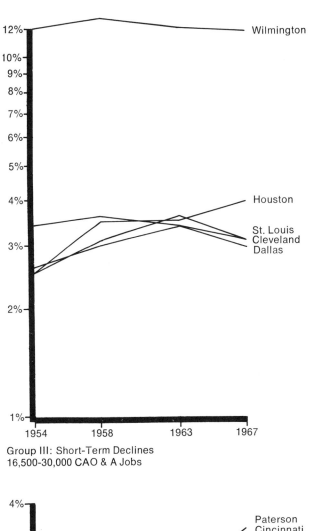

Group III: Short-Term Declines
16,500-30,000 CAO & A Jobs

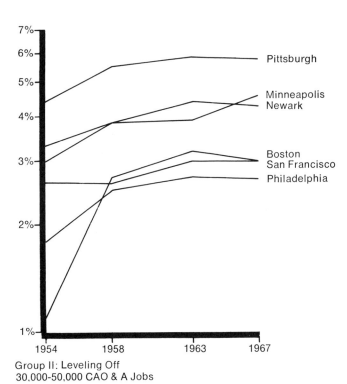

Group II: Leveling Off
30,000-50,000 CAO & A Jobs

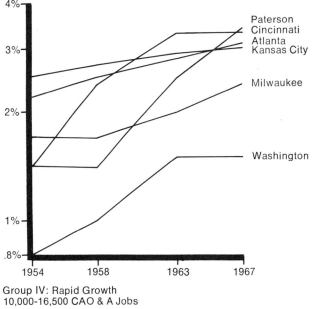

Group IV: Rapid Growth
10,000-16,500 CAO & A Jobs

Figure 2.2 Growth in headquarters employment as a share of total employment in metropolitan areas

Table 2.5. Industry Composition of CAO&A Employment in the Nation and the Major Metropolitan Areas, 1954, 1958, 1963, 1967 (in thousands)

Year	Manufacturing			Nonmanufacturing		
	Total jobs	Interim change		Total jobs	Interim change	
		Absolute	%		Absolute	%
The nation						
1954	451.2			320.0		
1958	602.2	+150.9	33.5%	384.8	+64.7	20.2%
1963	726.5	124.3	20.6	486.9	102.2	26.6
1967	829.5	103.1	14.2	586.5	99.6	20.5
The SCAs and SMSAs						
1954	325.7			208.2		
1958	430.4	+104.7	32.1%	242.3	+34.1	16.4%
1963	493.9	63.4	14.7	306.9	64.6	26.6
1967	558.9	65.0	13.2	366.4	59.5	19.4

Source: U.S. Census, *Enterprise Statistics: 1963 and 1967*, Part 2.
Notes: Detail may not add to totals because of rounding. See footnote in Table 2.3 for qualifications of data.

Trends in Headquarters Activity by Industry

In the nation as a whole, about three-fifths of the central administrative employment belongs to manufacturing industries, and two-fifths to nonmanufacturing. Since 1958, however, administrative nonmanufacturing jobs have been growing at a faster rate, so that in absolute numbers, the two sectors are increasing about equally. The de-emphasis of manufacturing in the national growth of administrative activity began during the late 1950s, with the successive years showing a steadily declining absolute volume of this employment being generated by the production sector while nonmanufacturing CAO&A expanded on a somewhat erratically enlarging course, shown in Table 2.5.

In the major SMSAs there has been an even stronger shift favoring the growth of central offices that belong to nonmanufacturing industries over those that belong to manufacturing (Figure 2.3). Through the mid-1950s, the group of 21 metropolitan areas being considered here captured only 53 percent of the nation's growth in nonmanufacturing central administrative jobs. In 1958–1963, this share jumped to 63 percent and then settled down to 60 percent in the most recent 1963–1967 period. Nonmanufacturing central administrative employment climbed from 36 percent of all CAO&A jobs in these metropolitan areas to 40 percent between 1958 and 1967. Pretty much the opposite has been happening to central administrative jobs in manufacturing industries.

Between 1954 and 1958, the selected metropolitan areas captured over 69 percent of the nation's increment in administrative jobs in manufacturing. In 1958–1963 this share declined to 51 percent, and even though it rebounded to 63 percent in 1963–1967, it is doubtful that most of these large metropolitan areas will fully reacquire their former attractiveness as locations for new manufacturing administrative activity.

In fact, it appears that within metropolitan areas, growth rates of manufacturing headquarters employment decline as the size of the area increases. As Table 2.6 shows, many of the smaller SMSAs, those that experienced the fastest growth rates in central office employment, expanded a heretofore underrepresented sector of their employment, while the larger SMSAs had slow rates of growth or even declines in manufacturing headquarters jobs. A notable exception to this pattern is the New York standard consolidated area (SCA).

Although the New York SCA enlarged its nonmanufacturing administrative base significantly between 1963 and 1967, it differed from other large metropolitan areas in a strong companion growth of manufacturing CAO&A employment. Part of the New York Region's manufacturing office growth is attributable to increases in the smaller metropolitan and nonmetropolitan areas that lie within the confines of its SCA, but a substantial part is due to the rather unique gains made by the New York SMSA. As Table 2.6 shows, Detroit and Pittsburgh may also be said to have gained exceptionally in manufacturing CAO&A jobs over the recent period, but the heterogeneity of the New York area's mix of manufacturing offices, as contrasted with the more narrow industry profile of Detroit and Pittsburgh, conveys the singular export status of the New York manufacturing office concentration.

Summarizing recent location trends of central administrative employment by size of metropolitan area, we can see that

1. Of the 1958–1967 national increment in manufacturing CAO&A jobs, 44 percent went to all the areas of generally less than 1 million, 39 percent to those of the 21 metropolitan areas located outside the New York SCA, and 17 percent to the New York SCA.

2. Of the 1958–1967 national increment in nonmanufacturing CAO&A jobs, 39 percent went to the smaller urban areas, 48 percent to the larger areas outside the New York SCA, and 13 percent to the New York SCA.

It appears that manufacturing administrative jobs are either decentralizing gently to smaller metropolitan areas, in the wake of their production plants or, if they have to be centralized, prefer to locate in or near New York. Most large metropolitan areas outside New York seem to hold little appeal for the expansion of central offices in manufacturing. To compensate, these areas, notably Chicago, Los Angeles, and Philadelphia, are capturing the fast-growing nonmanufacturing administrative employment.

Headquarters Composition by Geographic Area

Twenty-one major metropolitan areas contain two-thirds of the national CAO&A employment in manufacturing. However, the census data that present this index of headquarters activity do not break it down industry by industry for each of the metropolitan areas. Rather, industrial detail is given only for nine broad multistate regions, seven of which, those with headquarters metropolitan areas, are shown in Table 2.7. If one assumes that the industrial composition of manufacturing headquarters activity in the individual metropolitan areas is not too different from that of the broader multistate regions in which they are located, the data in Table 2.7 shed some light on the type of headquarters located in the different metropolitan areas. The table shows the regions, ranked by size of CAO&A employment in manufacturing, their degree of specialization, measured by the relative dominance of the largest two industry groups in each case, and the share of each region's CAO&A manufacturing employment that is located within the metropolitan areas in question.

Quite plausibly, it appears that the largest region—that

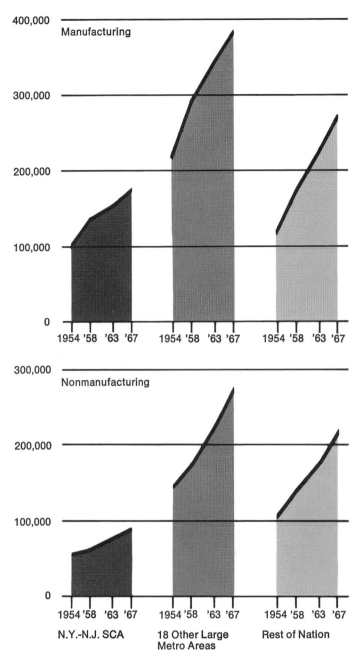

Figure 2.3 Growth of headquarters employment by industry by size of metropolitan area, 1954–1967

Table 2.6. Growth in Manufacturing and Nonmanufacturing Employment in CAO&A Units in Major Metropolitan Areas, 1958–1967

| | 1958–1963 | | | | 1963–1967 | | | |
| | Growth rate 1958–1963 | | Share of nation's growth | | Growth rate 1963–1967 | | Share of nation's growth | |
	Mfg.	Nonmfg.	Mfg.	Nonmfg.	Mfg.	Nonmfg.	Mfg.	Nonmfg.
United States	20.6%	26.6%	100.0%	100.0%	14.2%	20.5%	100.0%	100.0%
New York–N.E. N.J. SCA	12.3	21.6	13.5	13.5	14.0	16.5	20.8	12.9
New York SMSA	3.4	12.7	3.0	6.8	9.2	10.6	10.1	6.6
Newark SMSA	34.7	.0	5.3	.0	1.6	49.8	.4	2.2
Paterson SMSA	156.4	64.9	2.8	1.6	66.2	39.4	3.7	1.7
Chicago–N.W. Ind. SCA	18.9	22.1	6.9	8.2	7.4	25.1	3.9	11.7
Chicago SMSA	20.4	21.9	7.1	8.1	8.8	24.9	4.4	11.6
Los Angeles SMSA	12.8	61.3	1.6	10.2	3.3	24.2	.6	6.7
Philadelphia SMSA	5.7	15.3	1.0	2.2	4.6	23.7	1.0	4.1
Detroit SMSA	14.7	33.8	7.4	4.5	11.0	24.9	7.6	4.5
San Francisco SMSA	27.9	38.0	3.2	3.4	−5.9	42.9	*	5.4
Boston SMSA	20.0	42.2	2.9	4.1	−2.6	11.2	*	1.6
Pittsburgh SMSA	−2.4	12.4	*	.8	16.9	−4.5	5.7	*
St. Louis SMSA	13.8	31.3	1.5	2.4	13.4	−1.1	2.0	*
Washington SMSA	235.3	65.9	1.8	3.9	−37.3	35.4	*	3.5
Cleveland SMSA	20.9	13.9	2.5	.9	.5	7.2	.1	.5
Minn.–St. Paul SMSA	28.8	4.7	2.6	.4	58.9	13.3	8.1	1.2
Houston SMSA	53.8	10.5	1.7	1.2	84.4	17.7	4.9	2.2
Milwaukee SMSA	32.1	23.6	1.2	.6	49.9	15.4	2.9	.5
Dallas SMSA	−11.6	36.3	*	3.0	31.8	3.8	1.2	.4
Cincinnati SMSA	41.3	31.6	2.2	.9	18.1	22.8	1.7	.8
Kansas City SMSA	43.1	13.3	1.0	1.0	4.0	23.3	.2	1.9
Atlanta SMSA	173.0	20.2	1.5	1.5	85.2	21.5	2.4	1.9
Wilmington SMSA	−1.1	287.6	*	.8	15.7	21.9	2.6	.2
Total SCAs and SMSAs	14.7	26.6	51.0	63.2	13.2	19.4	63.1	59.8

Source: U.S. Census, *Enterprise Statistics: 1963 and 1967*, Part 2.
Notes: Detail may not add to totals because of rounding. (*) Indicates declining absolute employment. 1967 data are preliminary and contain, for the first time, CAO&A reportings of the construction industry in addition to the regularly reported minerals, manufacturing, and business groups. All data based on 1964 areal definition of selected metropolitan areas.

containing New York, Philadelphia, and Pittsburgh—is also the most diversified: its two largest headquarters employers, the electrical machinery and chemical industries, account for only 36.2 percent of its total CAO&A employment in manufacturing. By contrast, one of the smaller regions—that containing Houston and Dallas—is the most specialized: its two top headquarters employers, the petroleum and chemical industries, account for 80.2 percent of its total CAO&A employment in manufacturing. However, the East North Central region, containing Chicago, and the New England region, even though very different in size, appear about equally diversified: the two top industries account for about 42 percent of their total CAO&A employment in manufacturing. In the former case the top two are transportation equipment (mostly motor vehicles) and nonelectrical machinery, in the latter electrical machinery and transportation equipment (mostly aircraft engines). Of the remaining regions, the West North Central, the Pacific, and the South Atlantic, in that order, are progressively more specialized in the composition of their manufacturing headquarters activity, but in none of them do the top two industries account for more than half of all headquarters employment.

Generally (and with the exception of New York), there is a fairly close correspondence between the industrial composition of all manufacturing jobs in a broad geographic region and the industrial composition of central administrative manufacturing jobs. This is so because historically headquarters activity in manufacturing was often initiated and developed in a region by the major goods producer. Thus it is that we find a single producer, or a set of competitive producers, such as the petrochemical firms in the South, dominating the central office function.

However, a basic precept of long-term growth in office activity in a region would seem to be, aside from the scope of its market area, balance and diversity in the composition of its office employment. A well-balanced central office sector not only can weather the fluctuations in demand or the effects of automation within a single industry's operation but can also extend greater support to a broad-based mix of ancillary business services.

While diversity in types of headquarters employment best prepares an area to accommodate new growth and support ancillary activity, certain present-day benefits, nevertheless, do arise from specialization. Metropolitan areas most dominated in their central office and related sector by a few manufacturing industry groups usually contain firms with the largest employment. Quite often, the massive office requirements of such industries place their SMSAs among the leaders when ranked by share of CAO&A activity in total employment. These measures are only partially indicative, however, since CAO&A

Table 2.7. Manufacturing Headquarters Specialization in Multistate Regions, 1963

Region and metropolitan areas contained in it	Region's share of national CAO&A employ. in mfg.	Dominance of the hdqrs. sector by two top industries	Share of region's CAO&A mfg. employ. located in metropolitan areas listed
Middle Atlantic (New York SCA, Philadelphia, Pittsburgh)	34.0%	36.2% (electrical machinery, chemicals)	80.2%
East North Central (Chicago SCA, Detroit, Cleveland, Cincinnati, Milwaukee)	28.9	41.8 (transportation equipment, nonelectrical machinery)	72.2
Pacific (Los Angeles, San Francisco)	8.0	47.1 (petroleum, food)	68.1
South Atlantic (Washington, Atlanta, Wilmington)	7.9	47.4 (chemicals, petroleum)	40.9
West South Central (Houston, Dallas)	6.1	80.2 (petroleum, chemicals)	37.2
West North Central (St. Louis, Minn.–St. Paul, Kansas City)	5.8	43.1 (food, petroleum)	85.0
New England (Boston)	5.7	41.7 (Electrical machinery, transportation equipment)	46.9

Source: U.S. Census, *Enterprise Statistics: 1963*, Part 2.
Note: Data in columns two and three are for employees classified by industry category of owning company, in column four by industry category of establishments serviced.

Table 2.8. Characteristics of Employment in Central Administrative Offices and Auxiliary Units in Major Headquarters Metropolitan Areas, 1963

	Average jobs per CAO&A estab.	Share of nonagr. employ. in CAO&A	Share of CAO&A employ. in mfg.	Speciali- zation of mfg. hdqrs. employ.*	CAO† (×1,000)	CAO as a % of CAO&A
United States	69	2.1%	59.9%		838.5	69.1%
New York–N.E. N.J.						
SCA	103	3.9	66.4	19.0%	178.3	77.2
New York SMSA	101	4.0	64.7	18.0	153.0	87.5
Newark SMSA	128	4.4	85.2	57.0	11.0	36.6
Paterson SMSA	76	2.5	57.3	33.0	5.6	56.2
Chicago–N.W. Ind.						
SCA	101	3.7	53.6	26.0	70.3	70.4
Chicago SMSA	102	3.9	53.0	26.0	70.1	71.3
Los Angeles SMSA	58	1.9	39.6	25.0	34.2	75.3
Philadelphia SMSA	93	2.7	57.1	25.0	28.8	71.6
Detroit SMSA	229	7.4	79.9	47.0	53.5	59.7
San Francisco SMSA	60	3.0	59.1	29.0	23.5	76.8
Boston SMSA	100	3.2	60.4	20.0	19.8	55.9
Pittsburgh SMSA	149	5.8	81.8	39.0	27.2	63.6
St. Louis SMSA	90	3.4	60.3	29.0	18.1	71.2
Washington SMSA	50	1.5	23.7	—	7.1	54.1
Cleveland SMSA	90	3.6	70.7	29.0	17.8	71.2
Minn.–St. Paul SMSA	88	3.9	60.7	50.0	18.2	77.9
Houston SMSA	77	3.5	32.5	67.0	14.4	77.4
Milwaukee SMSA	78	2.0	63.5	50.0	7.0	73.7
Dallas SMSA	49	3.4	25.2	50.0	11.8	78.2
Cincinnati SMSA	88	3.3	72.1	50.0	8.9	67.4
Kansas City SMSA	49	2.9	32.5	50.0	9.3	75.3
Atlanta SMSA	47	2.8	24.9	—	8.8	74.2
Wilmington SMSA	405	12.2	94.1	67.0	9.3	50.9
Total SCAs and SMSAs	95	3.6	61.7		566.3	70.7

Sources: U.S. Census, *Enterprise Statistics: 1963*, Part 2; "The Fortune Directory," 1964.
* Percentage of manufacturing headquarters in one major industry group as reported by *Fortune*.
† Includes central administration, direct sales to customers, and trading stamp redemption offices.

activity does not represent all headquarters employment generated by all industry groups.

Table 2.8 presents further data on CAO&A characteristics by SMSA. Detroit and Pittsburgh, two large specialized areas, rank second and third in average employment per office establishment and in share of central office and related activity in their total employment. The small and highly specialized Wilmington area ranks first. However, as was earlier shown in Table 2.2, these areas are weak exporters of overall office activity. It is quite likely that the large specialized firms in Detroit and Pittsburgh internalize and import ancillary types of office activity. The New York SCA, on the other hand, combines its highly diversified headquarters sector with a high ranking in average firm size (fourth in the metropolitan distribution), a strong placement of CAO&A activity in its total employment structure (fourth in order), and a strong indication of the exportation of office activity (second in rank).

"Elite" Headquarters Location

An alternative way of analyzing office activity in view of the incomplete nature of CAO&A data consists of examining the locational preferences of "elite" office employers. By taking into account the financial power of resident corporations, their varying product mixes, and the growth and development of major offices in industries not reported in CAO&A statistics, a more complete picture of office activity may be formed. Elite firms with their massive office complexes make an exceptional contribution to the creation of an environment which is amenable to the success of smaller firms in the same, related, or supporting industries.

Fortune magazine annually lists the top 500 industrials by location of the firms' headquarters. Ranking them by sales, it cites each firm's corporate assets, net profit, invested capital, and number of employees for the preceding year. While "the 500" represent merely a fraction of one percent of all industrial corporations in the nation, they consistently account for more than half of the total sales and nearly three-fourths of the profits earned each year. In 1965, for instance, they directed the efforts of 11.3 million workers, a major share of the nation's employment in manufacturing and mining.[6]

Our selected group of SMSAs provided locations for 348 headquarters, or 70 percent of the 1965 total. This 70 percent share is slightly in excess of the group's com-

6. The subsequent discussion of trends in the *Fortune* headquarters listing will focus, for the most part, on activity over the period 1958 to 1965. This period, and more particularly the year 1963 which corresponds with a census benchmark, was the time frame chosen for initial research. For publication purposes, we have updated the series with inclusion of data for 1969. The reader will note that the same general trends are evident over the extended period.

parable share of CAO&A employment.[7] Table 2.9 outlines the current distribution of elite headquarters and indicates changes over the recent period. These data buttress our earlier finding showing a slight tendency for manufacturing front offices to move out of the major metropolitan areas.[8]

In 1963, the New York SCA was the home of the head offices of 33 percent of the "top 500" firms, accounting for 38 percent of their sales and roughly 40 percent of their assets, net profit, and invested capital. (The New York Region, which encompasses considerable land area outside of the SCA, contained 34 percent of the firms.) Chicago, Detroit, and Pittsburgh together housed the head offices of only 17 percent of the "top 500" industrial firms, and accounted for 27 percent of their sales. Thirteen other metropolitan areas housed 24 percent of the firms, and accounted for 18 percent of the sales. The remaining 26 percent of the firms, with 18 percent of the sales, were located in small metropolitan areas, generally under 1 million in population. Thus, the largest firms seem to have an affinity for each other and for a few selected large metropolitan areas. There is also an affinity for firms dealing in the same product to cluster together.

However, between 1958 and 1969 the number of "elite" industrial firms headquartered in the largest metropolitan areas—with the one exception of Los Angeles—declined somewhat, notably in Chicago, Philadelphia, Detroit, and especially Pittsburgh. This trend paralleled their sluggish growth in central administrative employment. The New York SCA also declined, while the New York Region held its own; the major changes between 1963 and 1965, however, are attributable to mergers and not to an exodus of firms from the area. In the meantime, some cities in the middle range, such as Minneapolis and Milwaukee, increased their share.

One should note that trends in the geographic distribution of headquarters are somewhat obscured not only by mergers and acquisitions within the industries, but also by other limitations of the *Fortune* data. For instance, between 1958 and 1965, the sales volume of the cutoff firm (the 500th corporation) rose from $62 to $110 million, a 77 percent increase. Many firms, however, did not experience a growth in sales commensurate with the growth of the aggregate group and thus were eliminated from the *Fortune* listing. The "dropped" firms were then replaced by rapidly gaining firms previously

7. While the degree of concentration may be roughly comparable in the aggregate here, disparities appear between such measures of office intensity when one examines particular SMSAs.
8. It must be noted that, in the instance of *Fortune* data, one is dealing with an arbitrarily defined "establishment" which includes branch and other out-of-town operations. This arises from an allocation of firm, that is, establishment employment to an SMSA based on sales alone.

Table 2.9. The Location of Headquarters for the Largest Industrial Corporations 1958, 1963, 1965, 1969

	Corporate headquarters				CAO&A establishments *	
	1958	1963	1965	1969	1963	% in corp. hdqrs.
United States	500	500	500	500	17,569	2.8%
New York–N.E. N.J. SCA	151	163	151	148	2,246	7.3
New York SMSA	142	147	137	131	1,738	8.5
Newark SMSA	4	7	7	7	235	3.0
Paterson SMSA	3	6	3	7	131	4.6
Chicago–N.W. Ind. SCA	50	50	48	49	987	5.1
Chicago SMSA	50	50	48	49	965	5.2
Los Angeles SMSA	17	16	14	21	780	2.1
Philadelphia SMSA	17	16	16	14	431	3.7
Detroit SMSA	16	15	15	13	392	3.8
San Francisco SMSA	13	12	12	11	512	2.3
Boston SMSA	7	10	9	9	355	2.8
Pittsburgh SMSA	23	22	22	14	287	7.7
St. Louis SMSA	14	14	12	10	282	5.0
Washington SMSA	—	—	—	1	264	—
Cleveland SMSA	15	14	16	17	276	5.1
Minn.–St. Paul SMSA	7	10	10	11	264	3.8
Houston SMSA	1	3	2	2	242	1.2
Milwaukee SMSA	6	8	10	11	122	6.6
Dallas SMSA	6	6	5	7	306	2.0
Cincinnati SMSA	4	4	4	4	149	2.7
Kansas City SMSA	3	2	2	2	251	.8
Atlanta SMSA	—	—	1	3	252	—
Wilmington SMSA	4	3	3	3	45	6.7
Total SCAs and SMSAs	354	368	352	350	8,443	4.4

Sources: "The Fortune Directory," 1959, 1964, 1966, and 1970; U.S. Census, *Enterprise Statistics: 1963*, Part 2.
Notes: Excludes large privately owned companies that do not publish sales. All 500 companies must qualify by deriving 50% of their revenues from mining or manufacturing for fiscal years ending not later than December 31 of year stated.
* Total central administrative offices and auxiliaries.

Table 2.10. Metropolitan Areas with Major Corporate Headquarters Locations: Their Share of the Nation's Top 500 Industrials and Their Corporate Wealth, 1963

	Hdqrs.	Sales	Assets	Net profit	Invested capital	Employees
United States	100.0%	100.0%	100.0%	100.0%	100.0%	100.0%
New York–N.E. N.J. SCA	32.6	37.8	41.5	40.4	41.0	38.0
New York SMSA	29.4	36.4	40.2	39.0	39.5	36.5
Newark SMSA	1.4	.5	.4	.6	.5	.5
Paterson SMSA	1.2	.6	.7	.7	.7	.7
Chicago–N.W. Ind. SCA	10.0	8.3	7.1	5.3	7.3	7.2
Chicago SMSA	10.0	8.3	7.1	5.3	7.3	7.2
Los Angeles SMSA	3.2	3.7	3.0	2.4	2.6	3.2
Philadelphia SMSA	3.2	1.9	2.0	2.0	2.3	1.7
Detroit SMSA	3.0	13.4	10.3	16.2	10.0	12.7
San Francisco SMSA	2.4	2.1	3.3	3.1	3.4	1.8
Boston SMSA	2.0	.7	.7	.6	.6	1.1
Pittsburgh SMSA	4.4	4.9	6.3	5.2	6.6	4.8
St. Louis SMSA	2.8	1.9	1.7	1.5	1.6	2.1
Washington SMSA	—	—	—	—	—	—
Cleveland SMSA	2.8	1.9	1.8	1.5	1.9	2.1
Minn.–St. Paul SMSA	2.0	1.4	1.0	1.2	1.0	1.3
Houston SMSA	.6	.6	.9	.7	.8	.2
Milwaukee SMSA	1.6	.6	.6	.3	.6	.8
Dallas SMSA	1.2	.6	.4	.3	.3	.9
Cincinnati SMSA	.8	.8	.7	.9	.7	.6
Kansas City SMSA	.4	.2	.1	.1	.1	.1
Atlanta SMSA	—	—	—	—	—	—
Wilmington SMSA	.6	1.3	1.6	3.4	2.1	1.2
Total SCAs and SMSAs	73.6	82.0	82.9	85.0	82.9	79.7

Source: "The Fortune Directory," 1964.
Notes: Detail may not add to totals because of rounding. Includes sales of subsidiaries when they are consolidated. Includes service and rental revenues of industrial corporations. Excludes excise taxes collected by manufacturer.

excluded. Quite often, the rapid gainers were located outside the selected metropolitan areas. Moreover, other headquarters were dropped from the listing because in changing their product mix they fell below (or above) the required share of revenues derived from manufacturing/mining which qualifies *Fortune* "industrials." Despite these caveats, the data in Table 2.9 are of interest.

Comparing the distribution of the 500 series with CAO&A statistics, one observes, in both cases, a positive correlation between participation in elite headquarters functions and the size of metropolitan area. The New York metropolitan area stands at the apex of this relationship, having 8 percent of its detached central administrative and auxiliary units listed among the major corporate offices.[9] New York's office specialization, as measured by corporate headquarters and CAO&A establishments, is roughly three times the national average of 2.8 percent. Interestingly, however, New York's degree of specialization is not representative of office activity in the other metropolitan areas characterized by office-type economies. Indeed, the companion areas with higher than average shares of major corporate establishments in the central office sectors rightfully belong among those we previously cited as production centers (such as Chicago, Detroit, and Pittsburgh).

Table 2.10 presents a summary by metropolitan area of the financial reportings of the corporations listed among *Fortune*'s 500. While the data are not to be interpreted as representing wealth or employment generated within an area by location of corporate headquarters, they are suggestive of the control of the nation's production capacity stemming from the administrative office sector of respective areas. Though disproportionate shares of major corporations seek large urban environs for the location of their administrative facilities, an even greater share of the nation's largest, most prosperous firms are headquartered in the selected metropolitan areas. Seventy-three percent of the front offices in the SMSAs earned 82 percent of the group's total sales and 85 percent of net profits, while controlling 83 percent of assets and invested capital. The most prosperous of the giant firms appear to be highly selective in their locational choice. Two metropolitan areas, New York and Detroit, more than account for the aggregate discrepancy between shares in headquarters location and financial power. Both have an above average share of the nation's sales leaders (a combined 50 percent of the top "500" sales), though corporate offices in New York outnumber those in Detroit roughly ten to one.

9. Because of the insufficiency of published data, we are restricted from analyzing the share of corporate headquarters in a more proper framework, central administrative offices in mining and manufacturing.

Of the 500 industrial corporations cited by *Fortune,* 90 recorded sales in excess of $600 million in 1963, 72 of which were located in our SMSA group.[10] Table 2.11 presents the relevant data. They suggest that major sales leaders have an apparent locational affinity for one another. Nearly half of the group's participation is represented by corporate locations in the New York area. Chicago, the second ranking area, contains only one-fourth of the elite headquarters activity of New York, while the Detroit area, with its command of corporate sales, has one-seventh the firm locations of New York. In New York, moreover, most of the region's sales leaders are located within a few blocks of one another in midtown Manhattan. This locational phenomenon reinforces one's general impression that the Manhattan CBD is a key source of the region's attractiveness, but it also suggests that the quality of "nearness" extends clear through to the microscale.

Corporate affinity manifests in yet another form. A tendency exists for the elite sales sector of a metropolitan area to be dominated by headquarters administering the production of like goods and generally the major goods produced in the area. For instance, four of the five sales leaders in the Detroit area are automotive producers, while three out of four headquarters in Los Angeles administer aerospace enterprises. New York is an exception to this tendency, however. Here the sales leaders are unique in the diversity of product mix. They are drawn from fifteen industrial sectors and represent, in many cases, administrative units that are far removed from the place of production.

Major headquarters activity in nonmanufacturing industry groups may well be judged the dominant growth sector of central office activity for metropolitan areas in the future. As we have seen, the selected trade and service industries reporting central administrative offices and auxiliaries have grown over the past two periods at a nationwide rate that exceeds manufacturing offices, while the major metropolitan areas have enjoyed a still stronger shift to this sector, being the preferred locations for such activity. These trends are further enforced by the changing overall composition of employment, in which the predominance of the goods-handling function is yielding to that of servicing industries, and by significant alterations taking place within the manufacturing sector. We have witnessed a long-term concentration of goods production in the corporate hands of relatively

10. The cutoff determination of $600 million annual sales was chosen to isolate strong CBD headquarter candidates, based upon the findings of an unpublished dissertation which analyzed postwar trends in manufacturing headquarters mobility. Lawrence Schwartz, *An Econometric Study of the Relocation of the Central Office and Its Workers,* thesis submitted in partial fulfillment of the Ph.D. requirement, Department of Economics, Harvard University, 1963.

Table 2.11. The Headquarters Location of the Nation's Industrial Corporations with Sales over $600 Million, 1963

	Hdqrs. with sales over $600 million	As a percentage of			% of sales leaders in largest industry
		Fortune's 500 hdqrs.	Hdqrs. with sales over $600 million	*Fortune*'s 500 located in the metropolitan areas	
United States	90	18.0%	100.0%	18.0%	14%
New York–N.E. N.J. SCA	36	7.2	40.0	22.1	19
New York SMSA	35	7.0	38.9	23.8	20
Newark SMSA	—	—	—	—	—
Paterson SMSA	1	.2	1.1	16.7	100
Chicago–N.W. Ind. SCA	8	1.6	8.9	16.0	50
Chicago SMSA	8	1.6	8.9	16.0	50
Los Angeles SMSA	4	.8	4.4	25.0	75
Philadelphia SMSA	3	.6	3.3	18.8	67
Detroit SMSA	5	1.0	5.6	33.3	100
San Francisco SMSA	2	.4	2.2	16.7	50
Boston SMSA	—	—	—	—	—
Pittsburgh SMSA	6	1.2	6.7	27.3	50
St. Louis SMSA	2	.4	2.2	14.3	50
Washington SMSA	—	—	—	—	—
Cleveland SMSA	1	.2	1.1	7.1	100
Minn.–St. Paul SMSA	2	.4	2.2	20.0	50
Houston SMSA	1	.2	1.1	33.3	33
Milwaukee SMSA	—	—	—	—	—
Dallas SMSA	—	—	—	—	—
Cincinnati SMSA	1	.2	1.1	25.0	100
Kansas City SMSA	—	—	—	—	—
Atlanta SMSA	—	—	—	—	—
Wilmington SMSA	1	.2	1.1	25.0	100
Total SCAs and SMSAs	72	14.4	80.0	19.6	17

Source: "The Fortune Directory," 1964.
Note: Detail may not add to totals because of rounding.

few firms. Mergers, acquisitions, and conglomerations can effectively reduce the number of key headquarters locational decisions being made by manufacturers. Moreover, the manufacturing office sector, characterized by large establishment size, massive informational requirements, and a familiarity with production time-saving devices, emerges as an activity highly susceptible to a dampening of white-collar growth by the pervasive influence of electronic data processing.

Because of its great diversity, nonmanufacturing headquarters activity has tended to be overlooked as a growth sector. Severe data limitations have also discouraged researchers from dealing with this grouping properly. As a result, analyses of the major headquarters distributions of transportation, utilities, merchandising, insurance, banking, and other business classifications are too abbreviated. Even so, crude data often support theoretically based conclusions or suggest new insights. For instance, Table 2.12 shows the distribution of major nonmanufacturing headquarters by SMSA and by type of industry; it suggests that these activities locate their headquarters facilities in a more discrete pattern than do major industrial firms.

In transportation and utilities, it is apparent that, while both activities are linked to population, their headquarters operations are not directly linked to SMSA size. Though somewhat constrained by the scope of their service areas, transportation headquarters tend to cluster in centers that provide external economies. Thus, they favor historic break-of-bulk points such as New York, Chicago, and San Francisco. Production areas, on the other hand, are generally quite underrepresented. The New York area has the greatest concentration with one-fifth of the nation's top transportation companies, 90 percent of which are located in Manhattan.

The metropolitan listing of major utility headquarters consists primarily of firms with regional markets under regulation, though some offices are distinctly resource-based. The leading national-market utilities, such as American Telephone and Telegraph, are all located in the New York area. Together with the local utilities, the New York area contains 26 percent of the nation's top companies and the Manhattan CBD, 22 percent. Three of the nation's major radio and television broadcasting establishments are headquartered in New York, with annual receipts amounting to 84 percent of the industry's top sales. In the production and distribution of motion pictures, the New York area ranks first with six of the ten leading film companies (annual sales $800 million) locating here.

Major insurance headquarters display a lesser degree of preference for location in the top metropolitan areas. The selected SMSAs contain slightly over one-half of the fifty largest life insurers. But significantly, smaller regions such as Hartford or Omaha support disproportionately sized shares. Life insuring is a consumer-oriented business whose initial establishment was governed by state regulation and whose present location is more a function of historical decisions taken as to effective market location, than any current response to the rewards of interfirm communication or labor specialization of large metropolitan areas. Some national insurance firms have developed out of a local area's insurance needs, and, though considerably enlarged, they retain a historical preference for their original location. In general, the big life insurance firms are located in areas more oriented toward office economies than toward production. However, centers such as Newark and Philadelphia bear strong exception to this. The New York area contains slightly less than its average share of headquarters in the life insurance grouping, but it does better than the other SMSAs on our list.

Nearly all of the major merchandising firms are located in the selected SMSAs. Their locational decisions are perhaps guided more by market criteria than any other force, though externalities on their production side (for example, concentrations of buyers) may influence the firms' decision makers. Areas such as Cincinnati and Minneapolis–St. Paul share disproportionately in major retailing activities with respect to their population size. The New York area with 34 percent of the top fifty merchandisers is decidedly the nation's leader. This participation in national distribution is roughly proportional to New York's manufacturing headquarters share. The office components of major merchandising—department, food, and apparel stores, eating and drinking places, and miscellaneous retailing—are drawn to New York in different degrees. Two-thirds of major retail apparel establishments are headquartered in New York while one-third of the leading department stores and restaurant chains in the nation are New York based.

The fifty largest commercial banks, though more intensely concentrated in the selected areas than any other major office employer except merchandising firms, are tending to increase assets at a less rapid rate than the smaller urban area banks. This is largely attributable to the population growth in smaller metropolitan and suburban areas. In 1963, 86 percent of the top fifty banks were housed in our SMSAs; 66 percent were in the areas that also contained a branch of the Federal Reserve Bank. Twenty percent of the top fifty institutions were located in the New York area, with nine banks in Manhattan's financial district and one in the suburban ring, in 1965.

Of the top 300 commercial banks in the nation, 49 percent are located in the SCAs and SMSAs. Forty-eight major commercial banks are located in the entire New York Region and are, on average, more than twice as

Table 2.12. The Location of Major Nonmanufacturing Headquarters and of Miscellaneous Business Service Establishments in the Nation, 1958, 1963, 1965

	Transportation			Utilities			Life insurance			Merchandising			Commercial banks				Business services Miscellaneous		EDP†
	1958	1963	1965	1958	1963	1965	1958	1963	1965	1958	1963	1965	1958	1963	1965	1966*	1958	1963	1965
United States	50	50	50	50	50	50	50	50	50	50	50	50	50	50	50	300	113,920	147,670	217
New York–N.E. N.J. SCA	10	8	10	13	14	13	9	9	9	16	19	17	13	12	10	40	18,800	20,130	30
New York SMSA	10	8	10	12	13	12	7	7	7	15	16	16	13	12	10	26	15,700	16,160	19
Newark SMSA	—	—	—	1	1	1	2	2	2	—	—	—	—	—	—	5	1,540	1,930	2
Paterson SMSA	—	—	—	—	—	—	—	—	—	1	1	1	—	—	—	5	950	1,270	4
Chicago–N.W. Ind. SCA	8	8	8	2	2	3	2	2	2	8	9	9	4	4	4	27	6,100	7,790	9
Chicago SMSA	8	8	8	2	2	2	2	2	2	8	9	9	4	4	4	14	5,940	7,530	9
Los Angeles SMSA	—	2	2	1	1	1	2	2	—	3	—	1	2	3	3	6	9,250	11,680	13
Philadelphia SMSA	2	2	2	1	1	1	3	3	3	4	2	2	3	3	4	8	2,940	3,190	7
Detroit SMSA	—	—	—	1	1	1	—	—	—	1	2	2	3	3	3	9	2,650	3,490	9
San Francisco SMSA	4	5	5	2	2	2	—	—	—	1	3	3	6	4	4	8	3,680	4,480	7
Boston SMSA	1	—	—	2	1	1	2	2	2	2	2	2	1	1	1	5	2,560	2,880	9
Pittsburgh SMSA	—	—	—	1	—	—	—	—	—	1	1	1	2	2	2	5	1,110	1,410	2
St. Louis SMSA	3	3	2	1	1	1	1	1	1	1	1	1	2	2	2	4	1,380	1,650	3
Washington SMSA	1	1	1	1	1	1	1	1	1	—	—	—	—	—	—	5	1,840	2,310	4
Cleveland SMSA	3	3	3	1	1	—	—	—	—	—	—	—	3	3	3	5	1,620	2,100	3
Minn.–St. Paul SMSA	3	4	4	1	1	1	2	2	2	2	2	3	—	1	—	3	1,170	1,540	4
Houston SMSA	—	—	—	3	4	3	—	—	—	1	1	1	1	1	1	4	1,160	1,600	1
Milwaukee SMSA	—	—	—	1	1	1	1	1	1	—	—	—	1	1	1	3	870	1,170	1
Dallas SMSA	2	1	1	1	1	2	1	2	2	—	—	1	2	2	2	4	1,060	1,400	2
Cincinnati SMSA	—	—	—	—	—	—	2	2	2	2	2	2	—	—	—	4	670	980	2
Kansas City SMSA	1	—	—	—	—	—	1	1	1	1	1	1	—	—	—	3	850	1,020	1
Atlanta SMSA	1	1	1	1	1	1	—	—	—	1	1	1	—	1	1	3	740	1,090	3
Wilmington SMSA	—	—	—	1	1	1	—	—	—	—	—	—	—	—	—	2	230	240	—
Total SCAs and SMSAs	39	38	39	34	34	33	27	28	26	44	46	47	43	43	41	148	58,670	70,140	113

Sources: "The Fortune Directory," 1959, 1964, and 1966, for data on the 50 largest transportation, utilities, life insurance, merchandising, and commercial bank establishments; *American Banker*, 1966, for data on the 300 largest commercial banks; U.S. Census, *Census of Business: 1958 and 1963 Selected Services* for miscellaneous busin ss services; *Directory o Data Processing Service Centers, 1967*, for EDP establishments.

* The 300 largest commercial banks.

† Electronic data processing centers.

Table 2.13. The Location of 500 Leading National Nonmanufacturing Establishments* in Major Metropolitan Areas, 1966

	Agr.	Contr. constr.	RR transp.	Pass. transp. & serv.	Trucking	Shipping	Airlines	Tel. & tel.	Broadcasting radio & tv	Pub. util.	Whsle. trade	Dept. stores	Food stores
Part I. The Number of Establishments													
United States	7	12	23	3	17	3	25	9	8	40	76	61	51
New York–N.E. N.J. SCA	2	3	2	—	2	2	5	4	3	10	16	22	7
New York SMSA	1	3	2	—	1	2	5	3	3	9	15	20	6
Newark SMSA	—	—	—	—	1	—	—	1	—	1	—	—	—
Paterson SMSA	1	—	—	—	—	—	—	—	—	—	1	1	1
Chicago–N.W. Ind. SCA	—	—	5	1	1	—	1	—	—	3	13	7	1
Chicago SMSA	—	—	5	1	1	—	1	—	—	3	13	7	1
Los Angeles SMSA	—	1	—	—	1	—	3	—	1	2	7	1	3
Philadelphia SMSA	—	—	2	1	—	—	—	—	—	1	2	2	3
Detroit SMSA	—	—	—	—	—	—	—	—	—	2	1	2	2
San Francisco SMSA	1	1	1	—	2	1	1	—	—	2	—	2	4
Boston SMSA	1	1	—	—	—	—	1	—	—	3	1	1	1
Pittsburgh SMSA	—	1	—	—	—	—	—	—	—	—	1	1	1
St. Louis SMSA	—	—	2	—	—	—	1	—	—	1	2	1	—
Washington SMSA	—	—	1	—	—	—	1	—	—	—	1	3	—
Cleveland SMSA	—	1	2	—	1	—	—	—	—	—	4	2	2
Minn.–St. Paul SMSA	—	—	2	—	—	—	2	—	—	1	1	1	2
Houston SMSA	—	—	—	—	—	—	1	—	—	3	2	—	1
Milwaukee SMSA	—	—	—	—	—	—	—	—	—	—	1	—	—
Dallas SMSA	—	—	—	1	—	—	1	—	—	1	3	—	—
Cincinnati SMSA	—	—	—	—	—	—	—	—	—	—	—	1	1
Kansas City SMSA	—	—	—	—	1	—	1	1	—	—	1	1	1
Atlanta SMSA	—	—	—	—	—	—	1	—	1	1	2	1	2
Wilmington SMSA	—	—	—	—	—	—	—	—	1	—	—	—	—
Total SCAs and SMSAs	4	8	17	3	8	3	19	5	6	30	58	48	31

Part II. The Sales, Assets, or Deposits of Establishments

Sales of nonfinancial establishments in millions

	Agr.	Contr. constr.	RR transp.	Pass. transp. & serv.	Trucking	Shipping	Airlines	Tel. & tel.	Broadcasting radio & tv	Pub. util.	Whsle. trade	Dept. stores	Food stores
United States	$1,106.4	$1,458.5	$9,535.5	$743.1	$1,320.3	$419.0	$5,611.3	$13,803.3	$1,704.0	$15,698.8	$10,800.2	$29,234.1	$25,262.5
New York–N.E. N.J. SCA	103.4	363.7	1,259.3	—	137.1	292.6	2,191.2	13,044.7	1,427.5	4,118.3	2,045.2	12,558.2	6,950.0
New York SMSA	61.3	363.7	1,259.3	—	104.1	292.6	2,191.2	12,540.6	1,427.5	3,556.9	2,004.8	12,107.6	6,113.8
Newark SMSA	—	—	—	—	33.0	—	—	504.1	—	561.4	—	—	—
Paterson SMSA	42.1	—	—	—	—	—	—	—	—	—	40.4	318.6	836.2
Chicago–N.W. Ind. SCA	—	—	1,792.1	545.9	73.9	—	856.9	—	—	1,271.8	1,867.4	9,638.8	1,190.5
Chicago SMSA	—	—	1,792.1	545.9	73.9	—	856.9	—	—	1,271.8	1,867.4	9,638.8	1,190.5
Los Angeles SMSA	—	53.4	—	—	66.4	—	400.2	—	65.9	835.5	626.8	249.6	641.9
Philadelphia SMSA	—	—	1,244.8	69.9	—	—	—	—	—	357.9	125.8	422.1	2,576.6
Detroit SMSA	—	—	—	—	—	—	—	—	—	633.7	41.6	1,234.3	761.1
San Francisco SMSA	267.3	98.4	930.5	—	340.1	126.4	50.1	—	—	1,432.8	—	243.7	4,258.5
Boston SMSA	439.8	124.6	—	—	—	—	62.3	—	—	564.6	78.2	106.0	641.9
Pittsburgh SMSA	—	146.3	—	—	—	—	—	—	—	—	84.3	315.0	139.4
St. Louis SMSA	—	—	584.8	—	—	—	30.3	—	—	229.7	262.1	979.1	—
Washington SMSA	—	—	316.3	—	—	—	43.4	—	—	—	66.1	230.3	—
Cleveland SMSA	—	150.0	1,063.7	—	68.9	—	—	—	—	—	342.3	150.3	450.0
Minn.–St. Paul SMSA	—	—	492.0	—	—	—	350.9	—	—	254.4	638.7	657.5	385.5
Houston SMSA	—	—	—	—	—	—	27.5	—	—	1,876.8	599.7	—	169.6
Milwaukee SMSA	—	—	—	—	—	—	—	—	—	—	88.2	—	—
Dallas SMSA	—	—	—	127.3	—	—	187.8	—	—	310.2	678.3	—	—
Cincinnati SMSA	—	—	—	—	—	—	—	—	—	—	—	1,408.6	2,660.0
Kansas City SMSA	—	—	—	—	104.6	—	681.6	107.4	—	—	65.5	74.9	81.8
Atlanta SMSA	—	—	—	—	—	—	318.9	—	37.7	486.9	223.5	148.0	654.3
Wilmington SMSA	—	—	—	—	—	—	—	—	70.6	—	—	—	—
Total SCAs and SMSAs	810.5	936.4	7,683.5	743.1	791.0	419.0	5,201.1	13,152.1	1,601.7	12,372.6	7,833.7	28,416.4	21,561.1

Source: *News Front* 1967.

* 525 firms in 23 non-manufacturing industry classifications; 446 firms outside the financial grouping are ranked by sales, banking institutions are ranked by deposits and insurance establishments by admitted assets. For year ending 1966. The categories of industrial activity excluded from the analysis are: transportation services, retail trade in building materials, automotive dealers and gasoline service stations, retail trade in furniture, personal credit institutions, and amusement and recreation services.

	Apparel	Eating & drinking places	Misc. retail	Holding cos.	Bus. serv.	Motion pictures	Engr. & arch. serv.	Total non-fin.	Coml. banks	Mutual svgs. banks	Life ins.	Fire & casualty ins.	Total fin.	Grand total
United States	19	11	21	22	22	10	6	446	39	7	26	7	79	525
New York–N.E. N.J. SCA	13	4	3	8	9	6	3	124	9	6	7	1	23	147
New York SMSA	12	4	3	7	9	6	2	113	9	6	5	1	21	134
Newark SMSA	—	—	—	1	—	—	1	5	—	—	2	—	2	7
Paterson SMSA	—	—	—	—	—	—	—	4	—	—	—	—	—	4
Chicago-N.W. Ind. SCA	—	3	1	—	4	—	1	41	4	—	1	1	6	47
Chicago SMSA	—	3	1	—	4	—	1	41	4	—	1	1	6	47
Los Angeles SMSA	—	1	3	1	—	4	1	29	3	—	1	—	4	33
Philadelphia SMSA	—	1	1	—	—	—	—	13	3	1	2	1	7	20
Detroit SMSA	1	—	1	—	1	—	—	10	3	—	—	—	3	13
San Francisco SMSA	—	—	1	—	1	—	—	17	4	—	—	—	4	21
Boston SMSA	1	—	—	1	1	—	—	12	1	—	2	—	3	15
Pittsburgh	—	—	1	1	—	—	—	6	2	—	—	—	2	8
St. Louis SMSA	1	—	—	1	—	—	—	9	—	—	—	—	—	9
Washington SMSA	—	1	1	—	2	—	—	10	—	—	—	—	—	10
Cleveland SMSA	—	1	2	1	—	—	—	16	2	—	—	—	2	18
Minn.-St. Paul SMSA	—	—	—	1	—	—	—	10	—	—	—	—	—	10
Houston SMSA	—	—	—	2	—	—	—	9	—	—	—	—	—	9
Milwaukee SMSA	—	—	—	—	1	—	—	2	—	—	1	—	1	3
Dallas SMSA	1	—	—	—	—	—	—	7	2	—	—	—	2	9
Cincinnati SMSA	—	—	—	—	—	—	—	2	—	—	1	—	1	3
Kansas City	—	—	1	—	—	—	—	7	—	—	—	—	—	7
Atlanta SMSA	1	—	—	—	1	—	—	10	—	—	—	—	—	10
Wilmington SMSA	—	—	—	1	—	—	—	2	—	—	—	—	—	2
Total SCAs and SMSAs	18	11	15	17	20	10	5	336	33	7	15	3	58	394

	Sales of nonfinancial establishments in millions								Financial establishments					
									Deposits in millions			Assets in millions		
	Apparel	Eating & drinking places	Misc. retail	Holding cos.	Bus. serv.	Motion pictures	Engr. & arch. serv.	Total non-fin.	Coml. banks	Mutual svgs. banks	Total fin. deposits	Life ins.	Fire & casualty ins.	Total fin. admit. assets
United States	$1,869.3	$785.2	$2,941.7	$4,100.5	$2,271.1	$1,325.2	$847.6	$130,837.6	$134,690.5	$10,989.1	$145,679.6	$127,322.0	$9,882.0	$137,204.0
New York–N.E. N.J. SCA	1,204.4	347.1	960.0	1,717.1	1,016.8	841.7	417.4	50,995.7	57,125.0	9,298.9	66,423.9	75,827.0	1,516.8	77,343.8
New York SMSA	1,135.6	347.1	960.0	1,309.4	1,016.8	841.7	112.8	47,746.8	57,125.0	9,298.9	66,423.9	49,975.7	1,516.8	51,492.5
Newark SMSA	—	—	—	407.7	—	—	304.6	1,810.8	—	—	—	25,851.3	—	25,851.3
Paterson SMSA	—	—	—	—	—	—	—	1,237.3	—	—	—	—	—	—
Chicago-N.W. Ind. SCA	—	136.0	487.2	—	692.5	—	86.8	18,639.8	11,752.3	—	11,752.3	1,281.8	1,440.7	2,722.5
Chicago SMSA	—	136.0	487.2	—	692.5	—	86.8	18,639.8	11,752.3	—	11,752.3	1,281.8	1,440.7	2,722.5
Los Angeles SMSA	—	48.0	333.2	43.6	—	483.5	293.3	4,141.3	8,770.8	—	8,770.8	1,279.8	—	1,279.8
Philadelphia SMSA	—	51.0	48.5	—	—	—	—	4,896.6	4,175.4	1,690.2	5,865.6	3,241.2	1,714.7	4,955.9
Detroit SMSA	39.4	—	69.6	—	59.1	—	—	2,838.8	5,904.5	—	5,904.5	—	—	—
San Francisco SMSA	—	—	78.3	—	46.0	—	—	7,872.1	24,730.5	—	24,730.5	—	—	—
Boston SMSA	91.7	—	—	44.2	81.3	—	—	2,234.6	2,506.0	—	2,506.0	11,361.1	—	11,361.1
Pittsburgh SMSA	—	—	57.7	55.0	—	—	—	797.7	4,288.9	—	4,288.9	—	—	—
St. Louis SMSA	175.0	—	—	81.1	—	—	—	2,342.1	—	—	—	—	—	—
Washington SMSA	—	123.9	154.2	—	108.1	—	—	1,042.3	—	—	—	—	—	—
Cleveland SMSA	—	79.2	134.2	166.9	—	—	—	2,605.5	2,947.4	—	2,947.4	—	—	—
Minn.-St. Paul SMSA	—	—	—	42.6	—	—	—	2,821.6	—	—	—	—	—	—
Houston SMSA	—	—	—	358.3	—	—	—	3,031.9	—	—	—	—	—	—
Milwaukee SMSA	—	—	—	—	61.2	—	—	149.4	—	—	—	5,229.0	—	5,229.0
Dallas SMSA	58.5	—	—	—	—	—	—	1,362.1	2,538.6	—	2,538.6	—	—	—
Cincinnati SMSA	—	—	—	—	—	—	—	4,068.6	—	—	—	1,510.9	—	1,510.9
Kansas City SMSA	—	—	64.5	—	—	—	—	1,180.3	—	—	—	—	—	—
Atlanta SMSA	42.6	—	—	—	111.4	—	—	2,023.3	—	—	—	—	—	—
Wilmington SMSA	—	—	—	1,218.6	—	—	—	1,289.2	—	—	—	—	—	—
Total SCAs and SMSAs	1,611.6	785.2	2,387.4	3,727.4	2,176.4	1,325.2	797.5	114,332.9	124,739.4	10,989.1	135,728.5	99,730.8	4,672.2	104,403.0

wealthy as their counterparts in the other metropolitan areas (16 percent of the nation's 300 largest commercial banks which are in the 31-county region control 32 percent of the aggregate deposits). The next leading competitive region in commercial banking, San Francisco–Oakland, controls 12 percent of the aggregate deposits in eight major commercial banks, of which half rank among the nation's top 50. Detailed statistics on the location of the leading 500 national nonmanufacturing establishments are given in Table 2.13.

Miscellaneous business services, which include such activities as advertising, employment agencies, public relations, and management consulting services, are normally not considered as headquarters "establishments," but their relations with headquarters operations are especially close. A detailed distribution of business service establishments, employment, and receipts in the selected metropolitan areas for 1963 is shown in Table 2.14.

Nationally, business services grew vigorously and numbered 148,000 offices in 1963. This represents a 30 percent increase over 1958. The selected SMSAs accounted for 47 percent of the economy's business service establishments, 71 percent of their annual receipts, and 60 percent of their employment in 1963. In the growth of new establishments, the SMSAs experienced a less than representative expansion, although they shared in one-third the net national gain, or 11,000 new business services. The New York area contains 14 percent of the nation's business service outlets, or nearly double the share of the next leading regional contender, the Los Angeles SMSA. In measures of business volume, New York's office-serving activities earn 30 percent of national receipts while employing 21 percent of the industry's workers. This represents more than the combined receipts of all establishments located in Los Angeles, Chicago, Philadelphia, Detroit, San Francisco, and Boston.

Data processing service centers represent a service specialization that is anticipated to grow very rapidly over the near future, as computer use becomes more and more pervasive. Of the 217 establishments in the nation, the New York area contains 14 percent, the same share as business service activity. The next leading regional competition in data processing centers comes from the Los Angeles SMSA with 6 percent of the nation's establishments. Chicago, Detroit, and Boston come next, each with 4 percent of the nation's data processing service centers in 1965.

This should conclude our necessarily somewhat sketchy review of the wealth of descriptive data on specific types of "elite" office establishments presented for the inquisitive reader in Tables 2.9 through 2.14. These are given in part as a reference, in part as an indication of the type of data that are available for further research in the field.

Office Construction and Occupancy Characteristics
So far, we have reviewed the distribution of selected office activities, such as headquarters or business services, between the major metropolitan areas of the nation. Before concluding this chapter with a look at office location within metropolitan areas, it is useful to see recent trends in office activity in the aggregate, as expressed in the construction of new office buildings over the 1960–1969 decade. Since data measuring new construction in square feet of floor space are not readily available by metropolitan area, Table 2.15 shows the dollar value of building permits authorized for 12 SMSAs. This index is admittedly imperfect, mostly because of cost variations from city to city and inflation over time: nationwide, a square foot of office space cost about $20 to build in 1960–1964, whereas by 1968 the cost was up to about $24 nationwide, and up to $32 in the New York SMSA. Nevertheless, useful conclusions can be drawn from the data. In line with previously used concepts, Table 2.15 indicates both the absolute volume of office construction and its relative intensity. The latter is measured by the share of office construction in all nonresidential construction.

It is evident that, of the $15 billion spent nationwide over a decade for new private office buildings, $6.7 billion or 44 percent went into only 12 metropolitan areas listed in the table, which account for 25 percent of the nation's population. In fact, these areas increased their share of the nation's office construction market from 40 percent in the first five-year period to 46.6 percent in the second one, suggesting a trend toward centralization. Most prominent among the metropolitan areas that increased their share of the nation's office construction are New York, Detroit, San Francisco, Boston, Washington, and Chicago. Los Angeles and Milwaukee declined noticeably, while other areas more or less held their own.

Comparing the last column in Table 2.15, which shows office construction as a percentage of total nonresidential construction for each metropolitan area, with similar measures of intensity listed previously in Table 2.2, reveals that the two are closely related. Metropolitan areas that have a high proportion of office occupations in export activities quite plausibly also have a high proportion of their nonresidential construction in office buildings. Washington and New York, which rank first and second in Table 2.2, have 49.7 and 41.1 percent, respectively, of their new nonresidential construction in office buildings. Smaller or more manufacturing-oriented metropolitan areas have substantially less, and the national average is 17.6 percent.

Table 2.14. Major Metropolitan Areas Activity in Business Services, 1963

	SMSA total							Central city*			Suburban ring*		
	Estab.	Employ.	Receipts (× $1,000)	Average employ. per estab.	Average receipts per estab.	% of U.S. employ.	% of U.S. receipts	% of SMSA estab.	% of SMSA receipts	Average receipts per estab.	% of SMSA estab.	% of SMSA receipts	Average receipts per estab.
United States	147,668	995,920	$15,192,622	6.7	$102,900	100.0%	100.0%	64.3%	82.0%	$150,000	35.7%	18.0%	$ 59,100
New York–N.E. N.J. SCA	20,127	206,214	4,502,028	10.2	223,700	20.7	29.6	63.7	88.0	308,800	36.3	12.0	74,100
New York SMSA	16,164	172,768	4,140,672	10.7	256,200	17.3	27.3	79.3	95.7	308,800	20.7	4.3	53,900
Newark SMSA	1,925	17,378	168,705	9.0	87,600	1.7	1.1	26.3	48.4	161,400	73.7	51.6	61,300
Paterson SMSA	1,266	10,194	141,625	8.1	111,900	1.0	.9	21.2	18.7	98,700	78.8	81.3	115,400
Chicago–N.W. Ind. SCA	7,788	73,082	1,550,398	9.4	199,100	7.3	10.2	63.3	85.5	269,100	36.7	14.5	78,500
Chicago SMSA	7,533	71,856	1,539,977	9.5	204,400	7.2	10.1	65.4	86.1	269,100	34.6	13.9	82,200
Los Angeles SMSA	11,682	77,471	1,063,246	6.6	91,000	7.8	7.0	57.1	60.8	96,900	42.9	39.2	83,200
Philadelphia SMSA	3,189	31,405	392,642	9.8	123,100	3.2	2.6	51.6	80.2	191,400	48.4	19.8	50,300
Detroit SMSA	3,486	25,859	628,031	7.4	180,200	2.6	4.1	51.5	81.9	286,400	48.5	18.1	67,500
San Francisco SMSA	4,481	31,633	483,721	7.1	107,900	3.2	3.2	54.8	66.3	130,700	45.2	33.7	80,400
Boston SMSA	2,878	24,445	322,348	8.5	112,000	2.5	2.1	40.9	61.8	169,400	59.1	38.2	72,300
Pittsburgh SMSA	1,407	11,369	206,973	8.1	147,100	1.1	1.4	50.1	85.6	251,400	49.9	14.4	42,300
St. Louis SMSA	1,649	13,101	229,833	7.9	139,400	1.3	1.5	44.5	83.7	262,500	55.5	16.3	40,800
Washington SMSA	2,309	23,363	269,965	10.1	116,900	2.3	1.8	55.0	55.2	117,300	45.0	44.8	116,400
Cleveland SMSA	2,104	15,126	236,094	7.2	112,200	1.5	1.6	49.8	84.3	190,100	50.2	15.7	35,000
Minn.–St. Paul SMSA	1,539	13,734	253,904	8.9	165,000	1.4	1.7	70.8	92.5	215,700	29.2	7.5	42,200
Houston SMSA	1,603	11,537	143,828	7.2	89,700	1.2	.9	86.7	96.5	100,000	13.3	3.5	23,300
Milwaukee SMSA	1,167	8,144	111,841	7.0	95,800	.8	.7	66.2	91.2	132,200	33.8	8.8	24,800
Dallas SMSA	1,401	9,747	130,456	7.0	93,100	1.0	.9	85.5	95.6	104,100	14.5	4.4	28,300
Cincinnati SMSA	977	7,339	107,247	7.5	109,800	.7	.7	59.1	85.3	158,500	40.9	14.7	39,500
Kansas City SMSA	1,019	7,806	91,831	7.7	90,100	.8	.6	63.6	87.5	124,000	36.4	12.5	30,900
Atlanta SMSA	1,090	10,166	124,732	9.3	114,400	1.0	.8	72.7	92.0	145,000	27.3	8.0	33,500
Wilmington SMSA	240	1,929	15,471	8.0	64,500	.2	.1	58.3	78.9	87,200	41.7	21.1	32,600
Total SCAs and SMSAs	70,136	603,470	10,864,589	8.6	154,900	60.6	71.5	61.7	83.4	211,300	38.3	16.6	67,800

Source: U.S. Census. *Census of Business: 1963 Selected Services.*

Notes: Detail may not add to totals because of rounding. The business service category includes data for advertising, public relations, credit, building maintenance, and other establishments.

* Figures for the United States totals are the average of all SMSAs (217) used in central city-suburban profile of nation. Figures for New York–N.E. N.J. SCA and Chicago–N.W. Ind. SCA are for only the major central city.

Table 2.15. Valuation of New Private Office Space Authorized for Construction in Selected SMSAs, 1960–1969 (in millions of current dollars)

Rank	SMSA	1960–1964	1965–1969*	10-year total*	New office constr. as % of all nonres. priv. constr.
1.	New York	$565.1	$1,094.6	$1,659.7	41.1%
2.	Los Angeles	548.7	671.9	1,220.6	25.7
3.	Washington	271.3	541.2	812.5	49.7
4.	Chicago	244.1	466.3	710.4	20.3
5.	San Francisco	171.7	429.5	601.2	30.7
6.	Boston	101.3	292.4	393.7	23.8
7.	Detroit	61.5	266.1	327.6	16.2
8.	Atlanta	107.7	171.6	279.3	25.4
9.	Philadelphia	72.8	177.7	250.5	15.1
10.	Cleveland	68.8	104.1	172.9	15.9
11.	Seattle	57.9	111.3	169.2	19.1
12.	Milwaukee	57.2	44.3	101.5	15.7
U.S. Total†		5,806.0	9,390.0	15,196.0	17.6
12 SMSAs as percentage of U.S. total		40.1%	46.6%	44.1%	

Source: U.S. Department of Commerce, *Construction Statistics 1915 to 1964*, 1966, and *Construction Review*, 1965 to 1970.
* First eight months of 1969.
† National office valuation adjusted to represent 13,000 building permit issuing places which report 85% of all residential construction and a greater share of nonresidential construction.

Office construction in the private sector occurs in response to market demand, some dimensions of which are indicated in Table 2.16. The sample on which the table is based may be questionable, but the data are of illustrative interest. Notable is, first of all, the sharp overall decline in vacancy rates, compared to pre-World War II years. More recently, metropolitan areas with the highest volume of new construction nevertheless have very low vacancy rates, such as the 0.1 percent reported for New York, or the improbable 0.0 percent reported for Washington. Substantial vacancy rates are reported for some smaller metropolitan areas with an older office stock, such as St. Louis, Cincinnati, Kansas City.

The square feet of office space per employee show an upward trend, reflecting room added for comfort, for prestige, and for new office machines. Nationally, for the buildings reported in the table, the standard appears to have risen by 24 percent, from 113 square feet per employee in 1948–1949 to 140 square feet in 1967. In New York City, the corresponding rise is reported as 63 percent, from 109 square feet to 178 square feet. The greater amount of indoor room per employee in New York reflects the increasingly more "elite" and headquarters-oriented character of its offices: *Fortune* estimated in 1963 that the average in Manhattan was 165 square feet per employee, whereas one highly executive-oriented building had as much as 337. Undoubtedly, increasing standards of space per employee alone account for much of the new office building construction nationwide. For example, if the figures in Table 2.16 were representative averages, most of the 1950–1969 increment in office space in Manhattan—a 77 percent increase in stock shown earlier in Table 1.3—could be explained by increased floor space per employee alone.

Finally, the third section of Table 2.16 illustrates some rentals per square foot over a period of three decades. The figures are in current dollars, and the increase reflects inflation, rather than a rise in real costs; recalculated in constant dollars the rents would be stable, or even slightly declining. Among the buildings surveyed by the Building Owners and Managers Association International in the selected metropolitan areas, New York, Washington, San Francisco, Philadelphia, and Dallas stand out in their low recent vacancy rates and high levels of occupancy per employee. Rents vary from over $7 per square foot per year in New York, to about $5 per square foot in Chicago or Philadelphia, to about $4 in the smaller metropolitan areas, in 1967 prices. New York rentals were nearly half again as high as the mean rate of the four areas and 60 percent greater than the national average. This is only partially explained by the disparate rates of operating and construction. In 1964, two of the four SMSAs ranked higher than New York in total costs, while New York's operating costs of office

Table 2.16. Major Metropolitan Area Trends in the Vacancy, Occupancy Standards, and Rentals of Selected Central City Office Buildings

	Average vacancy rates					Average square footage occupancy per employee					Average rental per square foot				
	1941–1942	1948–1949	1958–1959	1963–1964	1967	1941–1942	1948–1949	1958–1959	1963–1964	1967	1941–1942	1948–1949	1958–1959	1963–1964	1967
United States	14.8%	1.2%	3.2%	4.7%	3.6%	110.2	113.0	120.9	129.5	139.5	$1.78	$2.67	$3.96	$4.45	$4.80
New York	(6.2)	(.2)	.9	.9	.1	(136.7)	109.1	109.8	126.2	177.6	(2.47)	3.42	5.15	7.04	n.a.
Chicago	18.2	3.2	3.0	4.2	2.5	112.6	123.2	119.6	118.1	123.2	1.94	3.00	4.26	4.90	5.30
Los Angeles	17.6	1.7	4.0	4.2	n.a.	113.4	108.0	137.1	127.5	n.a.	1.56	2.84	3.72	4.31	n.a.
Philadelphia	16.8	.7	7.6	1.0	.4	110.7	128.7	141.4	153.8	137.8	2.26	2.86	4.51	4.67	5.19
Detroit	26.2	3.1	2.5	7.8	8.1	88.4	93.0	112.9	107.7	103.3	1.68	2.72	3.63	4.28	4.42
San Francisco	11.6	.2	.8	1.7	2.3	133.2	127.4	128.0	121.8	124.2	1.73	2.93	4.43	5.00	5.46
Boston	19.2	n.a.	n.a.	n.a.	n.a.	165.1	(111.2)	n.a.	n.a.	n.a.	1.46	(2.61)	n.a.	n.a.	n.a.
Pittsburgh	11.8	.2	2.2	6.7	2.1	107.2	85.2	145.2	133.6	156.7	2.64	3.74	4.87	5.31	5.71
St. Louis	21.9	1.2	8.4	16.6	16.4	85.9	84.0	74.3	59.2	55.9	1.66	2.16	3.11	3.56	4.20
Washington	(.0)	.0	(.0)	.0	.0	(92.7)	117.6	(261.8)	171.4	101.1	(2.33)	2.74	3.94	4.82	4.72
Cleveland	16.0	.9	1.5	2.2	2.4	135.0	124.0	128.0	137.0	154.3	1.30	2.59	3.61	3.58	4.05
Minn.–St. Paul	20.9	.9	3.9	5.1	2.4	103.0	100.9	118.6	127.8	142.2	1.47	2.57	3.57	4.29	4.71
Houston	n.a.	n.a.	2.5	8.8	8.1	n.a.	n.a.	130.0	138.9	170.3	n.a.	n.a.	4.11	4.65	5.26
Milwaukee	n.a.	n.a.	4.3	3.7	4.4	n.a.	n.a.	186.4	196.9	198.7	n.a.	n.a.	3.13	3.24	5.31
Dallas	6.9	.0	(1.3)	.5	.0	107.7	79.7	97.6	94.6	110.9	1.93	2.94	3.98	4.66	4.76
Cincinnati	14.7	(.8)	3.7	18.3	8.1	94.2	144.0	153.0	174.9	120.8	1.73	2.27	3.60	3.22	3.41
Kansas City	20.4	(1.4)	4.0	2.3	21.8	110.0	(116.8)	105.3	106.9	82.1	1.63	(2.40)	3.36	3.13	4.40
Atlanta	5.4	.0	2.2	5.9	6.7	110.0	123.6	132.3	163.8	223.6	1.87	2.52	3.44	3.88	4.45
Wilmington	n.a.	n.a.	n.a.	n.a.	.0	n.a.	n.a.	n.a.	n.a.	149.2	n.a.	n.a.	n.a.	n.a.	6.61

Source: Building Owners and Managers Association International, *Office Building Experience Exchange Report.*
Notes: The data in this table refer to buildings reporting to the Building Owners and Managers Association International, and should not be construed to represent city-wide averages, but only the averages of those buildings reporting to the survey. () Data are for one year, rather than the two-year period indicated.

buildings were exceeded by two of the 17 reported areas.

The dynamics of the construction market in private office building are primarily the result of (1) the growth of the white-collar labor force brought about by overall business expansion, as previously discussed; (2) the change in occupational composition of the work force and in the nature of office functions which directly influences the demand for space per employee; (3) the depreciation of existing office stock through either structural or functional change.

As construction began to catch up with labor demand for office space, rates of occupancy were kept high by a simultaneous expansion of space demands per worker. Upgrading of the skills of office workers ordinarily results in decreased density of a given space. Witness the growing executive corps with its need for larger offices, reception rooms, and conference areas. Finally, construction of office space in the postwar period was kept high by the need to replace physically deteriorating office structures and those buildings of prime location which had become technically obsolete by developments in lighting, temperature control, and internal movement of people.

With the exception of Manhattan, the postwar space provisions of the central business districts have been made largely in response to custom building demands. Important single users of office space, such as the federal government and corporate headquarters, are responsible for significant additions to the stock of space in many downtowns. Activity in the market for office space in Manhattan has been much broader as well as more speculative, as many private building concerns have responded to the huge demand. Also, in Manhattan the boom started earlier, around 1950, while large-scale construction of office buildings in most other downtowns —especially older ones—did not get underway until about 1955.

Outside the downtowns, the impact of suburban construction can be seen in building statistics reported for the nation as a whole. A surprisingly small average size of structure infers the extent of low-rise office building that is occurring in low-density urban areas, and at such a rate as to dwarf the downtown booms. Suburban office developments, which frequently locate on vacant tracts of land adjacent to major arterial roads, distinguish the postwar boom from previous years of building activity by their low rates of demolition, high-floor-space provisions per employee, and extensive demands for parking and ancillary facilities such as cafeterias and shops.

Office Location within Metropolitan Areas
In the absence of a national census of buildings, or at least of a comprehensive nationwide inventory of space in office buildings, there are no firm data on exactly how the existing stock of office buildings is distributed within metropolitan areas, or how large it is for that matter. Nor are data on the increment in new construction collected and presented in a manner that would make their detailed locational pattern within the nation's metropolitan areas apparent. For the New York Region, such detail is available and will be presented in Chapter 4. For the metropolitan areas outside the New York Region, this section attempts to provide some estimates, focusing on existing stock.

In 1960, the 21 selected SMSAs, for which CAO&A employment data were presented earlier, contained a total of 6 million office workers, as indicated in Table 2.17. Two-thirds of them were employed in central cities, one-third in the suburban ring. An estimated 40 percent, or 2.44 million, worked in the downtown business districts of the 21 metropolitan areas. More than a third of the downtown office jobs, however, were accounted for by Manhattan; leaving Manhattan and the New York SMSA out produces a fairly even allocation between the dowtowns and the suburbs: 1.84 million office jobs in the suburban ring, as against 1.60 million in the downtowns, with the remainder—some 1.28 million office jobs—located in the central cities outside the downtown business district, at various office, factory, institutional, and commercial sites, or in smaller subcenters.

Taken together, the central business districts of the 21 metropolitan areas represented roughly half a billion square feet of office space, 38 percent of it in Manhattan in 1960. Between 1960 and 1970, over 200 million square feet or one-fifth of the nation's net addition to office building floor space, was erected in the 21 central business districts (Figure 2.4). One-third of this gain was accounted for by Manhattan, which put in place over the decade the equivalent of the office floor space gains in the 5 next largest downtown areas: Chicago, Washington, Philadelphia, Boston, and Los Angeles. Although only marginal advances were made in several central business districts, notably those midranked with respect to metropolitan size, the group as a whole appears to be sustaining its position in the nation despite strong pressures for suburbanization. In 1960, the 21 central business districts contained an estimated 16 percent of the nation's office work force, including those located in nonoffice buildings, and 24 percent of its detached office floor space; by 1970, after acquiring roughly 20 percent of the net addition to the national office inventory, they contained 23 percent of the office building floor space.

The central business districts truly represent "environments of high interaction." Here, an average of 40 percent of a metropolitan area's office employment is concentrated on a fraction of 1 percent of its land area. The majority of the central business districts in question are about one square mile in extent, allowing for relatively easy pedestrian access within. The downtowns of Chicago, Philadelphia, and Washington are larger—about two square miles each. The central business district of New York, conventionally defined for simplicity as Manhattan south of 60th Street, is close to 9 square miles, but about half of it is in residential use. The office concentrations are confined within about 2 square miles in midtown and 1 square mile in downtown. Office buildings share this tight space with many other uses. While office skyscrapers dominate the skyline, the central business districts have only 30 to 40 percent of their entire floor space in office buildings. In the 9 square mile Manhattan CBD, office space in office buildings averaged 28 percent of the total floor space in 1963, though it reached about 65 percent in the densest square mile around Grand Central by 1970.

The degree to which office floor space is centralized in the downtown, or spread throughout the metropolitan area, varies over a fairly broad range. Table 2.17 shows that metropolitan areas with over 60 percent of their office employment in the central business district in 1960 are Washington, New York, Houston, and Dallas. Areas with less than 30 percent include some proverbially dispersed cities, among them Wilmington, Kansas City, Cleveland, Detroit, St. Louis, Los Angeles, and the Newark and Paterson metropolitan areas, which contain several older centers outside the central city and much suburban office development generated by the proximity of New York. The other nine metropolitan areas—large and small—fall in the middle range, with some 30 to 50 percent of their office jobs located in the downtown central business district. It appears that the degree to which office employment is concentrated downtown is in no way related to urban size; nor does it seem to be related to such likely factors as the presence or absence of rapid rail transit, as is shown in Figure 2.5. One factor to which the degree of downtown office concentration does seem to be mildly related is the office orientation of the economy. On the average, the higher the ratio of office workers per population, the higher the percentage of office workers located in downtown. The relationship is statistically somewhat weak (perhaps due to the approximate nature of the downtown employment estimates), but nevertheless significant. Of course, the absolute amount of downtown office employment, as measured by office floor space in the central business district, is strongly related to total office employment in a metropolitan area. The relationship is portrayed on a logarithmic scale in Figure 2.5.

Having looked at the degree to which total office employment and office space are concentrated in downtown central business districts, it will be interesting to see the pattern for headquarters locations. Table 2.18

Table 2.17. Total Office Employment in Selected SMSAs and Estimated Intraregional Distribution

	Office employ. in thousands, 1960*				% office employ. in downtown	Est. gross priv. and pub. office space in downtown (× 1 million sq ft)	
	SMSA	Central city	Suburban ring	Down-town		1960	1970
New York SMSA	1,334	1,113	221	840	63%	179	247
Los Angeles SMSA	703	376	327	100	14	16	33
Chicago SMSA	688	488	200	275	40	47	63
Philadelphia SMSA	397	240	157	120	30	26	34
Detroit SMSA	316	183	133	80	25	16	23
San Francisco SMSA	306	175	131	100	33	16	26
Boston SMSA	297	142	155	120	40	24	34
Pittsburgh SMSA	188	79	108	70	37	15	22
St. Louis SMSA	188	110	78	35	19	4	8
Washington SMSA	288	199	89	180	63	36	54
Cleveland SMSA	183	126	57	50	27	8	11
Newark SMSA	178	85	93	50	28	12	14
Minn.–St. Paul SMSA	168	124	44	65	39	10	12
Houston SMSA	118	100	18	80	68	13	22
Milwaukee SMSA	120	90	30	60	50	12	14
Paterson SMSA	97	24	72	5	5	1	1
Dallas SMSA	124	93	31	80	65	16	22
Cincinnati SMSA	106	71	35	45	42	10	12
Kansas City SMSA	113	76	37	30	27	6	9
Atlanta SMSA	111	77	34	45	41	8	17
Wilmington SMSA	34	17	17	10	29	2	3
Total SMSAs	6,055	3,990	2,065	2,440	40	477	681

Sources: Employment estimates constructed by Regional Plan Association from data in U.S. Census, *Census of Population: 1960 Detailed Characteristics*, and *Journey to Work*. Floor space estimates from a survey of respective city planning agencies and, when not locally available, constructed by Regional Plan Association.

Notes: Detail may not add to totals because of rounding. The data on downtown office employment are estimates rounded to the nearest five thousand and apply to major central business districts only.

* Office employment located at office, factory, store, institution, and other sites. Does not include sales workers in offices except for downtown estimates.

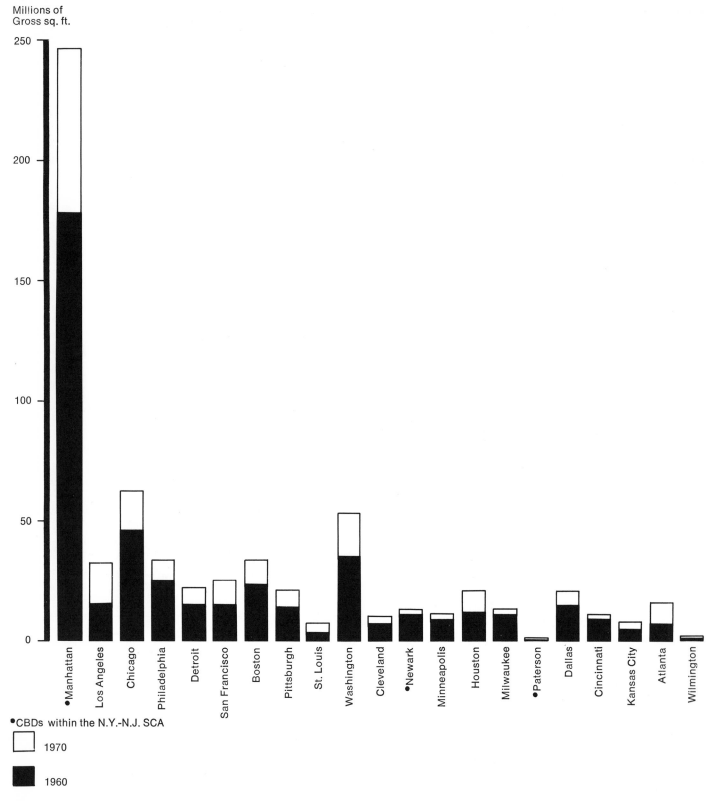

Millions of
Gross sq. ft.

•CBDs within the N.Y.-N.J. SCA

☐ 1970

■ 1960

Figure 2.4 Office floor space in selected CBDs, 1960–1970

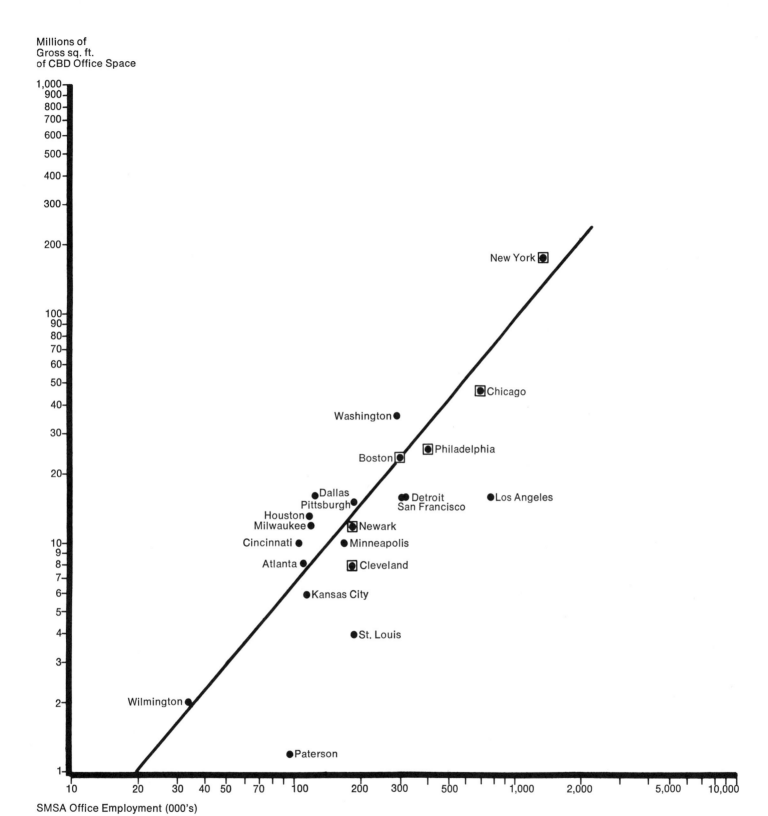

Figure 2.5 Metropolitan office employment and CBD office floor space in 1960

Table 2.18. The Intraregional Location of Corporate Industrial Headquarters in Selected SMSAs, 1965 and 1969

	Central city		Suburban ring	
	1965	1969	1965	1969
New York	131	126	6	5
Los Angeles	7	13	7	8
Chicago	39	37	9	12
Philadelphia	11	10	5	4
Detroit	12	9	3	4
San Francisco	11	8	1	3
Boston	6	5	3	4
Pittsburgh	21	14	1	—
St. Louis	11	10	1	—
Washington	—	—	—	1
Cleveland	16	16	—	1
Newark	2	3	5	4
Minn.–St. Paul	9	10	1	1
Houston	2	2	—	—
Milwaukee	8	9	2	2
Paterson	—	—	3	7
Dallas	5	7	—	—
Cincinnati	4	4	—	—
Kansas City	2	2	—	—
Atlanta	1	3	—	—
Wilmington	3	3	—	—
Total SMSAs	301	291	47	56

Source: "The Fortune Directory," 1966 and 1970.

Table 2.19. The Distribution of Office Employment and Residence of the Labor Force for Selected Metropolitan Areas, 1960

	% of office employ. located in		Share of central city office jobs filled by commuters from suburban ring	% of all population in suburban ring
	central city	suburban ring		
New York	83.4%	16.6%	19.8%	27.2%
Los Angeles	53.5	46.5	18.3	58.1
Chicago	70.9	29.1	19.6	42.9
Philadelphia	60.5	39.5	31.5	53.9
Detroit	57.9	42.1	22.2	55.6
San Francisco	57.3	42.7	19.5	60.2
Boston	47.9	52.1	58.3	73.1
Pittsburgh	42.3	57.7	43.9	74.9
St. Louis	58.7	41.3	28.1	63.6
Washington	69.2	30.8	52.1	61.8
Cleveland	68.7	31.3	36.2	51.2
Newark	47.7	52.3	67.8	76.0
Minn.–St. Paul	73.8	26.2	24.4	46.3
Houston	85.1	14.9	11.2	24.5
Milwaukee	75.2	24.8	23.1	37.9
Paterson	25.0	75.0	53.0	76.4
Dallas	75.1	24.9	15.1	37.3
Cincinnati	67.0	33.0	29.8	53.1
Kansas City	67.6	32.4	27.1	54.3
Atlanta	69.4	30.6	46.9	52.1
Wilmington	49.1	50.9	64.0	73.8

Sources: U.S. Census, *Journey to Work: 1960*, and Regional Plan Association estimates.

presents the intraregional distribution of industrial headquarters operations for our 21 metropolitan areas in 1965 and 1969. Only one out of seven firms headquartered in these metropolitan areas chose to locate in the suburbs in 1965, and the suburbs of eight metropolitan areas in the table—mostly the smaller ones—had no headquarters. By 1969, nearly one in six headquarters were housed in the suburbs. It is apparent that industrial headquarters preferences for suburban locations are mounting within large metropolitan areas, and that they initially appear as the size of metropolitan area increases beyond a population of about 2 million.

The pattern of headquarters location is on the whole more centralized than that of all office employment. This is plausible: the high-level office functions performed in headquarters require environments of high interaction more than average office jobs. The cases where headquarters are more suburbanized than all office employment are few indeed. In the instance of Newark and Paterson, the unusual distribution is explainable by the proximity of New York, while in Los Angeles, a strengthening of the central city role is apparent in recent floor space and employment indicators.

Table 2.19 proceeds to give some further dimensions of the urban-suburban balance of office work. The first column shows the share of the metropolitan areas total office employment that is located in the central city as a whole; the second column shows the corollary suburban employment. The third column shows the extent to which office jobs in the central city are filled by commuters from the suburbs, and the last column shows the relative weight of the suburbs in the metropolitan area in terms of population.

It is evident that employment in the central city is closely related to downtown employment; on the average, it is about 65 percent greater than downtown employment. Substantial departures from that average arise mostly from random factors, such as whether boundaries of the central city are drawn tightly or loosely. The incidence of central city boundaries is reflected in the last column, showing the percentage of all population residing in the suburban ring.

In each of the metropolitan areas a substantially greater share of office jobs than resident population is located in the central city. This results in a stream of commuters, who fill from one-ninth to two-thirds of the cities' demand for office workers. Generally, the greater the share of the population in the suburbs, the more commutation across the central city line. San Francisco, Boston, Pittsburgh, St. Louis, Washington, Newark, Paterson, and Wilmington all had over 60 percent of their population residing in the suburbs in 1960. All of them, except San Francisco, Pittsburgh, and St. Louis imported more than 50 percent of the central city office workers from the suburbs. The exceptions imply an above-average concentration of office workers residing in the central city.

Other cities with a large white-collar labor pool residing within city limits are the giants—New York, Los Angeles, and Chicago, as well as Dallas and Houston. All of them import less than 20 percent of their office labor from the suburbs.

In 1960, suburban office employment exceeded central city office employment only in Boston, Pittsburgh, Newark, Paterson, and Wilmington. However, in addition to these, Los Angeles, Philadelphia, Detroit, San Francisco, St. Louis, Cleveland and Kansas City had more office jobs located in the suburbs than in the central business district. All of these metropolitan areas with a heavy suburban office component had more than 51 percent of their population residing in the suburbs. Their office location pattern has undoubtedly been influenced by considerations of access to the suburban labor market, given the fact that the suburbs have become the overwhelming residential choice of the white-collar worker. In general, those metropolitan areas with a high share of suburban office employment also exported commuters from the suburbs to the central city at a high rate.

In most of the smaller SMSAs, the suburban white-collar population has not evidenced as strong an influence on decentralization of office locations before 1960. Here, the supply of office jobs and the demand for office workers still appeared to be converging on the central city. The proximity of the central city to the suburban market, and the ease of travel without heavy congestion characteristic of the larger metropolitan areas seemed to obviate the need for decentralization. Minneapolis–St. Paul, Houston, and Atlanta are examples of cities in which the suburbanization of office employment has been quite weak.

The two most prominent exceptions—small metropolitan areas that have heavily suburbanized office employment—are, as noted before, Paterson and Newark. The unusually high saturation of their suburbs with office employment appears to be related to the proximity of New York, just as a similar condition in the suburbs of Wilmington appears to be related to the proximity of Philadelphia. One can either say that the attractiveness of the main central business districts in New York and Philadelphia is so strong as to suppress the emergence of pronounced subcenters in their shadow, or that their generation of suburban-type office activities is so extensive that they invade the suburbs of neighboring metropolitan areas, which otherwise would have a much weaker office orientation.

Chapter 3

Headquarters Location in the New York Region

Issues and Historical Trends

Having reviewed the distribution of office activity between and within the nation's major metropolitan areas, we can now turn our attention to New York—the nation's largest office concentration, as well as the most intensive. In the mid-sixties, the New York Region contained slightly under 10 percent of the nation's population, but over 13 percent of its office-type occupations, over 14 percent of its office workers, and over 15 percent of its jobs in office buildings, as previously defined in Chapter 1.

The intensity is even more pronounced with regard to headquarters offices, as is evident from material in Chapter 2. The New York Region is the seat of one-third of the nation's top 500 industrial corporations, which control roughly 40 percent of the corporate wealth of the nation, and one-fifth of the top 50 banks. In 1967 the New York–Northeastern New Jersey standard consolidated area (SCA), which covers the 17 inner counties of the 31-county Region,[1] contained 18.7 percent of all of the nation's headquarters jobs and 21.1 percent of its manufacturing headquarters jobs, as measured by employment in central administrative offices and auxiliary units (CAO&A). As previously shown, between 1963 and 1967 the SCA maintained its position remarkably well by capturing 16.9 percent of the nation's increment in central administrative jobs, including 20.8 percent of the nation's central administrative jobs in manufacturing. Of course, one must realize that it will never again reach the degree of preeminence it enjoyed during the first third of this century, simply because the rest of the nation has since been growing at a faster rate.

Nevertheless, the continued importance of the Region as a headquarters location, and the importance of headquarters jobs for the Region, make the issue of headquarters placement within the Region of obvious interest. Headquarters jobs are the peak of a pyramid: they strongly affect the location of other office jobs, as will be shown in subsequent chapters, and help determine regional structure and regional form. Alternative ways of structuring the Region have alternative public costs attached to them, not only immediately, in terms of investment in transportation and utilities, but also recurrently, in terms of job opportunities, the convenience and the richness of the environment, and the performance of the headquarters operations themselves.

Thus, it is no wonder that the issue of headquarters location within the New York Region has been a matter of public debate for quite some time. It has usually been

1. The SCA is a Census definition of the New York Region which unites the four standard metropolitan statistical areas (SMSAs) of New York, Newark, Jersey City, Paterson-Clifton-Passaic, and two outside counties. Its relation to the 31-county Region as defined by Regional Plan Association is shown on Map 3.1.

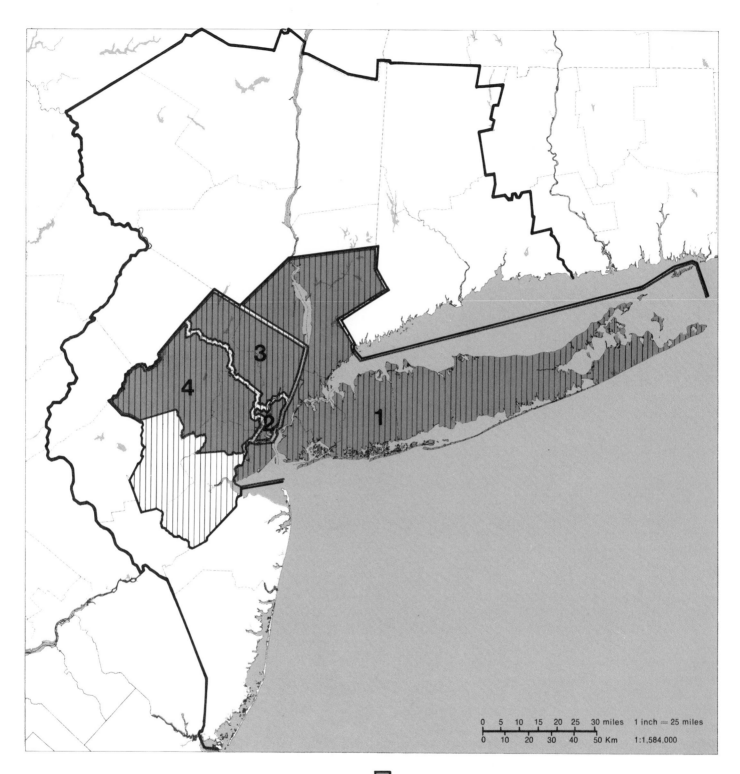

— Region Defined by Regional Plan Association

New York — Northeastern New Jersey
Standard Consolidated Area   (SCA)

Note: SMSA's outside the SCA not shown.

Standard Metropolitan Statistical Areas (U.S. Census)
1 New York SMSA
2 Jersey City SMSA
3 Paterson — Clifton — Passaic SMSA
4 Newark SMSA

0   5   10   15   20   25   30 miles   1 inch = 25 miles
0   10   20   30   40   50 Km   1:1,584,000

phrased as "Manhattan versus the suburbs." The suburbs, of course, have grown to extend quite a long distance from Manhattan and to become a "Spread City" in their own right, rather autonomous from Manhattan. For greater precision, the concept of "rings of development" is used in subsequent discussion, as defined in *The Region's Growth* (New York: Regional Plan Association, 1967). There are five:

The Manhattan CBD (central business district), the roughly 9 square miles south of Central Park, that part of New York City which was built up before the 1860s, which, in the early 1960s, housed about 3 percent of the Region's resident population at a developed land density of about 70,000 per square mile and contained about 28 percent of the Region's total employment, but 40 percent of its employment in the top 8 percent income bracket.

The remainder of the core, the roughly 300 square miles comprising the rest of New York City without Staten Island, plus Hudson County and the City of Newark in New Jersey. This was almost fully built up by 1950 and by 1960 housed some 46 percent of the Region's population at a developed land density of 36,000 per square mile and contained 31 percent of the Region's employment. This is the area in which most of the Region's social problems are concentrated today.

The inner ring of about 1,000 square miles, comprising Staten Island and six truly suburban counties in whole or in part. Around 1960, these housed 25 percent of the Region's population at a developed land density of 7,600 per square mile, and contained 19 percent of the Region's employment. This area is the Region's wealthiest ring of development.

The intermediate ring of about 4,000 square miles, extending east to include New Haven, Connecticut, and a large part of Long Island, and west to include Trenton, New Jersey. Around 1960, it housed 21 percent of the Region's population at a developed land density of 3,500 per square mile, and contained 17 percent of the Region's employment. This is the fastest growing belt of the Region.

The outer ring of over 7,000 square miles of largely rural land mostly north and south of the intermediate ring, with 6 percent of the Region's population and 5 percent of its employment. The five rings of development are shown on Map 3.2.

Historically, the Region's population growth has occurred almost exclusively on vacant land, rather than by rebuilding to higher densities. Thus, the relative weights of these rings of development—the proportions of the total population they contain—have been steadily moving outward. Moreover, Manhattan began to experience absolute declines in resident population after 1910, and the core as a whole has had a stable or declining population since 1950. The dynamics of employment growth have been rather different—through the later decades of the nineteenth century and until 1929, Manhattan not only grew precipitously in absolute numbers but for many decades also increased its relative weight, or its share of the Region's total, as an expanding rapid transit system provided it with a unique position of accessibility. Places of employment were—and still are—being provided by rebuilding to higher densities, by growing vertically rather than horizontally.

However, the size of an employment concentration is basically limited by its accessibility to the residences of potential workers. Accessibility depends on the capacity and the tributary area of a transportation system. Capacity is the ability to deliver so many people in a given unit of time, such as the peak hour. Tributary area has to do with the speed of the system, and the area it covers. The predominant mode of access to Manhattan is by rail, yet the number of railroad and transit tracks entering Manhattan—50 tracks—has been approximately stable since 1924. What was added by the construction of new subways during the thirties was later subtracted by the removal of old elevated lines, so aside from operational improvements, capacity has been virtually stable. Some improvement in rapid transit speeds was accomplished during the period and some new territory was covered, but neither was of dramatic proportions. Quite dramatically, 34 lanes of limited access highways, bridges, and tunnels were built into the Manhattan CBD between 1932 and 1958 for automobiles and buses, extending the tributary area far out. But, because of the system's inherently low capacity, they carry only 10 percent of the peak hour person trips into and out of the central business district, and have, in essence, merely diverted some traffic from rail.

In view of these facts, it is not surprising that the total employment in the Manhattan CBD has remained, apart from fluctuations due to business cycles, fairly stable since about 1929. As a consequence, because of the precipitous growth on the outskirts and because the rest of the nation grew faster than the Region in population since 1940, Manhattan has been obviously slipping in its share of the Region's and the nation's total employment. This is true of office employment as well, even though it has been growing in absolute numbers at the expense of blue-collar employment in Manhattan. A few random historical examples may be of interest.

When the First Regional Plan surveyed office activity in the New York area during the twenties, its field of focus was conveniently a narrow one, for the pattern was incredibly more centralized. Though more banks were located in the Region outside the financial district than

Map 3.1 Definitions of the New York Region

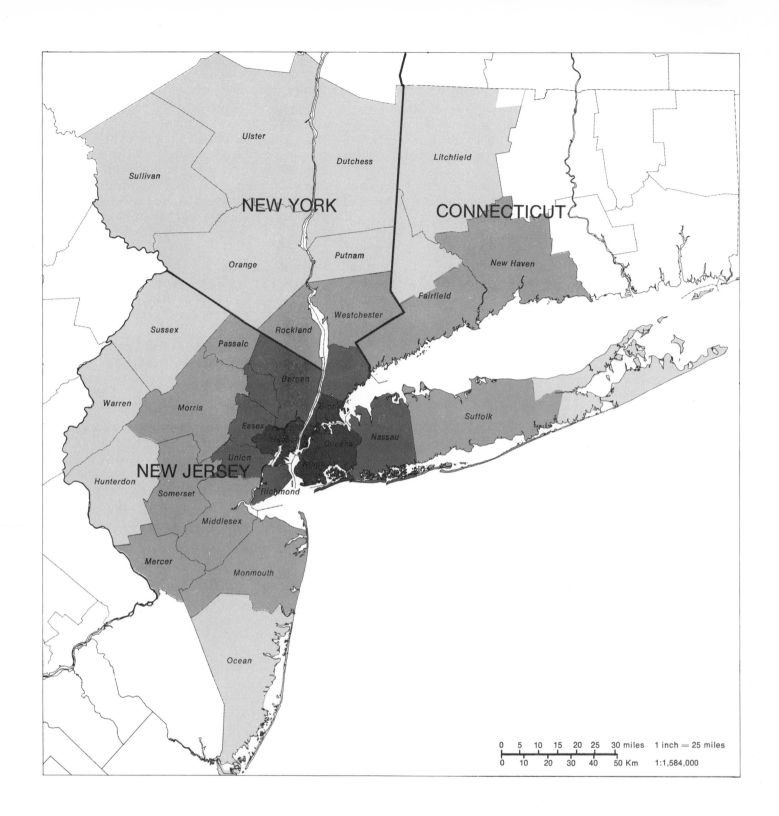

Manhattan CBD
Rest of Core
Inner Ring
Intermediate Ring
Outer Ring

in it, all banks of national or international importance conducted business from headquarters in the Wall Street section. Outlying banks, many of which were situated above 14th Street in midtown Manhattan, were comparatively small and served local markets. Nearly 90 percent of all stock exchange members in the nation were located in lower Manhattan, leaving less than one percent to be housed in the rest of the city. Other examples of the then far greater centralization of office activities in Manhattan abound.

Among the executive offices of major companies contributing to the stock index in 1926, 72 percent of the nation's total were located in New York City, all of them in Manhattan, and less than one-third of these were north of the financial district. The larger the corporation in size of assets, the greater appeared to be its need for frequent contact between executive and banker, and the stronger its headquarters alignment with the location of the nation's major financial institutions. Those that ventured north, in the early decades of the century, to the rapidly growing office center near Grand Central Station were primarily smaller concerns or those more actively engaged in supervisory sales or production work. Attesting to this split in character of administrative office work between downtown and midtown office centers, the First Regional Plan noted that, from 1900 to 1925, the share of accountants and lawyers working in the financial district changed in the following manner: accountants dropped from two-thirds to less than one-fourth of their total employed below Fulton Street, and lawyers shifted slightly from two-thirds to 60 percent of total located there.

It is hardly surprising, therefore, that the largest users of downtown floor space during this era were corporate headquarters. During the twenties, some observers believed that downtown Manhattan's attraction was transitory or, at least, could not be sustained. However, the affinity of various headquarters and other office operations for one another appeared so strong to the authors of the First Regional Plan that they concluded that there had been ". . . not a positive decline of the absolute importance of Wall Street, but a narrowing of the scope of the activities and a specialization of the functions performed in this district. . . . Some of the functions and agencies which can make less effective use of their location will continue to yield ground to those who can use them better. There will be relatively less storage and less low-grade clerical work in the financial district of today. Those corporation officers and professional men who reap relatively slight advantages from the proximity to this great center will find a more sat-

Map 3.2 Rings of development in the New York Region

isfactory location elsewhere." [2] In short, the authors felt that, despite Manhattan's magnetism and its ability to sustain office growth, maturation processes within industry would turn the attention of many to alternative locations. Many a more "satisfactory location" appeared to be in the other boroughs of New York City at this time. However, the suburbs also held a lure. The distribution of corporate headquarters between Manhattan and the rest of the nation in 1926 is illustrated in Table 3.1, and the gradual uptown movement of activity within Manhattan from 1912 to 1925, in Table 3.2.

As the state of the art of moving people—or ideas—became increasingly refined through modern technology, and as population growth spread the labor force further and further away from the center, ties to the central business district began to weaken. The central business district's declining relationship to the Region as a whole is equally true of New York City. Adjusting earlier estimates for changes in definition of the area, it appears that, in 1910, New York City had about 80 percent of the Region's total office employment (roughly 438,000 office jobs), which, by 1965, changed to 55 percent of the Region's employment (1,291,500 office jobs).[3] It should be noted that in 1910, one out of every six workers was employed in an office; by 1965, this relationship had changed dramatically with three out of every ten job holders being linked to offices (Figure 3.1). Although post-World War II growth in office employment has resulted in a great concentration of office jobs in Manhattan office buildings which today exceed in number all of the office jobs in plant, institutional, and commercial buildings sited throughout the entire Region in 1920, the Manhattan CBD presently has a smaller proportion of the Region's total office jobs than it had then. Manhattan, in 1965, had 52 percent of the Region's total office jobs in office buildings, as will be shown later. But only about three-eighths of the new office activity currently locates there, a fact masked by the highly visible and spectacular boom in office buildings.

In the process of the shifting balance between Manhattan and the other rings of development, Manhattan, despite substantial overall gains in office employment, has experienced some absolute losses as well. Initially, most of the office jobs that migrated outward consisted of

2. The Regional Plan of New York and Its Environs, *Major Economic Factors in Metropolitan Growth and Arrangement,* Regional Survey Volume 1, by Robert Murray Haig (New York, 1927), pp. 100–102.
3. Estimates for 1910 were derived from the earlier work done on offices as part of the Harvard Study on the New York Metropolitan Region. The figures for both years represent office employment at all sites, as no earlier estimates were made for employment in detached office buildings in the city which represented 68 percent of the Region's total in 1965.

Table 3.1. Location of Executive Offices of 232 Important Companies* of the Nation in New York City, 1926

Business	Total no. of cos. in the nation	Total no. with offices in New York City	No. with offices south of Fulton St.	No. with offices north of Fulton St.
Automobile	10	5	2	3
Auto accessory	8	3	3	—
Chain stores	11	4	—	4
Chemical	7	7	5	2
Coal	3	2	2	—
Copper	12	12	12	—
Electrical equipment	3	1	1	—
Farm machinery	3	—	—	—
Food	9	7	4	3
Leather and shoes	5	3	1	2
Machine manufacturing	5	2	1	1
Mail order	3	1	—	1
Metals, miscellaneous	12	9	9	—
Miscellaneous	18	13	6	7
Paper	3	3	—	3
Petroleum	17	11	10	1
Shipping	3	3	3	—
Steel	9	7	5	2
Sugar	6	5	5	—
Textile	5	4	—	4
Theater	3	2	—	2
Tire and rubber	7	7	1	6
Tobacco	7	6	1	5
Traction, gas and power	16	7	5	2
Telegraph and cable	5	5	4	1
Railroad equipment	11	11	10	1
Railroad	31	27	26	1
Total	232	167	116	51

Source: Regional Plan of New York and Its Environs, *Economic and Industrial Survey: The Retail Shopping and Financial Districts*, 1927.
* Major companies contributing to the stock index in 1926, classified according to the nature of their business.

plant-attached, head office activities which were carried along in the migration of factory from city to suburb. These offices were either too small to specialize and to separate, or too closely attached to their production operations, or, on the contrary, so large that they could internalize some of the external benefits or skills which the central business district offered. Thus, between 1924 and 1957, for example, the head offices of the Region's industrial establishments listed in Moody's *Industrial Manual* increased by 33 in 17 suburban counties, and declined absolutely in New York City, though some of the City's decline is attributable to mergers.

In 1963, the New York Region contained 168 headquarters or one-third of the nation's top industrial front offices, as defined by the *Fortune* "500" series. On an intraregional basis, 138 front offices of national firms (28 percent of the U.S. total) chose the Manhattan CBD, while the suburban counties which ring the CBD housed only 18 percent of the Region's total, or 6 percent of the nation. The Manhattan-based firms control a disproportionate share of total office activity, 39 percent of the nation's assets, 38 percent of its net profits, and 39 percent of its invested capital. Thirty-six of the ninety top industrial firms, or 40 percent of those that recorded sales in excess of $600 million, were located in the New York Region. Thirty-four of these firms (38 percent of the national total sales leaders) were Manhattan based.

The total number of the headquarters of *Fortune*'s 500 largest industrial corporations in the New York Region increased from 156 in 1958 to 168 in 1963, declined to 159 in 1965 largely because of mergers, and increased again to 161 by 1969. However, over the period, suburbanization of industrials accelerated, and particularly so to western Fairfield County in Connecticut, which is in the New York Region but outside the SCA.

Among the firms that migrated from Manhattan to various suburbs in 1954–1965 are some familiar names—General Foods, Continental Baking, Mack Trucks, Worthington, General Precision Equipment, Curtis Wright, American Cyanamid, Phoenix Steel, Foster Wheeler, International Business Machines. Their new suburban locations are not so easily remembered. Moves completed from 1965 through 1969 resulted in the loss of eight more major corporate headquarters from Manhattan to the Region's suburbs: Flintkote, AVCO, Bangor Punta, CPC International, Howmet, Lone Star Cement, Olin Mathieson, and Union Camp. However, no major losses were recorded over the period to places outside the Region. And at the same time, several industrial headquarters were introduced to the Region, among them Atlantic Richfield and Gulf and Western which are located in Manhattan.

What, on balance, made these firms favor one over the other? Speculation on the subject has b

Table 3.2. Location of the Executive Offices of Industrial and Miscellaneous Corporations in Manhattan, 1912 and 1925

Size of assets (millions of dollars)	South of Fulton St.		Between Fulton and 14th Sts.		Between 14th and 34th Sts.		Between 34th and 59th Sts.		Above 59th St.		Total	
	No.	%	No.	%	No.	%	No.	%	No.	%	No.	%
1912												
Under 25	143	66.9	32	15.0	20	9.3	17	7.9	2	.9	214	100.0
25 and under 50	19	65.5	2	6.9	2	6.9	5	17.2	1	3.5	29	100.0
50 and under 100	23	82.2	2	7.1	2	7.1	1	3.6	—	—	28	100.0
Over 100	10	83.4	—	—	1	8.3	1	8.3	—	—	12	100.0
Total	195	68.9	36	12.7	25	8.8	24	8.5	3	1.1	283	100.0
1925												
Under 25	161	35.3	69	15.1	76	16.7	138	30.3	12	2.6	456	100.0
25 and under 50	35	44.9	9	11.5	10	12.8	24	30.8	—	—	78	100.0
50 and under 100	20	57.1	4	11.4	1	2.9	10	28.6	—	—	35	100.0
Over 100	23	69.7	—	—	3	9.1	7	21.2	—	—	33	100.0
Total	239	39.7	82	13.6	90	15.0	179	29.7	12	2.0	602	100.0

Source: Regional Plan of New York and Its Environs, *Economic and Industrial Survey: The Retail Shopping and Financial Districts*, 1927.
Note: Only companies whose balance sheets were available (*Moody's Analysis of Investments: Industrials*) were included in this table.

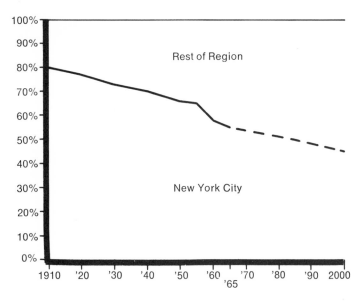

Figure 3.1 New York City's share of total office employment in the Region, 1910–1965

abundant. The subsequent pages will attempt to unravel some of the ties that link headquarters offices to a particular location. At best, this constitutes a "snapshot" view of a momentary equilibrium in a situation that, as we have just seen, has been continuously changing. Hopefully, it can expose certain spatial linkages within the office industry and between the office sector and other activities in the New York Region.

Headquarters Composition by Industry

Before delving into the location pattern of headquarters, their industrial composition should be reviewed. A special Census tabulation of jobs in the central administrative office category (CAO) permits us to investigate the New York standard consolidated area (SCA) in greater detail than was possible in Chapter 2.

The New York SCA has a massive concentration of CAO&A jobs; 19 percent of the nation's and 60 percent of the Middle Atlantic Area's total CAO&A employment is centered here. Measured by central administrative offices (CAO) alone, the Region enjoys an even more disproportionate concentration—22 percent of the nation's total; its detailed composition is shown in Table 3.3.

The manufacturing headquarters located in the New York Region specialize in nondurable goods: as one would expect, industry classifications such as apparel, or printing and publishing, clearly show New York's dominant position in these fields. The Region has roughly one-third of the nation's central office employment in apparel and printing. As one might not expect, however, New York also shows a comparable prominence in industries whose production component in the Region is small, such as chemicals and textiles; these can be managed from the Region by "remote control," so to say, made possible by air transportation and electronic communication.

The central office jobs of durable goods manufacturing in the Region are half as numerous while in the nation as a whole the ratio is more like one to one. Only electrical machinery and fabricated metals stand out, with about one-quarter of the nation's central office jobs. Over the 1958–1963 period, nondurable goods headquarters jobs in the Region kept pace with their nationwide rate of growth; durable goods slipped, in line with the general decentralizing tendency of durable goods manufacturing across the nation.

Within this overall picture, Table 3.3 shows some interesting variations by industry. In the nondurable goods category, New York increased its share of the nation's office employment in food, paper, chemicals, and petroleum—categories in which it has not been too strongly represented. It reduced its share of the nation's office employment in textiles, apparel, and publishing—

categories in which it was heavily overrepresented. The nationwide decentralization of the production facilities of these industries apparently induced related adjustments in the location of their office functions.

A similar dual trend, if less pronounced, occurred in the durable goods category. Fabricated metals—previously among the largest employment groups—declined rather drastically, while electrical machinery increased to emerge as the dominant group in this category.

Nonmanufacturing central office employment, related to New York's traditional strength in finance and trade, increased its concentration in the area, as the bottom part of Table 3.3 shows. During the five-year period, central office service jobs rose 76 percent in the nation with the New York area acquiring four out of every ten new jobs. Similarly, in wholesale trade, headquarters positions expanded 16 percent in the nation and 26 percent in the SCA. Stated in comparative terms, the New York SCA captured one out of every four new wholesale trade headquarters jobs. Retail trade performed even better, and where central office employment advanced 8 percent in the nation, it rose 19 percent in the SCA and, in so doing, diverted nearly half of the national economy's net gain to New York. These data show that the Region is sharing more favorably in the economy's rate of pure central office (CAO) growth than can be gleaned from overall changes reported in the CAO&A sector.

Another way to look at the industrial composition of the Region's headquarters is to assign the firms listed in the Fortune "500" series to the SIC industry groups[4] used previously. This is done in Table 3.4 for 1963, a year that corresponds with a CAO&A enumeration. The geographic base is the 31-county Region, rather than the 17-county SCA, but in 1963 the Region outside the SCA housed less than one percent of the nation's front offices (by 1969, this figure increased to nearly 3 percent).

The diversity of the New York Region's headquarters operations, as seen in Table 3.4, is remarkable. In contrast to other metropolitan areas, every manufacturing industry is represented in the Region's headquarters sector. Nonetheless, there is some specialization. Headquarters of predominantly nondurable goods producing industries account for 56 percent of total elite headquarters in the New York area. The leading industrial sector is the chemical products group which houses 25 front offices in Manhattan and 6 elsewhere in the Region. The petroleum industry, however, leads all manufacturing in terms of total financial and economic impact with five headquarters locations controlling more than one-fourth the assets, profits, and capital generated by the

4. The standard industrial classification code (SIC), used by federal and state agencies, classifies establishments by their principal product or service.

Table 3.3. Central Administrative Office Employment for Selected Industries in the New York SCA, 1958–1963

	1958		1963		
	Number	Share of nation	Number	Share of nation	% change 1958–1963
Manufacturing	107,831	23.9%	117,779	22.8%	9.2%
Nondurable goods	62,591	29.0	71,244	29.3	13.8
Food	11,912	21.9	13,578	22.5	14.0
Textile	7,221	58.6	6,174	38.3	−14.5
Apparel	3,015	46.8	3,101	36.1	2.9
Paper	5,566	26.7	6,366	27.8	14.4
Printing and publishing	2,892	52.1	3,178	34.0	9.9
Chemicals	20,893	32.5	27,045	36.7	29.4
Petroleum and coal	11,092	21.3	11,802	22.6	6.4
Durable goods	32,622	21.9	35,847	19.9	9.9
Stone, clay, glass	2,823	15.7	2,994	12.0	6.1
Primary metals	3,819	11.7	4,281	11.6	12.1
Fabricated metals	7,671	28.9	5,076	25.7	−33.8
Nonelectrical machinery	7,950	26.5	8,913	21.4	12.1
Electrical machinery	9,403	26.6	13,330	28.1	41.8
Instruments	956	15.6	1,253	13.1	31.1
All other manufacturing	12,618	14.7	10,688	11.6	−15.3
Selected services	4,453	29.6	9,310	35.2	109.1
Business services	1,576	35.8	3,642	42.1	131.1
Wholesale trade	14,858	14.5	18,752	15.8	26.2
Retail trade	27,374	18.4	32,505	20.3	18.7
Total	154,516	21.6	178,346	21.7	15.4

Source: U.S. Census, *Enterprise Statistics: 1958 and 1963*, Special tabulation.

The traditional location for detached industrial headquarters offices has been the central business district, epitomized here by midtown Manhattan, which still houses nearly one-quarter of the nation's major industrial front offices. The composite photograph shows midtown skyscrapers in elevation as of January, 1970, at a scale of 1 inch = 500 feet, exactly twice the size of maps 3.3 and 3.4.

65   HEADQUARTERS COMPOSITION BY INDUSTRY

New suburban headquarters locations are illustrated by American Cyanamid in Wayne (*facing page*) and Hess Oil in Woodbridge (*below*), both in New Jersey about 22 airline miles from Midtown Manhattan. The administrative offices of American Cyanamid shown do not include the consumer-related Fibers Division, or regional sales offices, which remain in Manhattan. The Hess Oil building on the New Jersey Turnpike (*foreground*) is related to the Eastern Seaboard's largest concentration of oil refineries.

Table 3.4. Industrial Headquarters in the New York Region, 1963

| Industry | Number of hdqrs. | Millions of dollars | | | | Total national employ. |
		National sales	National assets	National net profit	National invested capital	
Mining	4	$1,590	$1,830	$154	$1,483	55,210
Manufacturing	161	91,096	84,817	5,862	53,320	3,732,510
Nondurable goods	94	54,532	52,622	3,949	33,934	1,667,410
Food and kindred products	18	9,535	5,290	419	3,347	296,940
Tobacco manufacturing	5	1,773	2,047	153	1,372	48,730
Textile mill products	9	2,045	1,438	51	732	121,950
Apparel and related products	4	625	454	27	242	51,220
Paper and allied products	10	4,154	3,745	189	2,638	191,940
Printing and publishing	8	1,244	990	53	426	50,300
Chemicals and allied products	31	14,163	14,537	1,090	8,794	506,460
Petroleum and coal products	5	19,522	22,991	1,925	15,775	313,210
Rubber and miscellaneous plastics	3	1,352	1,018	34	534	79,160
Leather and leather products	1	119	112	8	74	7,500
Durable goods	67	36,564	32,195	1,913	19,386	2,065,100
Lumber and wood products	2	500	699	24	417	17,770
Furniture and fixtures	1	141	94	4	68	8,750
Stone, clay, and glass products	5	867	810	54	633	41,030
Fabricated metals	8	3,023	2,127	102	1,333	160,810
Primary metals	12	6,977	8,483	404	5,967	337,160
Nonelectrical machinery	15	4,647	4,342	395	2,614	234,660
Electrical machinery	12	15,584	12,732	734	6,661	1,022,630
Transportation equipment	8	4,082	2,317	161	1,252	206,280
Instruments and related products	3	653	527	31	398	30,760
Miscellaneous manufacturing	1	90	64	4	43	5,250
Other	3	625	464	7	255	35,600
Total	168	93,311	87,111	6,023	55,058	3,823,320

Source: "The Fortune Directory," 1964.
Note: Corporations were assigned to an industry group by Regional Plan Association, utilizing standard industrial classification codes for corporations as listed in *Poor's Register of Corporations, Directors and Executives*, 1967.

regional totals as shown in Table 3.4. Other significant industry groups with headquarters representation in the New York area are the food and electrical machinery sectors.

In aggregate terms, the top four industries cited comprise 39 percent of corporate front offices in the Region but control nearly two-thirds of the sales, assets, and invested capital. While not necessarily the fastest growing industries in the nation, they are, nevertheless, performing in an above-average manner, registering yearly gains in sales of 5–7 percent, profits of 4–15 percent, and invested capital of 9–15 percent. The remaining corporate sectors are not to be ignored, however, for their aggregate sales volume exceeds corporate sales for any other metropolitan area.

The Pattern of Manufacturing Headquarters

GEOGRAPHIC DISTRIBUTION

Certain kinds of office activity—specifically either the more routine, labor-intensive functions or the local-market or population-related activities—are comparatively insensitive to the benefits of location in the Manhattan CBD. They are, however, primarily responsible for the growth of outlying office activity. Hence, migration of these jobs within a region is primarily a natural consequence of growth and only rarely a symptom of a reduction in the external benefits offered by a CBD location. Nevertheless, some national market-oriented firms have moved their headquarters out of the CBD. Is this movement indicative of a growing "footloose" element in headquarters activity, or are they exceptions to the rule? Manufacturing-office activity was selected for research into this question because it is an important case and there was sufficient data to do an analysis. Manufacturing tends to be directed from a detached front office and has both strong inward (production) and strong outward (market) linkages. Furthermore, any large-scale decentralization of manufacturing headquarters could undermine the strength of the CBD as an office district.

Manufacturing office jobs located in detached office buildings account for one-tenth of total manufacturing employment. These jobs range in scope from central administrative headquarters jobs to those in local field offices. Our concern, however, is with the central office establishments which comprise the top three-quarters of this group. Nearly three-fourths of all manufacturing detached front offices in the Region are housed in the CBD, but not all industry types gravitate there to an equal degree, as indicated in Table 3.5. The range among industry types extends from 94 percent to 25 percent of headquarters establishments located in the CBD—a finding indicative of intense specialization in

Table 3.5. The Location of Manufacturing Headquarters Ranked by Descending Order of Centrality in the Region, 1963

| Industry | Central administrative offices by ring as a percentage of industry totals | | | | | |
	Man-hattan CBD	Rest of core	Inner ring	Inter-mediate ring	Outer ring	Total
Leather	94.1%	5.9%	—	—	—	100.0%
Apparel	93.7	2.5	1.3%	2.6%	—	100.0
Tobacco	90.0	—	10.0	—	—	100.0
Textile	84.6	4.6	4.6	6.2	—	100.0
Petroleum and coal	83.9	—	3.2	9.7	3.2%	100.0
Paper	83.8	8.1	2.7	5.4	—	100.0
Furniture and fixtures	83.3	8.3	8.3	—	—	100.0
Transportation	82.6	—	13.0	4.4	—	100.0
Primary metals	81.3	9.4	3.1	6.2	—	100.0
Rubber and plastics	80.0	6.7	—	13.3	—	100.0
Ordnance and miscellaneous	80.0	8.0	4.0	8.0	—	100.0
Total Manufacturing	72.4	7.2	11.2	8.8	.4	100.0
Chemicals	71.7	3.9	16.5	7.9	—	100.0
Fabricated metals	71.4	7.2	11.9	9.5	—	100.0
Printing and publishing	64.1	3.1	21.9	10.9	—	100.0
Food	62.8	11.6	19.8	5.8	—	100.0
Stone, clay, glass	62.2	10.8	16.2	8.1	2.7	100.0
Electrical machinery	55.6	15.9	7.9	19.0	1.6	100.0
Instruments	50.0	6.3	31.2	12.5	—	100.0
Nonelectrical machinery	48.9	10.6	12.8	27.7	—	100.0
Lumber and wood	25.0	50.0	25.0	—	—	100.0

Source: U.S. Census, *Enterprise Statistics: 1963*, Special tabulation.
Note: Detail may not add to totals because of rounding.

many industries choosing downtown locations. Eleven of the twenty industry types listed in Table 3.5 are more centrally oriented than the rest. Their product lines appear to offer a strong clue to their central locational preferences. Twice as many nondurable industries as durable locate greater than average shares of their headquarters offices in the CBD. The top six industry groups are all producers of nondurable items; the top three, with the exception of food, are the major producers of goods which earn the bulk of their receipts in consumer markets as shown in Table 3.6. Four of the remaining five groups produce durable goods. One is a processor of end-product durables while two, transportation and miscellaneous manufacturing, sell the leading, though not major, portion of their output to private consumers. The primary metals industry is unique in that it has a strong central orientation but does not have strong ties to the final consumer. Twice as many durable as nondurable goods sectors lie below the overall mean of central location tendency, and they produce items which usually sell to intermediate consumers, that is, industrial consumers.[5] Thus, one may conclude safely that *the more consumer oriented and/or nondurable is a firm's product, the stronger is its need or desire to be headquartered in a central location.*

There is another group of industries that are strongly associated with one another through interindustry purchases. The economic interrelationships characterizing these firms both demand proximity among headquarters operations and promote central location. But, even among these industries, the durable goods component, except for primary metals, is underrepresented among headquarters establishments in the Manhattan CBD.

Choice among the rings varies in these industries. Headquarters of *electrical* and *nonelectrical machinery* are more than twice as numerous in the intermediate ring than in the inner ring. The opposite relationship is true of headquarters for *instruments* and *stone, clay, and glass,* which gravitate toward the inner ring. Nonetheless, more than twice as many industries in the nondurable component of intermediary production exhibit a high preference for central location of headquarters. The bulk of those establishments manifesting weaker ties to the CBD, for example, *chemicals* and *printing,* locate in the inner ring.

Let us examine in detail the character of interindustry office relationships and their impact on promoting or diluting the influence and importance of centralized office location.

TIES TO THE PURCHASING ESTABLISHMENT
Spatial linkages in the Region's pattern of headquarters

5. We have defined consumer goods as those items for which more than half of total output demand arises from the household sector.

location may be examined according to input/output relationships that normally occur between industrial producers and suppliers. While detached headquarters do not engage in the physical transfer of goods, the verbal and written communication that precedes such a transfer occurs between head offices and is a vital component of the demand for face-to-face contact. Table 3.6 lists the manufacturing industries with headquarters establishments in the Region by central orientation of front offices and major purchasers of industrial product.

Let us first describe the organizational structure of purchasing sectors and expose our views regarding the force they can exert on the attractiveness of centralized headquarters location. The purchasing sector may range in number of decision-making units from a multitude of small households to a few giant, oligopolistic firms. Depending upon the number and accessibility of potential customers, a businessman will employ various communication techniques to reach and influence his market. Imagery or product identification through advertising best serve the businessman in overcoming the separation existing between a single headquarters as seller and numerous, dispersed households as purchaser. On the other hand, face-to-face contact, or personal communication, produces optimum results when the market is characterized by a few purchasers. Between these extremes is a stratum consisting of many small firms, more random in location than the corporate headquarters, yet less dispersed than those directly linked to a consumer market. Agriculture, construction, entertainment, and business services typify purchasing sectors in this stratum.

For the bulk of manufacturing activity (sixteen of twenty industrial groups), output is geared more toward other producing units (interfirm purchases) than toward private households, the government, or other elements of final demand. While final demand may account for a considerable part of the income earned by these manufacturing activities (none are over 50 percent), one would expect, nevertheless, the industry group to spend less per unit of output on media advertising than it would if it were more concerned with end products. That is, consumer taste does not assume the importance in interindustry transactions that it does in end-product sales. In the former, technological imperatives play a heavy role in determining seller-buyer relationships whereas, in the latter, the intangible effects of a contrived "image" may be the paramount factor influencing final or end-product demand. The concentration of advertising, marketing, and media services in Manhattan is an important "externality" for headquarters of firms with wide consumer markets and exerts, therefore, a pull toward the CBD on such firms. But for many manufacturing front offices, no such pull is felt since their market interests are promoted

Table 3.6. Major Purchasers of Manufacturing Groups Maintaining Headquarters in the Manhattan CBD

Headquarters industry group*	Major purchasers of product by industrial or market classification			% of product sold to leading purchaser†	Index of central force‡
	Leading	Second	Third		
Part I. Consumer goods producers§					
Strong central preference					
Leather	Households	Leather	Miscellaneous manufacturing	65.4%	93
Apparel	Households	Apparel	Government	76.2	96
Tobacco	Households	Tobacco	Entertainment	71.8	93
Furniture and fixtures	Households	Capital investment	Construction	52.7	53
Below average central preference					
Food	Households	Food	Agriculture	72.0	72
Part II. Intermediary and industrial goods producers					
Strong central preference					
Textile	Textile	Apparel	Households	39.3%	84
Petroleum and coal	Households	Transportation and warehousing	Construction	42.1	51
Paper	Paper	Printing	Food	30.0	30
Transportation	Households	Transportation	Government	25.4	50
Primary metals	Primary metals	Fabricated metals	Construction	26.4	26
Rubber and plastics	Households	Transportation	Construction	19.1	30
Miscellaneous manufacturing	Households	Miscellaneous manufacturing	Capital investment	48.0	53
Below average central preference					
Chemicals	Chemicals	Households	Textile	26.1	22
Fabricated metals	Construction	Transportation	Fabricated metals	32.6	18
Printing and publishing	Business services	Households	Printing	43.3	32
Stone, clay, glass	Construction	Stone, clay, glass	Food	49.9	11
Electrical machinery	Households	Electrical machinery	Capital investment	21.4	37
Instruments	Households	Government	Capital investment	16.1	16
Nonelectrical machinery	Capital investment	Nonelectrical machinery	Government	41.6	14
Lumber and wood	Construction	Lumber and wood	Paper	40.2	39

Source: Regional Plan Association.
* Ranked by descending order of industry centrality.
† An industry average based upon dollar flow transactions of the national input-output table for 1958.
‡ The index of central force represents the percentage of gross output sold to sectors exerting a centralizing pull, or strong force for high accessibility. The sectors are as follows: manufacturing industries with headquarters marked by a strong central locational preference in the New York Region; households, for selling purposes of advertising and image creation; nonmanufacturing groups with a major portion of headquarters establishments locating in Manhattan; and the same, or selling, manufacturing group for purposes of facilitating contact through accessibility. The purchasers regarded as having a neutral or negative central force on location in the New York Region are as follows: capital investment; government; manufacturing industries with headquarters bearing a below average preference for central location; and nonmanufacturing industries with a major portion of headquarters or office establishments locating in the Region outside Manhattan. The numerous small business service and construction establishments fall among the latter. Although the export sector might rightfully appear as a major purchaser in a few instances, it was omitted because the locational force it can exert may cut both ways—neutrally, or negatively, in that buyers often seek out customers, and positively, in that a central location at a port of export facilitates transactions with domestically based branches of foreign companies.
§ More than half of gross industrial output purchased by personal consumption expenditures.

by close contact with competitive and complementary firms and their purchasers and suppliers.[6]

The estimated indices of central force constructed for Table 3.6 provide an indication of the intensity with which firms seek central locations. For most headquarters in industries exhibiting stronger than average central tendencies—excepting paper and primary metals processors—the locational role of households and complementary and competing industry groups is almost self-evident. Accessibility to central offices of major industrial purchasers may be an especially significant or, at least, accommodating force in the location of head offices directing the production and sale of leather, apparel, and textile goods.

Therefore, the locational characteristics of the purchasing sectors with which a headquarters transacts its business exert a force over the locational decisions of the headquarters itself. Central offices exhibiting stronger than average preferences for central location derive most of their income from sectors either tending themselves to locate in the center or are, in some way, strongly identified with it. This identification may, as in the case of households, be derived through centralized services such as advertising and public relations, or it may be a function of the civic and business role played by a corporation. Those headquarters exhibiting weaker locational preferences for the center are exposed to lesser degrees of centralizing force from their purchasing sector. This may result from either the more dispersed intraregional location of purchasing headquarters or the lesser degree of product identification or corporate "imageability" which enters into the purchasing decisions. Most of the headquarters with weaker ties to the CBD are processors of intermediate durable goods destined for further processing by industrial purchasers. However, some of the headquarters—notably in the foods group—earn a significant portion of their income from a market that, by the locational criteria chosen, should characteristically manifest in a more centralized headquarters distribution. The nature of other ties, weakening this pull, will now be investigated.

TIES WITHIN THE PRODUCTION ESTABLISHMENT
Another critical linkage for the office industry occurs between offices and plant. Headquarters location patterns in the Region suggest that plant distribution has some influence on the location of front offices. According to such measures as factory employment, the processing of durable goods is predominant in manufacturing activity in the suburban rings, while in the CBD, nondurable production leads other forms of manufacturing by a wide margin. In the rest of the core, the mix of durable

6. Orientation to one's own production establishment is a factor that will be discussed later.

and nondurable activities appears much in balance. It is not surprising to find, therefore, that the heavier, durable goods producers account for 44 percent of detached central offices located in the suburban rings, while the core share of its total is only 34 percent. Because nondurable goods headquarters favor the city to the suburbs by four to one, the CBD houses a disproportionate share of them (68 percent), excelling especially in the Region's distribution of textile, leather, and apparel groups, which comprise nearly half of all production employment in the CBD.[7]

Underlying the similarity of location patterns between administrative and production work are myriad linkages among processing plants, research laboratories, and the central administrative offices. Large decentralized manufacturing firms often maintain separate facilities for headquarters, processing plant, and/or laboratory at the same location. But in New York, where there is a prodigious concentration of headquarters directing processing and research facilities that are located elsewhere, such proximity linkages between front offices and production are relatively rare. This is attributable not to a lack of large, decentralized manufacturers maintaining separate administrative facilities in the suburbs but to a surplus or influx of national headquarters in Manhattan which direct a network of processing and research facilities located throughout the Region and the nation (Figure 3.2). This pattern is evident when viewing the composition of production employment in the Region and the number of headquarters by industry located in the Manhattan CBD, as shown in Table 3.7.

Such evidence of those with direct linkages should be explored. For example, Johnson and Johnson has its headquarters adjacent to its plant for manufacturing of surgical, medical, and baby products in New Brunswick, N.J., and Merck also placed its head office and research laboratory next to a major chemical processing plant in Rahway, N.J. However, both firms made these locational decisions before World War II, and one may conclude that they represent an older suburbanizing trend in the Region. Recent departures of head offices from the CBD have primarily entailed the relocation of a national administrative office to a nonindustrial, suburban campus environment.

Among the 28 major industrial headquarters located in the Region's suburbs which were listed in Fortune's "500" series for 1963, only seven firms operated detached

7. Obvious exceptions exist to this association, however. The leading headquarters group, in numbers of central offices located in the CBD, is the *chemical and drug* industry. But this industry accounts for only one percent of total production employment in the CBD, while, on the other hand, the printing industry, which has fewer headquarters in Manhattan than do chemicals and drugs, generates 22 percent of total production employment in the CBD.

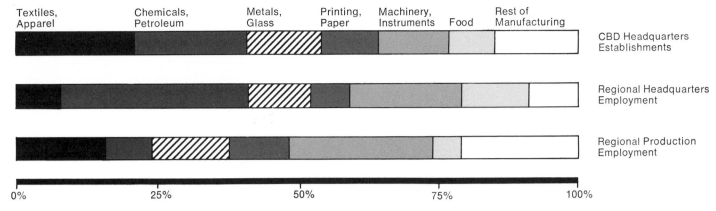

Figure 3.2 The composition of manufacturing headquarters and production activity in the New York Region

Table 3.7. Manufacturing Headquarters in the CBD and Production Employment in the Region: The Industry Composition as a Share of Total

Industry group	Regional production No. employed (× 1,000)	% of total	CBD central offices No. of hdqrs.	% of total
Food	87.8	5.0%	54	8.9%
Tobacco	.3	.0	9	1.5
Textile	65.6	3.7	55	9.1
Apparel	216.2	12.2	74	12.2
Lumber and wood	11.3	.6	2	.3
Furniture and fixtures	32.9	1.9	10	1.7
Paper	54.7	3.1	31	5.1
Printing and publishing	129.2	7.3	41	6.8
Chemicals	131.6	7.4	91	15.0
Petroleum and coal	6.6	.4	26	4.3
Rubber and plastics	42.2	2.4	12	2.0
Leather	45.4	2.6	16	2.7
Stone, clay, glass	41.6	2.4	23	3.8
Primary metals	79.0	4.5	26	4.3
Fabricated metals	128.0	7.2	30	5.0
Nonelectrical machinery	167.0	9.5	23	3.8
Electrical machinery	225.2	12.8	35	5.8
Transportation	109.6	6.2	19	3.1
Instruments	71.6	4.0	8	1.3
Miscellaneous manufacturing and ordnance	119.5	6.8	20	3.3
Total	1,765.3	100.0	605	100.0

Source: Regional Plan Association, based partly on special tabulations of the U.S. Census, *Enterprise Statistics: 1963.*

Table 3.8. Major Industrial Headquarters Located in the Region Outside New York City: The Number of Plant and Research Locations Maintained Outside the City in 1963

	No. of hdqrs.	No. in same county as hdqrs.		No. located in suburban counties other than hdqrs. county	
		Plants	Labs	Plants	Labs
Nondurable goods	12	9	6	16	5
Food	3	2	2	1	—
Apparel	1	1	—	—	—
Paper	1	1	—	1	—
Chemicals	6	4	4	14	5
Rubber and plastics	1	1	—	—	—
Durable goods	16	17	5	16	—
Stone, clay, glass	2	1	—	1	—
Primary metals	2	2	—	—	—
Nonelectrical machinery	3	2	—	3	—
Electrical machinery	2	1	1	4	—
Transportation	4	6	2	5	—
Instruments	2	4	2	3	—
Miscellaneous manufacturing	1	1	—	—	—
Total manufacturing	28	26	11	32	5

Sources: "The Fortune Directory," 1964; respective state research, industrial, and telephone directories.

headquarters from a suburban county location that did not also house, within county lines, a manufacturing establishment of the firm. In eleven instances, the county of headquarters location was also the locus of the firm's only regional processing establishments. Thus, a number of the major industrial headquarters were found to have a strong association with the location of production facilities. This association simply indicates that for some firms, benefits exist when headquarters and plant are located close to one another.

While every suburban headquarters in the "500" sample had one or more counterpart processing establishments located in one or more of the suburban counties of the Region, not all maintained research laboratories, either within or outside the Region. Ten headquarters were sited in the same county as their laboratory facility; three located labs in counties other than that of their headquarters; and only one had multiple county locations for research activity. Though a spatial association with research facilities does exist, it appears that the greater abundance of separate plant facilities influences the location of a larger number of physically detached head offices in the suburban rings. However, in the locational pattern of plants and laboratories engaged in durable goods production, we notice a uniformly closer linkage to suburban headquarters location than is the case with nondurable goods activity, and all research facilities of durable plants were found in the county of headquarters location as seen in Table 3.8.

Of 138 major headquarters listed in Fortune's series with home office locations in Manhattan, 35 maintained separate research facilities in the New York portion of the Region,[8] comprising 43 facilities of which 18 were housed within New York City itself. Most product research was conducted by laboratories of nondurable producers (31 research facilities for *food, chemicals and drugs, petroleum,* and *other*). Fourteen of these laboratories tied to the production of nondurable goods were located in New York City. By way of contrast, twice as many of the durable goods research facilities located in the New York suburbs, although suburban laboratories were also predominantly engaged in nondurable production (17 of a total 25).

Thus, viewed from a suburban perspective, nondurable goods activity shows a greater degree of freedom from spatial linkages to research and production facilities. It is perhaps this degree of freedom, favored by the more centralized distribution of nondurable production and coupled with the stronger ties of soft goods marketing to final demand, that attracts most nondurable adminis-

8. Data on research facilities for New Jersey were not available at the time of research, nor was a uniform source of information on plant locations of CBD headquarters.

trative offices and holds them in a central business district location.

TIES TO THE ADVERTISING WORLD

About half of the firms which spend the most on advertising are located in the New York Region. It is not surprising to find, therefore, that the Region, especially the Manhattan CBD, is nationally preeminent in advertising services. Of the 125 advertising leaders in the nation, 49 are located in Manhattan and another 13, elsewhere in the Region. The data in Table 3.9 indicate that the firms located outside the CBD generally tend to be smaller but, paradoxically, heavier spenders on advertising. Their aggregate sales account for 3 percent of the national figure, but advertising budgets represent 9 percent of the same total. Firms based in Manhattan spend slightly in excess of 2 percent of gross sales on advertising while their suburban neighbors spend more than 8 percent. What is the significance of this spending pattern?

It may be recalled from an earlier section that few soft goods producers chose suburban locations. In fact, *chemicals, printing,* and *food* producers provided the only exceptions to what was otherwise a CBD oriented group. However, *chemical* and *food* producers spend more on advertising than do other industry groups. Further, the two industries account for all of the nondurable goods producers located outside the CBD in the advertising survey and eleven of the thirteen top advertisers with suburban locations in the Region. And while the Manhattan-based headquarters in the same industry group are more representative of the nation in per unit expenditures, their suburban counterparts are heavier advertisers.

The inconsistency may be explained in terms of the locational freedom, or footloose quality of these headquarters. Their "footlooseness" comes at a price to the firm (or to the consumer) and is, in effect, purchased through the added costs of corporate image-building and product differentiation. Or, there is another way of explaining the large advertising outlays of suburban headquarters. The suburban headquarters are, on average, more representative of the extremes in a spectrum of firm size. Being either large or small producers, they tend to spend more per unit on advertising than do medium-sized firms.

That both very large and small firms can thrive in a suburban environment without apparent integration of advertising activity into their own corporate structure leads to another important conclusion. That is, the pull of intraregional locational ties to a concentration of supporting business services such as advertising is not infinitely strong. It is possible for the benefits of a decentralized location to outweigh the costs of spatial friction.

And this, of course, is precisely the argument of the "decentralists" who would strive to decant the city.

The data, however, firmly support the acknowledged importance of advertising linkages on an interregional basis. Indeed, it is perhaps a facility for using the media to influence national markets that constitutes a basic locational advantage of New York as a site for headquarters operation. But, perhaps intraregionally, linkages occurring within and between firms of the manufacturing sector are more important for selecting a headquarters site than demands for frequent, or facile, contact with supporting business services. No single determining location factor may be isolated, however, since a headquarters makes a plethora of demands upon a regional economy and responds reciprocally to a diverse set of locational benefits.

LOCATION BY SIZE OF FIRM

The data in Table 3.10 show that average size of a headquarters office is not significantly affected by distance from CBD, or ring location. In Manhattan the heterogeneous makeup of its headquarters operations is quite apparent. High-priced space is demanded here by both large and small front offices. Further, within industry groups, no consistent size pattern emerges.

Some tendencies may be observed, nonetheless. Manufacturing head office size appears to drop off gradually from the center to the intermediate ring, where it registers an increase before dropping again in the outer ring. Interindustry variation in average size of central office is quite marked, ranging from the small leather and apparel headquarters with less than fifty employees to the giant tobacco and petroleum offices with nearly four hundred workers per unit. This variation undoubtedly reflects different market structures in the respective industries.

Spatial factors exert pressure on head offices in relation to their relative size in the manufacturing group and the industry's disposition toward centrality. Head offices for any one industry group, when arrayed by size (to segregate the large administrative units over 150 employees per establishment), display a positive correlation between size variation by ring of development and central preference in headquarters location. In other words, large establishment industries such as *tobacco, petroleum,* and *paper,* which tend to place a relatively large share of head offices at the center, also have larger-sized CBD headquarters than do their suburban counterparts. Then too, industries with weak central tendencies, such as *chemicals, food,* and *nonelectrical machinery,* have CBD office operations that are dwarfed by their suburban counterparts.

A different pattern is evident for smaller head offices.

Table 3.9. The Region's Share of the Nation's Leading Advertisers, 1965

Industry group	Nationwide Firms	Nationwide $ Advert. (× $1 million)	Nationwide % of sales	New York Region Firms	New York Region $ Advert. (× $1 million)	New York Region % of sales	Manhattan CBD Firms	Manhattan CBD $ Advert. (× $1 million)	Manhattan CBD % of sales
Food	40	$1,151.5	4.7%	14	$536.8	5.4%	11	$385.3	4.9%
Food products	22	690.7	3.8	8	350.2	4.8	5	198.7	3.9
Gum and candy	3	52.5	11.5	1	21.0	10.4	1	21.0	10.4
Beverages	15	408.3	6.8	5	165.6	6.7	5	165.6	6.7
Tobacco	8	313.1	5.8	6	202.5	6.4	6	202.5	6.4
Apparel	2	35.0	7.3	2	35.0	7.3	2	35.0	7.3
Paper and allied	3	52.3	2.2	1	12.3	1.0	1	12.3	1.0
Chemicals and allied	33	1,259.9	8.2	22	776.6	9.5	14	572.6	9.3
Chemicals	5	163.0	2.1	3	86.6	2.4	2	39.8	1.4
Drugs and cosmetics	23	631.1	14.9	17	505.0	13.9	10	347.8	14.6
Soaps, cleansers	5	465.8	13.5	2	185.0	21.6	2	185.0	21.6
Petroleum and related	6	99.0	.3	4	63.5	.2	4	63.5	.2
Rubber and plastics	4	116.7	1.9	1	26.8	2.2	1	26.8	2.2
Tires	4	116.7	1.9	1	26.8	2.2	1	26.8	2.2
Stone, clay, glass	2	27.7	2.0	—	—	—	—	—	—
Primary metals	2	23.4	1.2	—	—	—	—	—	—
Fabricated metals	2	62.0	15.8	1	10.0	18.7	—	—	—
Electrical machinery	6	195.2	1.5	4	146.9	1.4	4	146.9	1.4
Household appliances	4	174.0	1.6	2	125.7	1.5	2	125.7	1.5
Communications equipment	2	21.2	.9	2	21.2	.9	2	21.2	.9
Transportation equipment	5	409.0	1.0	1	17.0	3.4	—	—	—
Motor vehicles	5	409.0	1.0	1	17.0	3.4	—	—	—
Instruments	2	55.0	4.7	—	—	—	—	—	—
Miscellaneous manufacturers	2	55.0	4.7	—	—	—	—	—	—
Air transportation	6	77.8	2.2	4	55.3	2.2	4	55.3	2.2
Communications	2	92.1	.8	2	92.1	.8	2	92.1	.8
General merchandise	1	86.0	1.3	—	—	—	—	—	—
Total	125	4,066.2	2.4	62	1,974.8	2.6	49	1,592.3	2.3

Source: *Advertising Age*, 1967. Reprinted with permission from the August 28, 1967 issue of *Advertising Age*. Copyright 1967 by Advertising Publications Inc.

For headquarters groups of 80 to 150 employees, the medium-sized operations, an inverse relationship generally exists between central locational tendency and size. Industry groups with a strong affinity for the CBD locate smaller-sized units there and larger operations in the rest of the core and the intermediate ring. For the few medium-sized groups which one would expect to have weak CBD ties, no pattern is evident. For instance, the *fabricated metals* industry locates its larger offices in the CBD while producers of scientific and photographic *instruments* site their big administrative units in core counties.

The smallest establishment size group (80 employees or less per headquarters unit) maintains undersized office operations in the CBD. An exception is the *lumber and wood products* industry, which manifests the weakest overall central tendencies by establishment distribution but locates its largest single offices in the center. The other small head office groups choose inner and intermediate ring locations when decentralizing their largest headquarters units.

In sum, one finds that size of headquarters and intra-regional locational tendency do not correlate simply or strongly. In the case of the largest firms, headquarters distribution appears to reinforce the pattern of locational preference within the Region, while in the middle and lower ranges, size tends to compensate for location. The end product of such relationships is, indeed, a mixed one. Because firms in the manufacturing sector exhibit varying demands for central and suburban office space, it is apparent that both the core and the environs of the Region must be prepared to offer, or accommodate, a variety of headquarters offices. No one area of the Region may be categorized as the appropriate location for exclusively small or large front offices. In absolute terms, however, the Manhattan CBD houses the greatest number of all three strata—67 percent of the large units, 78 percent of medium-sized offices, and 76 percent of small headquarters, or 72 percent of all central administrative offices in manufacturing.

MAIN VERSUS SECONDARY OFFICES
The importance of ties to the externalities provided within the CBD varies not only between different industry groups but also within any given group. Moreover, within the firm itself, it may be advantageous to sort out office functions with strong central linkages from the others and locate them so that location benefits received and rents paid are optimally balanced. Let us consider the behavior of these firms in respect to multiple office locations.

One of every five major manufacturing firms with headquarters in Manhattan maintains other office space in the CBD for separate aspects of its overall administra-

Table 3.10. Manufacturing Headquarters by Average Employment Size and by Ring in the Region, 1963

Industry*	Average employment size of central administrative offices					
	Manhattan CBD	Rest of core	Inner ring	Intermediate ring	Outer ring	Region
Leather	18	38	—	—	—	19
Apparel	41	12	10	106	—	41
Tobacco	408	—	10	—	—	368
Textile	96	146	98	53	—	95
Petroleum and coal	406	—	132	298	137	378
Paper	201	23	55	11	—	172
Furniture and fixtures	72	57	106	—	—	74
Transportation	89	—	105	7	—	87
Primary metals	139	228	10	153	—	144
Rubber and plastics	144	167	—	52	—	133
Ordnance and miscellaneous	48	21	159	350	—	74
Total manufacturing	151	106	132	192	52	149
Chemicals	219	133	210	249	—	216
Fabricated metals	143	23	68	120	—	123
Printing and publishing	61	15	36	122	—	61
Food	154	80	261	23	—	159
Stone, clay, glass	73	70	145	55	10	80
Electrical machinery	323	149	47	196	10	239
Instruments	21	668	41	164	—	86
Nonelectrical machinery	219	159	36	389	—	242
Lumber and wood	162	19	62	—	—	65

Source: U.S. Census, *Enterprise Statistics: 1963*, Special tabulation.
* Ranked by descending order of industry centrality.

tive work. Maps 3.3 and 3.4 depict the front office distribution of industrial firms reporting sales of $1 million and over in midtown Manhattan. The firms are graphically identified for sales volume and product type, and the maps detail other central office space purchased by the firm which is detached from the headquarters location. For these offices, the corresponding front office is not ascertainable, but the sites are differentiated by sales order and product type of the firm. The maps suggest a considerable degree of sales and product affinity in the location of headquarters in Manhattan. Firms with a greater annual volume of business bid more effectively for the higher priced, prestigious office locations along Park Avenue, in Rockefeller Center and the accessible Grand Central area, while smaller, less prosperous firms are found south and westward of the high rent district (areas of lower proximity to the suburban transit routes). Certain industry groups such as *chemicals, petroleum,* and *tobacco,* those with a high share of headquarters in the Region relative to production employment, cluster their head offices closely together, while industry groups with presumably a lower order of export activity (*metals* and *machinery* for instance) display more dispersive locational characteristics.

Firm size appears to be correlated with the maintenance of multioffice operations. Table 3.11 shows that the largest firms maintain the greatest number of other core and "rest of Region" operations. More than half the firms with sales of $600 million and over, that is, the office elites, maintain multiple offices in the central business district. On the average, nearly three separate offices are occupied in addition to the headquarters address. This contrasts with firms grossing under $60 million which have, in the aggregate, few secondary offices in Manhattan (less than 10 percent) outside of their primary CBD office operation. There is considerable circumstantial evidence to suggest that it is growth per se that is the driving force causing fragmentation in the office industry. Why is this so? Consider that, first, the locational pattern of secondary central space relates quite closely to that of headquarters space, and that, in operation, space users are structured along departmental or product, that is, marketing, lines. These factors suggest that it is not variations in rents within the CBD nor the desire to improve accessibility which chiefly determines the demand for secondary space or shapes its locational pattern. Instead, factors pertaining to the inability of firms to expand facilities incrementally or the drive to locate segments of operations in certain parts of the CBD which supply highly specialized benefits really provide a more adequate explanation of the locational pattern of secondary offices in the CBD.

For the elites, partial evidence shows that the nature of their office space demand in the rest of the Region is

Table 3.11. Secondary Offices of Manhattan Manufacturing Headquarters by Annual Sales Range, 1967

| Sales range | Major manufacturing headquarters reporting sales of $1 million and over | | | | |
	Total hdqrs.	No. with other Manhattan offices	Total other Manhattan offices	No. with other offices in rest of Region	Total other offices in rest of Region
$600 million and over	44	23	65	25	84
$300–600 million	34	12	20	16	27
$60–300 million	121	40	62	43	64
$30–60 million	52	8	9	7	13
$10–30 million	88	9	11	12	12
$1–10 million	192	7	7	8	8
Total	531	99	174	111	208

Source: Regional Plan Association, based primarily on *Poor's Register of Corporations, Directors and Executives,* 1967.

Map 3.3 Location of mid-Manhattan headquarters by annual sales volume

Annual 1965 Corporate Sales Volume

● $60–300 million

⬤ $300–600 million

⬤ $600 million and over

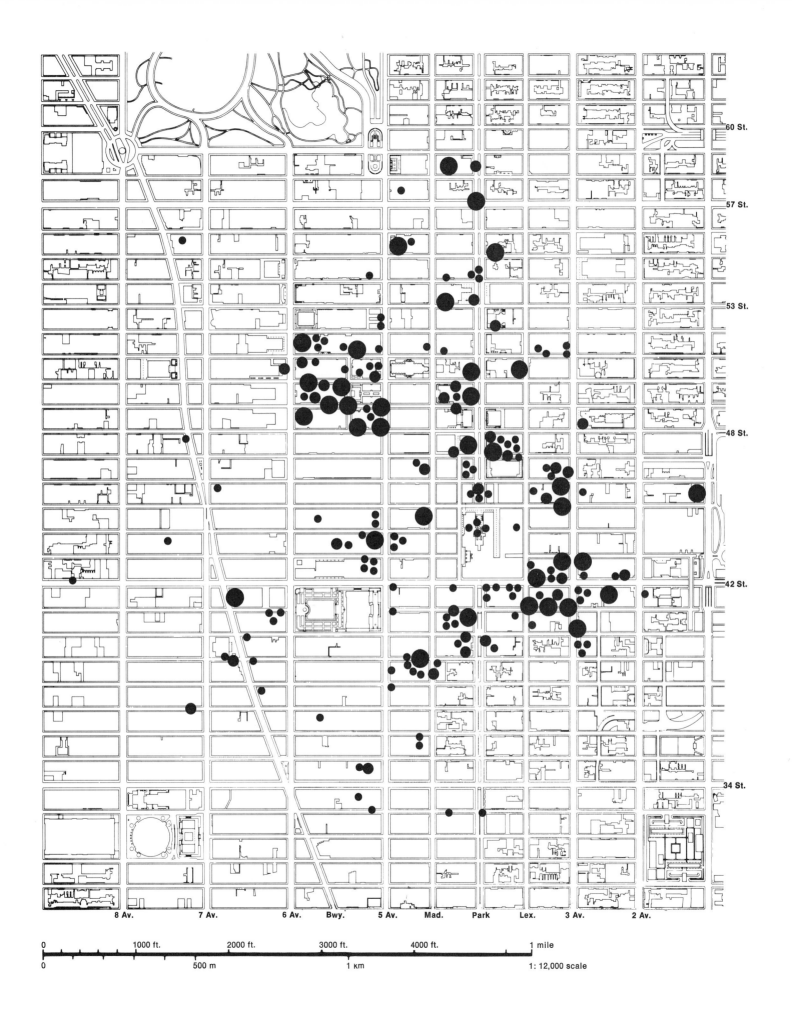

60 St.

57 St.

53 St.

48 St.

42 St.

34 St.

8 Av.   7 Av.   6 Av. Bwy. 5 Av. Mad. Park Lex. 3 Av. 2 Av.

0   1000 ft.   2000 ft.   3000 ft.   4000 ft.   1 mile

0   500 m   1 km   1: 12,000 scale

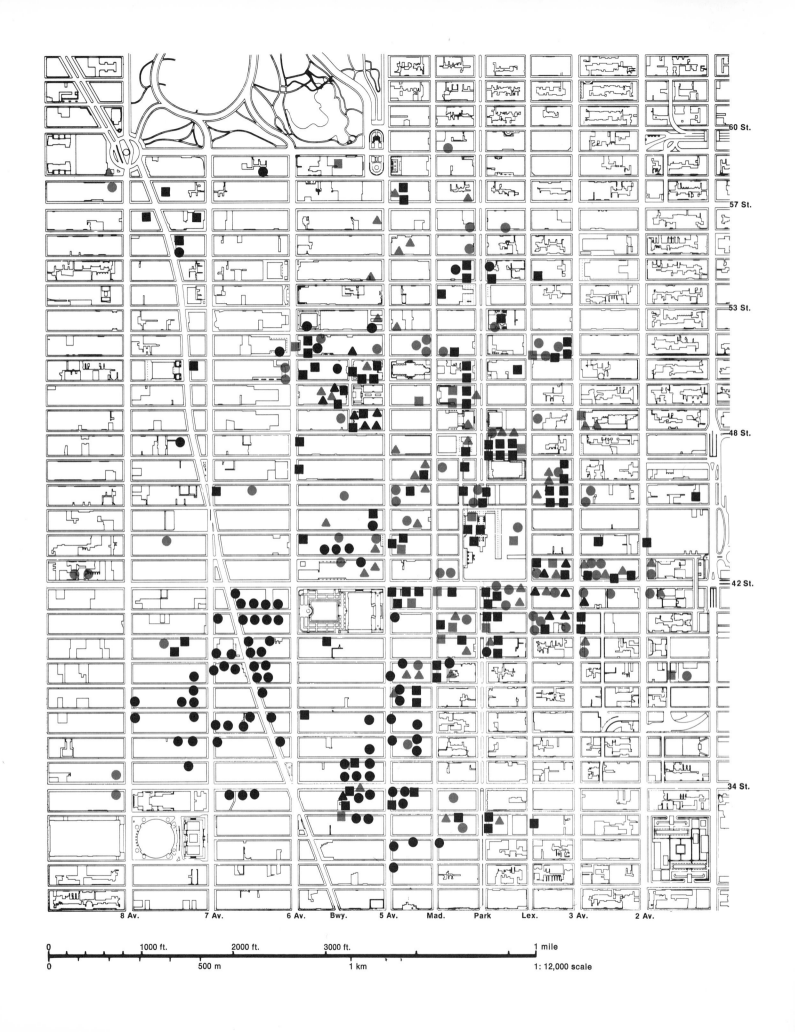

60 St.

57 St.

53 St.

48 St.

42 St.

34 St.

8 Av.   7 Av.   6 Av.   Bwy.   5 Av.   Mad.   Park   Lex.   3 Av.   2 Av.

0   1000 ft.   2000 ft.   3000 ft.   1 mile

0   500 m   1 km   1: 12,000 scale

clearly of another order. This demand responds to a number of locational benefits more characteristic of the suburbs than the core, such as (1) lower space costs per employee; (2) comparative flexibility in expanding per employee space allocations; (3) greater accessibility to a specialized or untapped labor force; (4) more amenable surroundings measured in terms of less congestion or an enhanced environment. Internal economies of production limit the efficient operating size of offices as they do production plants. As a result, diminishing returns to scale may provide a stimulus for secondary office deployment to suburban areas.

Table 3.11 also provides information regarding the secondary office pattern in suburban areas. Indications are that the tendency to purchase other space within the Region for detached office activity or plant-attached office space is only slightly greater than the demand for secondary space in the CBD. We note that firms earning over $300 million in annual sales account for more than half of all decentralized office activity in the sample, but that this overall demand is not too unlike comparable demands made by smaller-sized firms.[9]

Table 3.12 presents industry detail on the pattern of secondary office distribution. Three industry groups are seen to account for about half of the secondary manufacturing offices in the CBD. They are *chemicals* and *machinery (electrical* and *nonelectrical)*, sectors with weak links to the center. Indeed, most headquarters manifesting a greater tendency to maintain multiple offices in the CBD are also representative of those footloose industry groups with weak ties to the Region's center. Specifically, we find that, of those industries more oriented toward the CBD, only 16 percent maintain multiple offices accounting for 30 percent of total sec-

9. Nearly half of the decentralized portion of total headquarters activity consists of district sales and service centers while another fourth represents product divisional units. The former might be characterized as requiring lesser skilled white-collar operations and as being more labor intensive per unit of output than the more broadly based divisional offices or headquarters operations.

Map 3.4 Location of mid-Manhattan headquarters by product type

● Apparel, Textiles and Leather

● Paper, Printing and Publishing

▲ Petroleum

▲ Chemicals

■ Machinery, Instruments, Misc. Manufacturing,
Primary and Fabricated Metals, Transportation Equipment

■ Mining, Rubber, Stone, Clay, Glass, Lumber,
Furniture and Fixtures

ondary office demand. On the other hand, a footloose 20 percent generate 70 percent of the secondary manufacturing offices in the CBD.

The regional location pattern of secondary headquarters space indicates that those industries with a preference for headquarters location in the CBD also require relatively fewer office locations in the rest of the Region. Only 23 percent of the total secondary headquarters space demanded outside the CBD stems from strong CBD oriented firms, or less than their comparable tendency to maintain multiple offices within Manhattan. Conversely, those industry groups that generally tend toward a suburban headquarters location show an equally strong suburban pattern of secondary offices even when their front offices have chosen to remain in Manhattan.

Of those major headquarters ranked among Fortune's "500" which had suburban locations in the Region in 1963, only one-third did not maintain office space in the Manhattan CBD. Nearly another third occupied space at several locations in the midtown and downtown areas, separating such paperwork functions as export/international divisions and regional sales offices. Only three major soft goods manufacturers with suburban headquarters locations showed no indication of office ties to the Region's center. For two of these producers, the nature of their output suggests a stronger orientation to intermediary and industrial purchasers than to final consumer markets.

In conclusion, there is considerable circumstantial evidence to suggest that fragmentation of offices or the tendency for some back office operations to move out of the city into the suburbs is a function of growth per se. Many firms apparently have a great deal of difficulty expanding facilities incrementally. On the other hand, we have seen that the more footloose firms which retain head offices in the CBD also sustain 70 percent of the secondary manufacturing office demand in the center. This means that, for many firms, the cost of space in the CBD may not be the determining factor behind a move to the suburbs. Another factor, such as the "lumpiness" of space availability, may induce firms that characteristically experience lower benefits from central location to seek decentralized sites that promote access to their many other linkages. For other firms, however, the pressures of growth may fragment office operations in the center, where the costs of physical separation are attenuated by a central location.

The Pattern of Nonmanufacturing Headquarters

FINANCIAL INSTITUTIONS
Headquarters, or detached executive offices, arise in nearly every field of economic endeavor. The limitations

Table 3.12. Secondary Offices of Manhattan Manufacturing Headquarters by Industry, 1967

Industry group and sales range	Major manufacturing headquarters reporting sales of $1 million and over				
	Total hdqrs.	No. with other Manhattan offices	Total other Manhattan offices	No. with other offices in rest of Region	Total other offices in rest of Region
Food	34	8	9	13	27
$60 million and over	23	7	8	12	21
$1–60 million	11	1	1	1	6
Tobacco	9	2	3	1	1
$60 million and over	7	2	3	1	1
$1–60 million	2	—	—	—	—
Textile	38	7	8	—	—
$60 million and over	14	6	7	—	—
$1–60 million	24	1	1	—	—
Apparel	69	8	11	5	5
$60 million and over	9	2	5	1	1
$1–60 million	60	6	6	4	4
Lumber and wood	4	—	—	—	—
$60 million and over	2	—	—	—	—
$1–60 million	2	—	—	—	—
Furniture and fixtures	4	3	3	1	1
$60 million and over	1	1	1	1	1
$1–60 million	3	2	2	—	—
Paper	31	3	6	9	12
$60 million and over	12	3	6	6	9
$1–60 million	19	—	—	3	3
'rinting and publishing	74	8	9	4	4
$60 million and over	10	4	5	1	1
$1–60 million	64	4	4	3	3
Chemicals	65	15	23	25	65
$60 million and over	35	14	22	20	59
$1–60 million	30	1	1	5	6
Petroleum and coal	10	5	9	2	2
$60 million and over	8	5	9	2	2
$1–60 million	2	—	—	—	—
Rubber and plastics	6	1	1	3	4
$60 million and over	3	—	—	2	3
$1–60 million	3	1	1	1	1
Leather	8	1	1	2	2
$60 million and over	2	1	1	2	2
$1–60 million	6	—	—	—	—
Stone, clay, glass	8	1	1	4	5
$60 million and over	4	1	1	3	4
$1–60 million	4	—	—	1	1
Primary metals	25	4	6	9	11
$60 million and over	13	4	6	7	9
$1–60 million	12	—	—	2	2
Fabricated metals	22	5	8	4	6
$60 million and over	7	4	6	3	5
$1 – 60 million	15	1	2	1	1
Nonelectrical machinery	33	7	21	8	12
$60 million and over	16	6	18	6	10
$1–60 million	17	1	3	2	2
Electrical machinery	46	15	47	11	36
$60 million and over	17	10	42	10	35
$1–60 million	29	5	5	1	1
Transportation	14	3	4	4	8
$60 million and over	9	3	4	4	8
$1–60 million	5	—	—	—	—
Instruments	13	2	3	4	5
$60 million and over	5	2	3	3	4
$1–60 million	8	—	—	1	1
Miscellaneous manufacturing	18	1	1	2	2
$60 million and over	2	—	—	—	—
$1–60 million	16	1	1	2	2

Source: Regional Plan Association, based primarily on *Poor's Register of Corporations, Directors and Executives*, 1967

of data have restricted us to a locational investigation of a few industry types, such as the manufacturing groups. For most regions, this would suffice in outlining the major structural elements of headquarters location. In New York, however, the analysis must be broadened to encompass certain population-serving industries which have long been attracted to this area in disproportionate numbers. Such is the case of headquarters for the major communications networks. In addition, various local activities such as commercial banking contribute significantly to the head office component as they have grown up and become "exporters" of office services. Though the data is limited, some characterization of the present distribution of other headquarters types within the Region is in order. We shall first examine the financial sector.

BANKING. Over 2,400 commercial and savings bank establishments were located in the Region in 1964, with one in five institutions being a main office. As would be expected, the distribution of branch banking offices closely corresponds with the Region's pattern of residential settlement. The main banking facilities, however, which are headquarters and middle-market office functions, align themselves in roughly even proportions among the various rings of the Region. As the establishment count in Table 3.13 shows, the core area including the Manhattan CBD would appear to hold no competitive edge over the intermediate ring in main office location. As we shall see, this inference is misleading when the data is weighted by size of banking operations.

Trips to the bank are characteristically short trips. Main office establishments, being restricted by state law, have had to assimilate to a degree the locational preferences of business and households in their mandated markets. Thus, banking institutions with main offices that service predominantly subregional market areas entrust the scope of their office operations to the growth potential of the immediate environment. In doing so, they conform more conceptually to the middle-market strata of office activity. Headquarters banks, on the other hand, perform a nationwide service that is dependent on and a part of the Region's export base. The benefits of clustering in a headquarters environment becomes apparent in the configuration of all deposits within the Region.

While Manhattan contains only 14 percent of the main offices of commercial and savings banks in the New York area, it holds 66 percent of the deposits of the Region on account. Most of these savings are held by New York banks which rank uppermost among the nation's leading financial institutions. Table 3.14 presents the intraregional apportionment of the New York area's share of the nation's top 300 commercial and stock savings banks. The Region contains 16 percent of the major banks and

Table 3.13. Banking Establishments: The Location of Main Offices, Branches, and Total Deposits by Ring for Commercial and Savings Institutions in the New York Region, 1964

	Main office	Branch office	Deposits ($\times$ $1 million)
Core	130	853	$73,614
Manhattan	68	367	58,795
Rest of core	62	486	14,819
Inner ring	105	488	7,152
Intermediate ring	141	458	6,184
Outer ring	121	123	1,992
Region	497	1,922	88,942

Source: *Polk's Bank Directory*, 1964.

Table 3.14. The Location of the Region's Share of the 300 Largest Commercial Banks in the Nation, 1966

	Main office	Deposits ($\times$ $1 million)
Core	28	$61,311
Manhattan CBD	19	57,966
Downtown*	11	43,871
Midtown*	12	14,095
Rest of core	9	3,345
Inner ring	11	4,424
Intermediate ring	9	2,169
Outer ring	—	—
Region	48	67,904

Source: *American Banker*, 1966.
* Main offices in the midtown and downtown areas do not total to the CBD because four banking institutions maintain dual headquarters establishments, one in each district. Deposits have been allocated equally, however.

Table 3.15. The Location of the Region's Share of the 50 Largest Commercial and Mutual Savings Institutions in the Nation, 1964

	Commercial banks		Mutual savings banks	
	Hdqrs.	Deposits (× $1 million)	Hdqrs.	Deposits (× $1 million)
Core	10	$47,374.8	30	$18,042.0
Manhattan CBD	9	46,621.0	12	9,139.9
Rest of core	1	753.8	18	8,902.1
Inner ring	1	1,269.8	—	—
Intermediate ring	—	—	2	532.5
Outer ring	—	—	—	—
Region	11	48,644.6	32	18,574.5

Sources: "The Fortune Directory," 1965; *Polk's Bank Directory*, 1964.

32 percent of total deposits. Seven of the 10 largest banking houses are located in the financial district while 19 of the top 300 locate headquarters throughout the Manhattan CBD. These 19 institutions hold 85 percent of the deposits in the Region's major banks and 65 percent of all deposits on account in the New York Region. The midtown and downtown districts of the Manhattan CBD absorb major banking headquarters equally. Though a trend may be observed toward the establishment of home offices in the exclusive corporate headquarters district along Park Avenue, the Wall Street complex continues to lead the Region and the nation, handling one in every four dollars on deposit in the country's 300 leading banking institutions.

An even more detailed appraisal of headquarters banking can be made from the distribution of the Region's share of the fifty largest commercial banks in the nation, as listed by Fortune's "500" series, and the fifty largest mutual savings banks, as ranked by Polk's bank directory and shown in Table 3.15. Twenty-two percent of the major commercial banks with 40 percent of their deposits are New York based; 64 percent of the leading mutual savings institutions with 73 percent of comparable deposits are housed in New York. Manhattan excels in the location of commercial institutions with nine of the nation's fifty largest banks and 38 percent of the deposits. The rest of the core area leads as the home office location of eighteen mutual savings institutions (over half of the Region's share) while the Manhattan CBD maintains the lead in savings bank deposits. Such disproportion in financial activity on the part of the city banks suggests the continued concentration of headquarters banking in the Region's center and the considerable extent to which New York functions as the nation's banker.[10]

INSURANCE. The New York area's leadership in the financial world extends to a less renowned role in life underwriting. Of the fifty foremost life insurance companies that control five-sixths of all life insurance assets in the nation, nine have home offices in the Region and seven in the Manhattan CBD. The Region contains the top four national corporations that underwrote 47 percent of life insurance in force among the industry leaders in 1963. In the aggregate, the nine New York-based insurance giants, which are housed in Manhattan and Newark, command nearly half (46 percent in 1966) of total assets of all life insurance companies in the nation.

The locational preference of the 30 principal life insuring operations is distinctly an urban one. Though a few headquarters offices of smaller life insuring groups are situated in the Region outside the core, their operations are more regional than national, and their needs appear to be met best by such suburban centers as East

10. Average per capita deposits on account in the area are over 250 percent greater than the norm for the entire economy.

Orange, Mineola, and New Haven. The field offices of major headquarters, the function of which is middle market or local in scope, supplement the more population-related insuring services in noncentralized and suburban locations. Twenty-six of the headquarters or home offices of principal insuring firms continue to remain located in the Region's core cities, New York and Newark. These national activities are supported in major centers partially by the CBD's unique ability to assemble large pools of clerical and managerial skill. Table 3.16 indicates the present configuration of the Region's principal insuring establishments in terms of home office address and total firm assets. It should be noted that midtown Manhattan is the preferred location of life insuring activity in the Region and the nation, with the home offices of seventeen firms controlling 31 percent of industry assets.

Fire and casualty insurance has long been a specialized activity in which the Region excels. Nearly 20 percent of the 400 property insurers in the nation are located in the New York Region, with 61 firms (79 percent of the Region's total) located in the Manhattan CBD and five in Newark. The practice of insuring property represents a smaller business venture than life underwriting, with smaller demands for employment and space. The geographical segregation of activity within the firm is not as common a practice in property as it is in life operations. Indeed, the economies of firm agglomeration appear to be more effective with non-life offices. Hence, non-life headquarters continue to concentrate, much intact, in the insurance district of lower Manhattan, which provides them with easy access to clients, agents, and brokers. The nation's second largest home office is housed there in close proximity to seven other firms ranked among the fifty largest fire and casualty insurers. In total, forty-five principal home offices with 69 percent of the Region's property insurance assets are residents of lower Manhattan, while eight establishments operate from such outlying locations as Westbury, L.I., and Trenton, N.J.

Aside from insurance activities which are functionally linked to the financial world through assets that consist of major security holdings, certain other companies—not predominantly of an operating, but of a holding nature—share in similar ties through the ownership of large blocks of securities. More than one-third of the major holding companies in the nation are located in the New York Region; six of the top 22 establishments are based in Manhattan while the other two are to be found in suburban New York and New Jersey.

STOCK EXCHANGES. Before departing from this brief overview of financial headquarters distribution in the New York Region, mention must be made of the oft-discussed location of the securities industry. Though controversy has swirled on occasion around the issue of relocation

Table 3.16. The Location of the Region's Share of the 800 Principal Life and Property Insurers in the Nation, 1966

	Life insurers		Property insurers	
	Hdqrs.	Assets (× $1 million)	Hdqrs.	Assets (× $1 million)
Core	26	$77,993	69	$7,089
Manhattan CBD	23	52,112	61	6,617
Downtown	6	849	45	5,343
Midtown	17	51,263	16	1,274
Rest of core	3	25,881	8	472
Inner ring	3	164	6	434
Intermediate ring	1	11	2	223
Outer ring	—	—	—	—
Region	30	78,168	77	7,746

Source: *Moody's Bank and Financial Directory*, 1967.

Table 3.17. The Location of Wholesaling Headquarters Ranked by Descending Order of Centrality in the Region, 1963

Industry	Central administrative offices by ring as a percentage of industry totals					
	Manhattan CBD	Rest of core	Inner ring	Inter-mediate ring	Outer ring	Total
Scrap and waste	100.0%	—	—	—	—	100.0%
Tobacco	100.0	—	—	—	—	100.0
Beer, alcohol	100.0	—	—	—	—	100.0
Metals and minerals	83.3	16.7%	—	—	—	100.0
Dry goods, apparel	81.0	4.8	4.8%	4.8%	4.8%	100.0
Paper and products	71.4	—	14.3	14.3	—	100.0
Farm and raw materials	66.7	—	—	33.3	—	100.0
Machinery, equipment, and supplies	61.5	10.2	23.1	5.1	—	100.0
Wholesalers n.e.c.	59.1	22.7	18.1	—	—	100.0
Groceries and related	50.0	25.0	25.0	—	—	100.0
Total wholesaling	49.0	25.2	17.8	3.5	4.5	100.0
Drugs, chemicals	47.8	21.7	13.0	17.4	—	100.0
Lumber and construction materials	44.4	38.9	5.6	—	11.1	100.0
Motor vehicles and equipment	42.9	7.1	28.6	21.4	—	100.0
Furniture	35.7	35.7	14.3	14.3	—	100.0
Electrical goods	33.3	44.4	22.2	—	—	100.0
Bulk petroleum	27.1	40.0	25.7	5.7	1.4	100.0
Hardware and plumbing equipment	—	75.0	—	—	25.0	100.0

Source: U.S. Census, *Enterprise Statistics: 1963*, Special tabulation.
Note: Detail may not add to totals because of rounding.

Table 3.18. Wholesaling Headquarters by Average Employment Size and by Ring in the Region, 1963

Industry*	Average employment size of central administrative offices					
	Manhattan CBD	Rest of core	Inner ring	Inter-mediate ring	Outer ring	Region
Scrap and waste	30	—	—	—	—	30
Tobacco	30	—	—	—	—	30
Beer, alcohol	183	—	—	—	—	183
Metal and minerals	22	70	—	—	—	30
Dry goods, apparel	57	13	13	13	13	49
Paper and products	17	—	10	10	—	15
Farm and raw materials	25	—	—	10	—	20
Machinery, equipment and supplies	102	19	92	30	—	87
Wholesalers n.e.c.	69	19	42	—	—	53
Groceries and related	20	10	8	—	—	15
Total wholesaling	72	79	55	68	15	69
Drugs, chemicals	69	25	83	88	—	64
Lumber and construction materials	22	20	13	—	21	21
Motor vehicles and equipment	19	40	21	230	—	66
Furniture	20	6	7	30	—	14
Electrical goods	30	464	16	—	—	220
Bulk petroleum	136	47	73	10	8	75
Hardware and plumbing equipment	—	24	—	—	13	22

Source: U.S. Census, *Enterprise Statistics: 1963*, Special tabulation.
* Ranked by descending order of industry centrality.

within the Region, the exchange offices appear to retain their historic preference for lower Manhattan. Nationwide, the recent growth of regional stock exchanges in major headquarters cities has created some dispersal of New York business to areas outside the Region. The present exchange community remains strong and willing to make significant commitments for the future in the CBD.

The two stock exchanges represent a nominal source of office employment in themselves, but their main contribution arises from their ability to induce demands for office space among their members. The entire stock exchange community numbers approximately 50,000 personnel (roughly one-fourth of financial employment in lower Manhattan) and occupies over 6 million square feet of office space. Two out of three member organizations have executive offices in New York City, with the major concentration in lower Manhattan. In the conceptual framework of this report, only the exchange offices are considered as headquarters activity. Member organizations are classified among the headquarters-related middle-market functions. However, the spatial organization of the entire exchange community warrants some consideration here.

A recent boom in branch and some head office brokerage facilities has occurred with the corporate headquarters expansion along Park Avenue. Discussion of the spinoff of clerk intensive back office activity from the exchange community to a more spacious location elsewhere in the Region has been a frequent topic. While some dispersal of back office activity is probable in the future, a major dispersal of securities brokerage activity from the CBD does not appear likely despite the occurrence of two procedural changes by the Big Board which allow a greater degree of locational freedom to exchange-linked activities. First, with the substitution of bookkeeping entries, it is no longer necessary for the physical transfer of securities to take place between member firms at the end of each day's trading. Second, noncomputerized brokerage houses may now avail themselves of a data processing service provided by the exchange. This should tend to loosen many of the former ties of easy accessibility between member firms. As indicated in an earlier section of this book, however, the orientation of much of the financial industry appears primarily toward the business community at large. We might presume that, though the ties of member organizations weaken among one another, the executive functions of the securities industry as a whole will continue to structure its location around the major corporate headquarter concentrations in the Region.

TRADE AND SELECTED SERVICES
Aside from the financial institutions, major non-goods-

producing activities that generate employment in detached central offices are wholesale trade, retail trade, and selected services.[11] All three sectors are less centrally oriented in firms than manufacturing but show considerable variability. Measured by employment distribution, however, one sector (services) has a greater relative commitment to the CBD than does manufacturing. For non-goods-producing firms, the pull of centrality on headquarters location appears to be determined less by interfirm contact and more by the need for market aggregation. Front offices of selected services exhibit the strongest central attraction. Two-thirds of the Region's total service industries locate in the Manhattan CBD and four-fifths are situated within the confines of the core.

Though retailing headquarters concentration in the core approximates that for servicing offices, the CBD share amounts to under 60 percent of the total retail offices in the Region. Wholesale administrative activity exhibits the least preference for central location, with half of the Region's total located outside the Manhattan CBD. Wholesaling administration, however, cannot be considered a truly dispersive office activity since it performs a middle-market role vis-à-vis producers and consumers. This role keeps wholesaling relatively tied to the major central markets. This linkage is reflected in the fact that a major portion of wholesaling activity (43 percent) is located between the CBD and the intermediate ring, areas that provide fair access to the center but which are significantly less expensive. A strong correlation exists by industry between the location of wholesaling functions and their corresponding industrial producers. As Table 3.17 shows, tobacco, metals, and apparel rank among the office groups manifesting strong preferences for central location in regard to both manufacturing and wholesaling activity. The distribution of chemical and electrical goods offices provides examples showing a correlation between decentralized counterparts. In general, wholesaling offices employ fewer workers per establishment than do manufacturing. The largest wholesaling offices on average are found in the core area adjacent to the center, as shown in Table 3.18.

The administration of retailing outlets requires an average headquarters employment which is slightly larger than wholesaling and considerably more centralized in location. Unlike manufacturers or wholesalers, retailers as a group place their biggest central offices in Manhattan. Exceptions occur in the retail sectors that are primarily marketers of convenience goods, such as food stores, restaurants, jewelry, and toy shops. Tables 3.19 and 3.20 present the size and locational configuration of retailing headquarters in the Region.

11. Selected services consist of approximately one-half of total services, reporting only SIC 70 through 79.

Table 3.19. The Location of Retailing Headquarters Ranked by Descending Order of Centrality in the Region, 1963

| Industry | Central administrative offices by ring as a percentage of industry totals | | | | | |
	Manhattan CBD	Rest of core	Inner ring	Inter-mediate ring	Outer ring	Total
Apparel and accessories	82.6%	9.9%	5.6%	1.9%	—	100.0%
General merchandise	80.3	8.5	5.6	5.6	—	100.0
Total retailing	58.7	20.4	13.4	7.0	.5%	100.0
Eating and drinking places	43.3	26.7	16.7	10.0	3.3	100.0
Miscellaneous retail stores	34.8	26.1	23.9	15.2	—	100.0
Furniture	32.1	25.0	28.6	10.7	3.6	100.0
Food	20.7	53.4	17.3	8.6	—	100.0
Automotive	18.2	18.2	54.5	9.1	—	100.0
Building materials and hardware	18.2	27.3	27.3	27.3	—	100.0

Source: U.S. Census, *Enterprise Statistics: 1963*, Special tabulation.
Note: Detail may not add to totals because of rounding.

Table 3.20. Retailing Headquarters by Average Employment Size and by Ring in the Region, 1963

| Industry* | Average employment size of central administrative offices | | | | | |
	Manhattan CBD	Rest of core	Inner ring	Inter-mediate ring	Outer ring	Region
Apparel and accessories	57	51	15	15	—	53
General merchandise	223	72	99	56	—	194
Total retailing	95	56	55	37	15	77
Eating and drinking places	50	17	14	83	15	37
Miscellaneous retail stores	34	34	12	50	—	31
Furniture	64	28	21	19	15	36
Food	91	80	181	12	—	94
Automotive	30	93	51	13	—	51
Building materials and hardware	6	20	24	26	—	20

Source: U.S. Census, *Enterprise Statistics: 1963*, Special tabulation.
* Ranked by descending order of industry centrality.

Table 3.21. The Location of Selected Service Headquarters Ranked by Descending Order of Centrality in the Region, 1963

Industry	Central administrative offices by ring as a percentage of industry totals					
	Manhattan CBD	Rest of core	Inner ring	Intermediate ring	Outer ring	Total
Hotels and lodging places	87.5%	—	12.5%	—	—	100.0%
Miscellaneous business services	85.5	9.1%	3.6	—	1.8%	100.0
Total selected services	67.3	12.8	14.1	4.5%	1.3	100.0
Miscellaneous repair services	60.0	—	20.0	20.0	—	100.0
Amusement and recreation	60.0	10.0	30.0	—	—	100.0
Motion pictures	57.1	17.2	14.3	11.4	—	100.0
Personal services	51.7	17.2	24.1	3.5	3.5	100.0
Automobile repair	50.0	21.4	21.4	7.2	—	100.0

Source: U.S. Census, *Enterprise Statistics: 1963*, Special tabulation.
Note: Detail may not add to totals because of rounding.

Table 3.22. Selected Service Headquarters by Average Employment Size and by Ring in the Region, 1963

Industry*	Average employment size of central administrative offices					
	Manhattan CBD	Rest of core	Inner ring	Intermediate ring	Outer ring	Region
Hotels and lodging places	55	—	8	—	—	49
Miscellaneous business services	63	105	81	—	40	67
Total selected services	73	37	41	17	27	60
Miscellaneous repair services	17	—	20	13	—	17
Amusement and recreation	21	13	18	—	—	19
Motion pictures	100	22	28	23	—	68
Personal services	94	13	21	6	13	57
Automobile repair	96	5	121	5	—	75

Source: U.S. Census, *Enterprise Statistics: 1963*, Special tabulation.
* Ranked by descending order of industry centrality.

Next to extractive industries, headquarters of servicing activities locate the highest share of all central office jobs in the CBD (81 percent of total). With the few exceptions of automobile repair and miscellaneous business, detailed service activity strongly peaks (in terms of average and total employment) at the Region's center. There are, however, relative differences in the intraregional distribution of specific service industries. Notably, the range of population relatedness in service activity influences the location of headquarters functions as the more personalized services follow their establishments outward to suburban markets as indicated in Tables 3.21 and 3.22.

OTHER NONMANUFACTURING HEADQUARTERS

TRANSPORTATION, COMMUNICATION, AND UTILITIES. The New York Region contains many of the largest firms in the transportation, communication, and utility fields. The 29 companies headquartered in the area represent 23 percent of the foremost establishments and earn 47 percent of the annual sales in this industry group. The Manhattan CBD is the preferred location for such national activities and has the greatest concentration of transport and communications headquarters to be found anywhere in the nation. Twenty-three companies earning 44 percent of the leaders annual sales in 1966 are located in the CBD, with the greatest relative specialization present in telephone and telegraph communication and broadcasting enterprises. Outside the CBD, six headquarter locations in the Region administer rail, trucking, utility, and other operations of considerable earning power. The service markets of these endeavors are more regional and megalopolitan than national or international. Table 3.23 shows the pattern by headquarters location and annual sales.

THE EXTRACTIVE INDUSTRIES. Nearly four-fifths of all mining front offices located in the Region have selected the Manhattan CBD as their base of administrative operations, as shown in Table 3.24. Few choose to locate in the rest of the Region. The fifty-odd mineral headquarters provide over 2,000 office jobs and are, on the average, one-third the size of manufacturing front offices. Selected industry groups, such as metals and coal, chose CBD locations exclusively. Others are not so strongly attracted to the CBD. For instance, nonmetallic industries site less than half of their front offices in Manhattan.

A sample of mineral industries located in the CBD which report sales of $1 million and over—Table 3.25—offers scant evidence of multiple office locations either nearby or in the suburbs. Though firms range the full spectrum of industry sales, the extractive industries' administrative office employment demands are less, on average, than those of manufacturing.

	RR	Truck-ing	Ship-ping	Airlines	Tel. & tel.	Broad-casting radio & tv	Pub. util.	Total
Number of headquarters								
Manhattan								
CBD	2	1	2	4	3	3	8	23
Rest of core	—	—	—	1	1	—	1	3
Inner ring	—	1	—	—	—	—	1	2
Intermediate ring	1	—	—	—	—	—	—	1
Outer ring	—	—	—	—	—	—	—	—
Region	3	2	2	5	4	3	10	29
Annual sales in millions								
Manhattan								
CBD	$1,259.3	$104.1	$292.6	$2,137.9	$12,540.6	$1,427.5	$3,336.9	$21,098.9
Rest of core	—	—	—	53.3	504.1	—	561.4	1,118.8
Inner ring	—	33.0	—	—	—	—	220.0	253.0
Intermediate ring	125.6	—	—	—	—	—	—	125.6
Outer ring	—	—	—	—	—	—	—	—
Region	1,384.9	137.1	292.6	2,191.2	13,044.7	1,427.5	4,118.3	22,596.3

Source: *News Front*, 1967.

Table 3.24.   The Location of Mineral Headquarters Ranked by Descending Order of Centrality in the Region, 1963

Industry	Central administrative offices by ring as a percentage of industry totals					
	Man-hattan CBD	Rest of core	Inner ring	Inter-mediate ring	Outer ring	Total
Metal mining	100.0%	—	—	—	—	100.0%
Coal mining	100.0	—	—	—	—	100.0
Petroleum and gas	84.6	—	7.7%	7.7%	—	100.0
Total minerals	77.5	—	14.3	8.2	—	100.0
Nonmetallic mining	43.8	—	37.5	18.7	—	100.0

Source: U.S. Census, *Enterprise Statistics: 1963*, Special tabulation.
Note: Detail may not add to totals because of rounding.

Table 3.25.   Secondary Offices of Manhattan Mineral Headquarters by Industry, 1967

Industry group	Major mineral headquarters reporting sales of $1 million and over				
	Total hdqrs.	No. with other Man-hattan offices	Total other Man-hattan offices	No. with other offices in rest of Region	Total other offices in rest of Region
Metal mining	12	1	1	1	2
Coal mining	3	—	—	—	—
Petroleum and gas	9	—	—	1	1
Nonmetallic mining	2	—	—	—	—
Total	26	1	1	2	3

Source: Regional Plan Association, based primarily on *Poor's Register of Corporations, Directors and Executives*, 1967.

Chapter 4

Regional Pattern of Office Jobs and Office Space

Office Composition and Location by Industry

The previous chapter dealt in considerable detail with the location of headquarters offices within the New York Region and attempted to establish some relationships between types of industry and the locational requirements of their headquarters. Emphasis was deliberately placed on headquarters first, because they are the most important office activity economically, and because they are the most center-oriented activity geographically. However, jobs in headquarters offices represent only 29 percent of all office jobs in the New York Region and, of course, much less than that in the nation as a whole. In this chapter, we shall deal with the entire universe of office jobs in office buildings in the New York Region. First, we shall go briefly through an exercise similar to that performed in Chapter 3 with regard to headquarters —namely, seeing how office activity as a whole is distributed within the Region, by ring of development, by type of industry. Subsequently, the location of office employment by three classes—headquarters, middle market, and local—will be pinpointed, placing the earlier discussion of headquarters in a broader context. Finally, the distribution of existing office floor space and the increment in new floor space will be traced by rings of development and by subcenters in the Region.

It is important to stress that the data presented in this chapter—on where how many office workers work, by type of industry—has been synthesized for this study and has been otherwise unavailable. The standard industrial classification code (SIC), used by federal and state agencies to present statistics on economic activity and employment, classifies establishments by their principal product or service, not by the occupational composition of employees or the type of building they work in.

The starting point in deriving the data to be presented was the detailed occupational composition of the labor force by *place of residence,* as given by the U.S. Census. Summarizing the selected office occupations previously shown in Table 1.8 provided a control total for the Region as a whole, since the Region is a self-contained entity with regard to commuting: only a fraction of 1 percent of its workers commute in or out of the 31-county area. Unpublished data from the Census *Journey to Work* provided trip destinations arrayed by major occupational groups (professional and clerical, for example), to which estimated ratios of office workers in the selected occupations were applied. This provided the first approximation of total office jobs by *place of work* for counties and selected subcounty areas.

Next, major "industry" groups, as given in the SIC classification, were tabulated by county and by the types of occupations they employ. This "industry-occupation matrix" was developed on the basis of special Census tabulations and Tri-State Regional Planning Commission data. The matrix coefficients were then applied to estimates of county employment for 1959 and 1965, and this produced occupational profiles by industry for each county in the Region for these two years. This second approximation of office employment was reconciled with the previous estimate and prepared for the final step which was necessary to reduce total office employment to office jobs in office buildings.

Data on new office space, by county, started between 1957 and 1963, was obtained from the F. W. Dodge Division of McGraw-Hill Information Systems Co. Sampling of different areas of the Region produced estimates of average office space requirements per office worker at different locations. Additions to office space were matched against additions to office-type employment, lagged by the time period required for most building completions. The ratio of office employment increase in office buildings to the total office employment increase thus derived was used to estimate how much of the pre-1959 office-type employment was located in office buildings. In 1967, the results of the Tri-State Regional Planning Commission 1963 land-use inventory, including office floor space data, became available. These were matched with the results of Regional Plan Association field surveys of office space in selected centers of the Region and used to develop final estimates of employment in office buildings by small area. The latter are not presented fully in this report but were needed, among other things, to make estimates by ring of development, since ring boundaries do not always match county lines.

Existing employment in office buildings, by type of industry and by ring of development, derived from the analytical process just described, is shown in Tables 4.1 and 4.2. It is evident from the bottom part of Table 4.2 that, though all major industries perform some of their business in office buildings, not all of them demand space there with the same intensity. While on the average 20 percent of the Region's employment in 1965 was in office buildings, the finance, insurance, and real estate industry housed 70 percent of its workers in detached office buildings, and the transportation, communication, and utilities industry was second, with 38 percent. One should stress that these two industries are also the industries that, in the national picture, are most overrepresented in the New York Region, that is, those in which the Region is most specialized. Government is also a heavy user of office space—28 percent of its employment is in office buildings. Wholesale and retail trade, by contrast, show relatively few employees in office buildings—about 6 percent, though this is in part attributable to the definition of office workers adopted for this study; the definition, as noted in Chapter 1, excluded sales workers.

The proportions of an industry's employees who work in detached office buildings can vary quite substantially by ring of development. In the Manhattan central business district (CBD), 86 percent of all workers in agriculture and mining are office workers; in the inner through outer rings, where farms and gravel pits still exist, only 6 percent of the employees in agriculture and mining are office workers. Similarly, 33 percent of manufacturing employees in the Manhattan CBD actually work in office buildings; in the other rings the ratio varies from 2 to 6 percent; retail trade and government exhibit somewhat parallel patterns. By contrast, the ratio of office workers to total industry employment does not vary too much by ring for such categories as construction or utilities.

The largest office user, in absolute terms, is the finance, insurance, and real estate category, as is evident from the top part of Table 4.2. It accounts for 26 percent of the Region's office employment and is followed by services, government, manufacturing, and utilities, in that order; these five categories together account for almost 90 percent of all office building employment in the Region. Again, the proportions vary, quite plausibly, by ring of development. In the Manhattan CBD, finance, insurance, and real estate is the leading office user, followed by services and manufacturing. In the outer ring, government is the leading office user, followed by transportation, communication, and utilities, supporting the casual impression that local government and telephone company offices are the most prominent office buildings in rural areas.

Finally, with regard to the distribution of total office building employment in the Region, it is evident from the bottom part of Table 4.1 that, in 1965, almost 52 percent of it was in the Manhattan CBD. Other rings followed in neatly descending order: 22 percent in the remainder of the core, 13 percent in the inner ring, 10 percent in the intermediate ring, and 3 percent in the outer ring. Once again, proportions vary by industry: the highest concentration in Manhattan is achieved by manufacturing, which has 72 percent of its workers employed in detached office buildings located there; finance, insurance, and real estate comes second, with 61 percent; services and wholesale trade follow closely, with 59 percent each. By contrast, the office activities of construction, utilities, and government are much less centralized and more closely related to the resident population.

These variations in industry distribution within the Region lead to a conclusion. It is that, though all sectors contain a headquarters component, some industries respond more strongly to the benefits of locating front offices in the Region's business center. Others locate in patterns manifesting weaker external communication needs but stronger links to their own employment. The

Table 4.1. Estimated Office Employment in Office Buildings by Industry and by Ring in the New York Region, 1965

	Agr. & min.	Constr.	Mfg.	Trans., comm., util.	Whsle. trade	Retail trade	Fin., ins., real est.	Serv.	Govt.	Total
Jobs in office buildings										
Manhattan CBD	3,150	12,910	165,110	53,460	20,250	27,690	248,300	178,060	95,490	804,420
Rest of core	1,160	17,700	9,340	76,150	6,090	14,760	87,110	45,210	85,010	342,530
Inner ring	580	14,480	21,460	35,360	5,110	12,940	40,910	39,980	33,110	203,930
Intermediate ring	1,140	9,850	29,570	24,430	2,420	5,950	23,600	31,500	35,160	163,620
Outer ring	1,030	3,770	4,120	8,600	620	1,600	7,040	7,010	9,290	43,080
Region	7,060	58,710	229,600	198,000	34,490	62,940	406,960	301,760	258,060	1,557,580
As a percentage of Region										
Manhattan CBD	44.62%	21.99%	71.91%	27.00%	58.71%	44.00%	61.01%	59.01%	37.00%	51.65%
Rest of core	16.43	30.15	4.07	38.46	17.66	23.45	21.41	14.98	32.94	21.99
Inner ring	8.21	24.66	9.35	17.86	14.81	20.56	10.05	13.25	12.83	13.09
Intermediate ring	16.15	16.78	12.88	12.34	7.02	9.45	5.80	10.44	13.63	10.50
Outer ring	14.59	6.42	1.79	4.34	1.80	2.54	1.73	2.32	3.60	2.77
Region	100.00	100.00	100.00	100.00	100.00	100.00	100.00	100.00	100.00	100.00

Source: Regional Plan Association.

Table 4.2. Percentage Distribution of Office Building Employment by Industry and by Ring in the New York Region, 1965

	Agr. & min.	Constr.	Mfg.	Trans., comm., util.	Whsle. trade	Retail trade	Fin., ins., real est.	Serv.	Govt.	Total
As a percentage of office building employment										
Region	.45%	3.77%	14.74%	12.71%	2.22%	4.04%	26.13%	19.37%	16.57%	100.00%
Manhattan CBD	.39	1.60	20.52	6.65	2.52	3.44	30.87	22.14	11.87	100.00
Rest of core	.34	5.17	2.72	22.23	1.78	4.31	25.43	13.20	24.82	100.00
Inner ring	.28	7.10	10.52	17.34	2.51	6.35	20.06	19.60	16.24	100.00
Intermediate ring	.70	6.02	18.07	14.93	1.48	3.64	14.42	19.25	21.49	100.00
Outer ring	2.39	8.75	9.56	19.96	1.44	3.72	16.34	16.27	21.57	100.00
As a percentage of total industry employment										
Region	14.80%	18.35%	10.70%	38.02%	6.41%	5.58%	70.45%	20.18%	28.41%	19.98%
Manhattan CBD	86.47	17.67	32.91	38.26	7.78	16.17	73.42	39.06	74.69	38.35
Rest of core	69.34	25.09	1.60	37.19	5.21	3.67	75.49	9.31	24.26	14.54
Inner ring	6.66	15.91	4.46	40.79	5.26	4.78	60.53	14.75	18.76	13.01
Intermediate ring	6.85	15.73	6.44	36.88	4.71	2.75	53.95	14.45	18.49	12.22
Outer ring	6.04	16.59	3.49	36.73	4.99	2.40	55.11	10.83	14.62	10.59

Source: Regional Plan Association.

latter element of economic activity corresponds closely to the economic development concept of *nonbasic* (local population services like construction, utilities, and transportation). In the nationwide distribution of the headquarters establishments of nonbasic firms, it may be noted that they tended to locate in patterns conforming more clearly to the overall population configuration.

There are other distinctions that the data on office activity suggest. Some industries' office functions are centrally oriented because of organizational structure while others choose the CBD because of the special nature of their business. Both, however, thrive on external economies, although there is wide latitude in the types of externalities demanded. Consider some examples. Goods-handling office activity in an urban center is primarily of a headquarters nature. These activities are located in the center to facilitate the administration of goods production. Control of production is maintained through close contact with purchasers, suppliers, and competitors. Services, to cite a different example, is not as committed to maintaining detached head office operations, so many high-priced central locations must be indicative of other benefits. For the manufacturers, benefits are derived through linkages with their own kind and, secondarily, with their business servicers; while the non-goods-producing office activity is primarily oriented *outward* toward the business community as a whole and with lesser exception, *inward,* toward its own industry group. These are, of course, broad generalizations which mask the many exceptions in the way firms can be associated or linked.

The interrelation of these locational tendencies produces a varied mix of office activity. Figure 4.1, which illustrates Table 4.2, forcefully makes this point by summarizing the relative concentration of various types of office activity by ring. The commodity–goods-handling sector is prominent in the CBD. Its peaking, explainable by headquarters activity, appears to be so strong as to suppress development in the rest of the core and inner ring. Indeed, commodity–goods-handling office activity is weak and attenuated from the CBD outward to the intermediate ring where, some 40 miles from the Manhattan CBD, it rises again. The distribution of finance and services, industries that engage in many headquarters-serving functions, similarly peaks in the CBD but drops off more evenly and gradually as one moves toward the Region's periphery. The other industries—transportation, government, construction, retailing—generate office employment in greater relative amounts outside the CBD. These industries appear, therefore, to pattern their office locations more in line with the total population and employment distribution.

The different patterns of concentration of an industry's offices in the Manhattan CBD or their relatively even distribution throughout the various rings of development can be explained, in large part, by the Region's ability to attract the central administrative functions (that is, export the administrative services) of national-market firms whose production facilities are located elsewhere. Partial data on employment in central administrative functions by industry group and changes over a recent period are presented in Tables 4.3 and 4.4. The administrative and auxiliary employment shown there is similar in definition to the central administrative office and auxiliary employment used in previous chapters, though the coverage is somewhat more extensive. Keeping in mind all the limitations of these data, about which we previously cautioned, a sample of administrative jobs in the Region can still be meaningfully analyzed with comparable national data to expose regional strengths and weaknesses.

Over the six-year period 1959–1965, private wage and salary positions in the Region's central administrative establishments grew as a proportion of comparable total employment by 36 percent. Comparable data for the nation show a smaller 25 percent shift. Thus, a significant portion of central office employment may be considered a natural product of regional growth while another portion, about a quarter, is attributable to the Region's ability to capture a disproportionately larger share of headquarters activity.

A more precise view of this import phenomenon may be had by examining shares of administrative employment by industry related to the Region's salaried employment. As Table 4.3 shows, the Region's administrative and auxiliary employment is relatively overrepresented (see last column). If one then makes the reasonable assumption that industry in the New York area is comparable to the nation in terms of physical detachment of front offices, one can conclude that approximately one-third of the Region's headquarters establishments are not native to the area but have located in the Region presumably for external benefits of a central location.

From all appearances, the margin of export activity (that is, the influx of office functions) in the headquarters sector has widened the most in the administration of manufacturing and wholesaling activities. These industries presently account for three-fourths of total central administrative employment in the Region and slightly more than one-fifth of total national employment. As a share of salaried employment in the New York area, manufacturing and wholesaling contain the largest central administrative office sectors among major industry groups, with the exception of mining.

In both absolute as well as relative terms, the commodity–goods-handling sector in the Region dominates the field of headquarters activity. Deficiencies in the data, however, result in a probable understatement of

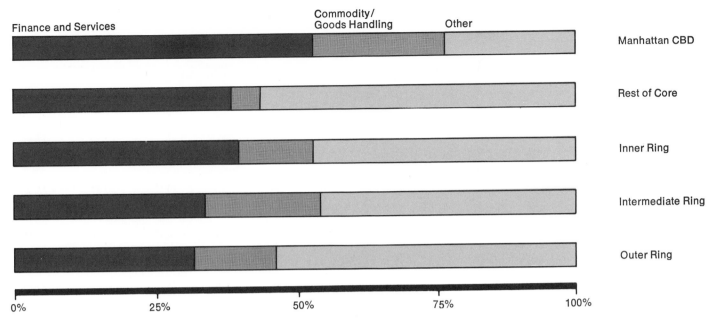

Figure 4.1 The industry composition of office employment by rings of development in the New York Region

Table 4.3. Characteristics of Administrative and Auxiliary Employment in the New York Region, 1959 and 1965

	Admin. & auxil. employ. *		As a % of nation's admin. & auxil. employ. by industry		As a % of Region's salaried employ. by industry		Nationwide share of admin. & auxil. employ. in salaried industry jobs		% of Region's admin. & auxil. employ. overrepresented in Region vis-à-vis the nation	
	1959	1965	1959	1965	1959	1965	1959	1965	1959	1965
Mining	1,730	2,540	4.44%	5.37%	23.31%	33.00%	5.52%	7.88%	76.32%	76.12%
Construction	2,290	2,750	15.58	11.21	.97	1.05	.59	.87	39.18	17.14
Manufacturing	95,750	161,570	19.98	21.33	4.65	7.65	2.96	4.31	36.34	43.66
Transportation, communications, utilities	4,080	3,360	11.44	11.72	.98	.68	1.22	.89	−19.67	−23.60
Wholesale trade	14,450	29,120	17.65	21.67	3.16	5.85	2.65	3.91	16.14	33.16
Retail trade	24,860	39,420	16.20	17.45	3.01	4.13	1.98	2.52	34.22	38.98
Finance, insurance, real estate	12,690	1,440	26.64	12.49	2.54	.26	1.90	.38	25.20	−31.58
Services	6,460	7,280	31.32	20.42	.75	.65	.36	.46	52.00	29.23
Total	162,310	247,480	18.61	19.56	3.02	4.11	2.08	2.65	31.13	35.52

Source: U.S. Department of Commerce, *County Business Patterns*, 1959 and 1965.
* The administrative and auxiliary classification of *County Business Patterns* is similar in definition to that employment classification used by *Enterprise Statistics* and entitled "central administrative and auxiliary employment." One difference exists in that *CBP* industry coverage is more extensive than the Business Census, the major groups of construction, transportation, communications, and utilities, finance and most services being included in the former and not in the latter. Unless specified, however, the job counts for both incorporate nonoffice activity at auxiliary units.

Table 4.4. Percentage Distribution of Administrative and Auxiliary Employment by Ring in the New York Region, 1959 and 1965

	Mining	Constr.	Mfg.	Trans., comm., util.	Whsle. trade	Retail trade	Fin., ins., real est.	Serv.	Total
1965, as a percentage of ring totals									
Region	1.02%	1.11%	65.29%	1.36%	11.77%	15.93%	.58%	2.94%	100.00%
Core	1.20	1.53	57.96	1.79	14.20	19.06	.67	3.59	100.00
Manhattan CBD	1.43	1.68	61.81	1.59	13.08	15.76	.75	3.90	100.00
Rest of core	—	.72	37.99	2.80	20.04	36.15	.29	2.01	100.00
Inner ring	.30	.30	71.89	.25	9.04	15.34	.08	2.80	100.00
Intermediate ring	.84	.21	86.17	.95	5.86	5.33	—	.64	100.00
Outer ring	2.45	1.11	86.95	—	1.97	1.99	4.82	.71	100.00
1959, as a percentage of ring totals									
Region	1.06%	1.41%	59.00%	2.51%	8.90%	15.32%	7.82%	3.98%	100.00%
Core	1.21	1.73	54.69	2.82	9.53	15.92	9.32	4.78	100.00
Inner ring	—	—	72.07	1.67	6.81	18.65	.80	—	100.00
Intermediate ring	.99	—	83.13	—	6.59	8.16	—	1.13	100.00
Outer ring	—	—	85.69	3.98	—	—	10.33	—	100.00

Source: U.S. Department of Commerce, *County Business Patterns*, 1959 and 1965.
Note: See explanatory note on Table 4.3.

the importance of certain noncommodity industries (for example, finance, insurance, real estate, and services).

The data in Tables 4.1 through 4.4 also shed some light on the commonly held hypothesis that the opportunity for face-to-face communication is a major reason for the clustering of office activity in Manhattan. If the face-to-face hypothesis is correct, one would expect to find that those firms at the center are also those generating the greatest number of central office workers relative to their total work force and/or those most dependent upon frequent personal contact between firms for the successful conduct of business. This appears to be so.

Table 4.3 indicates that mining, manufacturing, and wholesale trade are the industries with the highest ratios of administrative jobs to total employment in the New York Region. Table 4.1 has shown that they are also among the industries whose office employment is most highly clustered in the Manhattan CBD. The two industries that are most densely settled in Manhattan—finance and services—fall short in terms of measures of central administrative activity but are traditionally dependent on face-to-face linkages between themselves as well as to the central administrative functions of the three commodity-handling industry groups mentioned earlier—namely, manufacturing, mining, and wholesale trade.

Office Location by Class of Activity:
Headquarters, Middle Market, and Local

So far we have dealt either with headquarters employment alone, as in Chapter 3, or with total office employment, as just discussed. It is now time to pull these together and to take a brief look at the locational characteristics of nonheadquarters office jobs. As is apparent from Table 4.6, headquarters jobs amounted in 1965 to some 29 percent of all of the Region's jobs in office buildings. The remainder can be divided between middle-market jobs, which accounted for 47 percent, and purely local-market employment, which amounted to 24 percent. One may note that because of the initially assumed definition of office workers, which excluded sales occupations, the office building employment is somewhat underestimated.

Conceptually, this three-step graduation of office jobs is related to the notion of economic base and the export of office services as pointed out in Chapter 1. Headquarters jobs, defined here on the basis of U.S. Census *Enterprise Statistics,* selected industrial directories, and state and county employment data, are presumed to serve a national, or even international market. They represent, in large part, the export activity of the New York–New Jersey–Connecticut urban region taken as a whole. Local market jobs, by contrast, are those that are

Table 4.5. Office Employment in Office Buildings by Industry for Counties of the New York Region, 1965

	Mfg.	Trans., comm., util.,	Trade	Fin., ins., real est.	Serv.	Govt.	Other	Total
Connecticut	8,060	11,270	3,180	11,070	13,940	9,970	4,710	62,200
Fairfield	6,300	3,860	1,500	5,190	6,760	4,430	2,160	30,200
Litchfield	150	440	180	520	480	670	460	2,900
New Haven	1,610	6,970	1,500	5,360	6,700	4,870	2,090	29,100
New Jersey	37,360	52,170	22,200	66,600	46,220	47,230	16,140	287,920
Bergen	1,760	7,010	4,690	5,040	6,730	4,200	2,670	32,100
Essex	5,690	13,680	3,480	35,270	14,610	10,140	2,890	85,760
Hudson	3,030	11,840	5,420	8,310	4,070	5,500	1,570	39,740
Hunterdon	—	220	90	270	210	360	230	1,380
Mercer	4,060	2,200	620	2,540	4,190	12,690	920	27,220
Middlesex	3,230	3,010	1,420	2,080	3,050	2,450	1,230	16,470
Monmouth	2,080	1,980	640	1,950	1,870	1,960	1,060	11,540
Morris	6,340	1,480	440	1,320	1,810	1,640	760	13,790
Ocean	—	630	240	770	570	830	600	3,640
Passaic	2,420	3,110	1,650	3,500	4,160	2,700	1,440	18,980
Somerset	200	630	910	710	850	1,060	490	4,850
Sussex	—	540	70	430	210	330	200	1,780
Union	8,540	5,440	2,430	4,170	3,710	3,050	1,870	29,210
Warren	10	400	100	240	180	320	210	1,460
New York	184,180	134,560	72,050	329,290	241,600	200,860	44,920	1,207,460
New York excl. N.Y.C.	15,490	24,390	10,910	26,890	30,930	26,700	12,830	148,140
Dutchess	3,820	1,150	320	1,020	1,270	2,010	850	10,440
Nassau	1,300	8,370	4,000	11,480	12,040	8,610	5,130	50,930
Orange	90	2,340	410	1,190	820	1,400	710	6,960
Putnam	—	200	40	100	180	250	180	950
Rockland	10	1,110	200	840	910	1,550	590	5,210
Suffolk	270	3,410	1,290	3,780	5,970	5,010	1,970	21,700
Sullivan	—	180	60	290	210	550	80	1,370
Ulster	—	1,200	280	620	600	870	530	4,100
Westchester	10,000	6,430	4,310	7,570	8,930	6,450	2,790	46,480
New York City	168,690	110,170	61,140	302,400	210,670	174,160	32,090	1,059,320
Bronx	160	16,830	3,860	8,450	3,050	7,560	3,580	43,490
Brooklyn	1,930	15,190	4,720	20,050	11,710	42,110	5,770	101,480
Manhattan	165,110	55,660	48,070	261,300	186,190	101,850	16,060	834,240
Queens	1,210	20,850	4,200	11,300	8,570	16,760	6,020	68,910
Richmond	280	1,640	290	1,300	1,150	5,880	660	11,200
Region	229,600	198,000	97,430	406,960	301,760	258,060	65,770	1,557,580

Source: Regional Plan Association.

Table 4.6. Headquarters, Middle Market, and Local Office Employment by Ring in the New York Region, 1965

	Jobs in office buildings			As a percentage of total		
	Hdqrs.	Middle market	Local market	Hdqrs.	Middle market	Local market
Manhattan CBD	368,090	404,420	31,910	80.14%	55.46%	8.65%
Rest of core	27,860	148,590	166,080	6.07	20.37	45.01
Inner ring	29,580	87,550	86,800	6.44	12.00	23.52
Intermediate ring	28,670	75,600	59,350	6.24	10.37	16.08
Outer ring	5,110	13,100	24,870	1.11	1.80	6.74
Region total	459,310	729,260	369,010	100.00	100.00	100.00
All jobs in office buildings		1,557,580		29.5%	46.8%	23.7%

Source: Regional Plan Association.
Note: Detail may not add to totals because of rounding.

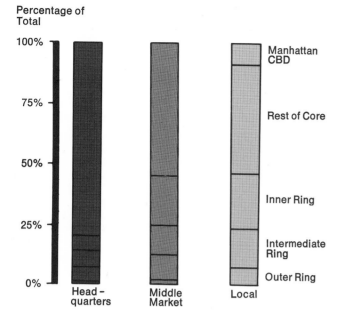

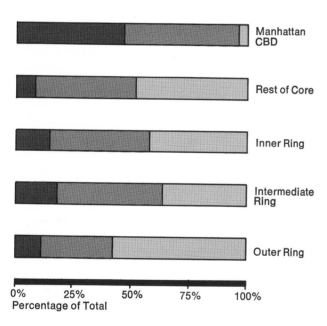

Figure 4.2 Class of office activity: the distribution between and within rings of the New York Region

necessary to serve a population of about 150,000 at their place of residence; they were calculated by taking small geographic areas—predominantly residential such as groups of municipalities—and seeing what the minimum requirement for office jobs at such locations was; it turned out to be roughly two office jobs in office buildings per 100 residents. Office job concentrations in excess of that were assumed to be serving either subregional markets in excess of 150,000 residents, or higher-level headquarters activity: this subregional or headquarters-subsidiary category was termed middle market.

While not the most numerous of office employers, headquarters operations are, on the average, the largest employment units and certainly the most region-shaping components in the industry. The clear preference of headquarters for the Manhattan CBD, where 80 percent of the Region's—and nearly 20 percent of the nation's—headquarters jobs are located, is underscored in these data (see Figure 4.2). Manpower and space demands in detached central offices range from fewer than 100 workers to over 15,000 and command from several thousand to over 2 million square feet of space. The determining locational factor here certainly would seem to be the facilitation of face-to-face communication by executive decision-makers in an "environment of high interaction."

The industry's largest office sector, the middle-market component, provides 47 percent of total office building employment and locates slightly more than half of its total jobs in Manhattan CBD office space. The other half is located primarily in the rest of the core and the inner and intermediate rings. Middle-market consumption of space per worker is somewhat less than that of the headquarters component, and size of establishment varies over a fairly wide range. The economic and social characteristics of middle-market activity help to explain its locational preferences. More specifically, middle-market activity is really a function of both population and other large office and job concentrations. That is, it needs to be near large supplies of manpower and have access to the subregional consumer or national office markets that it services. Thus, middle market is guided by an environment midway between headquarters activities and local activities. The former need manpower but have a national market, the latter have diffuse manpower needs and a local-market orientation.

Local-market office activity comprises the smallest sector of the office industry. Fewer than one out of every four workers is engaged in population-oriented office functions at the community level. It is quite reasonable, then, that only 9 percent of total local-market activity occupies space in the Manhattan CBD and that the remainder would disperse so as to optimize access to local consumer markets. Thus, 45 percent of local-market office jobs were located in the rest of the core, where 45 percent of the population lived, and 23 percent in the inner ring, which had 25 percent of the population. The intermediate and outer ring shares are similarly proportional to population.

One shortcoming of presenting data in terms of shares by ring of development is that the geographic extent of the rings is left out of the picture. As was pointed out at the outset of Chapter 3, the remainder of the core, as an example, is 33 times larger in area than the CBD; the inner ring, in turn, 3 times larger than the core; and the intermediate ring about 4 times larger than the inner. To take account of these huge and irregular variations, it is useful to "normalize" for area, that is, to present *densities* of office development in the different rings. This is done in Table 4.7 and Figure 4.3, which plot each ring's average distance from the center of the Region against density of development. To make the data more readable, both distance and density are compressed by taking the logarithm of each. A line connecting the plot of log distance versus log density is a density gradient, showing the rate at which density falls off with increasing distance from the center. A steeper or flatter density gradient shows how much more or less centralized one activity is than another. Changes in the density gradient over time are a useful reference for projecting future allocation of development.

Figure 4.3 shows that the density gradient of middle-market office jobs is virtually a straight line, going from some 50,000 jobs per square mile in the CBD to about 2 per square mile in the outer ring. The density gradient of headquarters jobs is much steeper, indicating their greater degree of centralization. It starts out at the same level in the CBD, drops off very sharply toward the rest of the core, exhibits a bulge in the inner and intermediate rings, indicating their attractiveness for suburban-type headquarters locations, and drops off to less than 1 in the outer ring. The local-market office employment gradient is predictably the flattest; local-market employment exceeds middle market in the predominantly residential rest of core and outer ring; the two are about equal in the inner ring; in the intermediate ring, the middle-market component is slightly higher than the local one, indicating that the area is, on the one hand, sufficiently far from Manhattan, and on the other, sufficiently dense to assume some leadership in subregional functions: a string of traditionally independent metropolitan areas, such as Trenton, Bridgeport, and New Haven, are located in this ring. Thus, some middle-market functions for the rest of core are provided by the Manhattan CBD, while some of those for the outer ring are provided by the intermediate ring. The distribution of the three employment classes by county is shown in Table 4.8.

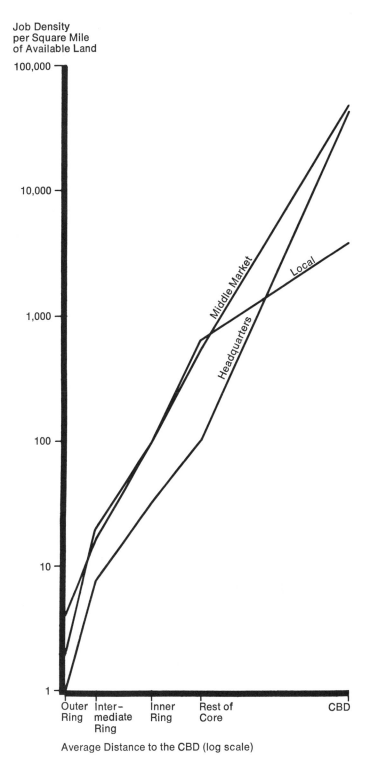

Figure 4.3 Density of office activity by rings of development in the New York Region

Table 4.7. Density of Office Employment by Class of Activity by Ring in the New York Region, 1965

	Average ring distance from center (miles)	Office jobs per square mile of available land*		
		Hdqrs.	Middle market	Local market
Manhattan CBD	1	44,188	48,550	3,831
Rest of core	9	105	562	628
Inner ring	19	32	96	95
Intermediate ring	44	8	21	17
Outer ring	70	1	2	4

Source: Regional Plan Association.
* Densities on "available land" are here defined on the basis of total area minus area under water and area in park land and reservations.

Table 4.8. Distribution of Headquarters, Middle Market, and Local Office Employment by County in the New York Region, 1965

	Jobs in office buildings			As a percentage of Region		
	Hdqrs.	Middle market	Local market	Hdqrs.	Middle market	Local market
Connecticut	10,310	32,550	19,340	2.25%	4.46%	5.24%
Fairfield	7,200	13,800	9,200	1.57	1.89	2.49
Litchfield	160	790	1,950	.04	.11	.53
New Haven	2,950	17,960	8,190	.64	2.46	2.22
New Jersey	45,100	143,560	99,260	9.82	19.69	26.90
Bergen	7,240	13,300	11,560	1.58	1.82	3.13
Essex	12,240	48,370	25,150	2.66	6.63	6.81
Hudson	5,550	21,060	13,130	1.21	2.89	3.56
Hunterdon	—	210	1,170	—	.03	.32
Mercer	2,660	18,430	6,130	.58	2.53	1.66
Middlesex	3,200	5,830	7,440	.70	.80	2.02
Monmouth	2,160	4,130	5,250	.47	.57	1.42
Morris	3,210	6,970	3,610	.70	.96	.98
Ocean	—	1,210	2,430	—	.17	.66
Passaic	2,660	8,280	8,040	.58	1.13	2.18
Somerset	520	2,120	2,210	.11	.29	.60
Sussex	290	370	1,120	.06	.05	.30
Union	5,370	13,080	10,760	1.17	1.79	2.92
Warren	—	200	1,260	—	.03	.34
New York	403,900	553,150	250,410	87.93	75.85	67.86
New York excl. N.Y.C.	23,860	49,030	75,250	5.19	6.72	20.39
Dutchess	4,280	2,380	3,780	.93	.33	1.02
Nassau	4,390	18,050	28,490	.95	2.47	7.72
Orange	370	1,950	4,640	.08	.27	1.26
Putnam	—	260	690	—	.04	.19
Rockland	220	1,670	3,320	.05	.23	.90
Suffolk	400	7,180	14,120	.09	.98	3.83
Sullivan	—	210	1,160	—	.03	.31
Ulster	—	1,060	3,040	—	.14	.82
Westchester	14,200	16,270	16,010	3.09	2.23	4.34
New York City	380,040	504,120	175,160	82.74	69.13	47.47
Bronx	3,330	9,530	30,630	.73	1.31	8.30
Brooklyn	4,570	40,420	56,490	.99	5.54	15.31
Manhattan	368,090	423,640	42,510	80.14	58.09	11.52
Queens	3,740	26,260	38,910	.81	3.60	10.55
Richmond	310	4,270	6,620	.07	.59	1.79
Region	459,310	729,260	369,010	100.00	100.00	100.00

Source: Regional Plan Association.
Note: Detail may not add to totals because of rounding.

Office Employment and Office Floor Space

Having examined the internal structure of the office industry and its pattern of location by ring of development, we can now summarize and relate both office jobs and office buildings to other activities in the Region. As previously mentioned, the Region in 1965 housed one out of every five employment opportunities, or 1,560,000 jobs in office buildings; this compared to 2,427,000 production-oriented, blue-collar jobs in manufacturing and warehousing, and 3,780,000 other jobs; of these "other" jobs, 780,000 were likewise office jobs, except that they were located not in detached office buildings, but at plant, institutional, and other attached sites. In round numbers, 20 percent of the labor force were white-collar workers in office buildings, 30 percent were blue-collar workers at production sites, and 50 percent consisted of white-collar, blue-collar, and service workers employed at a variety of office, factory, educational, institutional, retail, and other locations in the Region, including some that are not fixed, such as construction or transportation.

The relative degree of centralization of these three types of employment is evident from Table 4.9 and Figure 4.4. Nearly 52 percent of all office building employment is in the Manhattan CBD, compared to 24 percent of the production-oriented employment and 18 percent of all other employment. With the exception of a few highly specialized and numerically small activities, such as legitimate theaters, 76 percent of which are in the CBD, no other major type of employment is as highly centralized as jobs in office buildings. Compared to total employment, office building employment is overrepresented in the central business district by a factor of two, and underrepresented in all the other rings of development even more, the farther one moves from the center. Manufacturing-production employment, by contrast, is underrepresented both in the CBD and in the remainder of the core, and overrepresented in the three suburban rings, most strongly in the intermediate ring. The catch-all category of all other employment is overrepresented in the remainder of the core and in all of the suburban rings, and generally distributed very much like the population.

The floor space in nonresidential buildings generally follows a pattern not too different from that of employment. In 1963, the 31-county New York Region had a total of 8.9 billion square feet of floor space in buildings; of this total, 5.5 billion was in residential buildings, 3.4 billion in nonresidential ones. Of the nonresidential buildings, 400 million square feet were in office buildings, 1,200 million in manufacturing plants and warehouses, and nearly 1,800 million in a variety of other nonresidential structures, including schools, universities, hospitals, retail stores, and other functions. In round

Job Density
per Square Mile
of Available Land

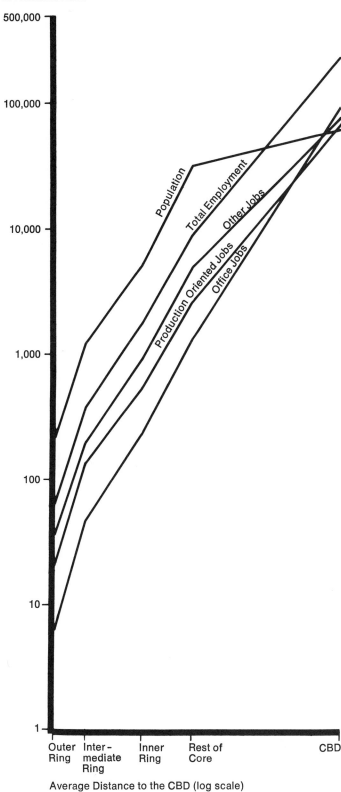

Average Distance to the CBD (log scale)

Figure 4.4 Density of major activities by rings of development in the New York Region

	Population	Total employ.*	Prod.-oriented jobs	Jobs in office bldgs.	Other jobs
Total in thousands					
Manhattan CBD	533.2	2,097.7	596.1	804.4	697.2
Rest of core	8,223.9	2,355.7	713.8	342.5	1,299.4
Inner ring	4,654.7	1,567.7	518.6	204.0	845.1
Intermediate ring	4,279.5	1,339.1	469.8	163.6	705.7
Outer ring	1,289.6	406.6	128.9	43.1	234.6
Region	18,980.9	7,795.6	2,427.2	1,557.6	3,782.0
Densities per square mile of available land†					
Manhattan CBD	64,010	251,825	71,561	96,567	83,697
Rest of core	31,102	8,909	2,699	1,295	4,914
Inner ring	5,106	1,720	569	224	926
Intermediate ring	1,201	376	132	46	197
Outer ring	189	59	19	6	34
Percentage by ring					
Manhattan CBD	2.8%	26.9%	24.5%	51.6%	18.4%
Rest of core	43.3	30.2	29.4	22.0	34.4
Inner ring	24.5	20.1	21.4	13.1	22.3
Intermediate ring	22.6	17.2	19.4	10.5	18.7
Outer ring	6.8	5.2	5.3	2.8	6.2
Region	100.0	99.6	100.0	100.0	100.0
Percentage of employment within ring					
Manhattan CBD		100.0%	28.4%	38.3%	33.3%
Rest of core		100.0	30.3	14.5	55.2
Inner ring		100.0	33.1	13.0	53.9
Intermediate ring		100.0	35.1	12.2	52.7
Outer ring		100.0	31.7	10.6	57.7

Source: Regional Plan Association.

* Detail does not add to totals because of undistributed regional employment.

† Total area less water, parks, and reservations.

Table 4.10. Office Floor Space, Residential Floor Space, Manufacturing, and Other Nonresidential Floor Space by Ring in the New York Region, 1963

	Total res. fl. space	Total nonres. fl. space	Mfg. & warehousing fl. space	Office bldg. fl. space	Other nonres. fl. space
Totals in thousands of square feet					
Manhattan CBD	193,000	528,390	193,080	202,600	132,710
Rest of core	2,470,310	987,650	350,750	77,560*	559,340
Inner ring	1,307,760	817,870	285,200	62,720	469,950
Intermediate ring	1,188,420	848,060	299,300	56,310	492,450
Outer ring	399,780	187,440	72,170	11,310	103,960
Region	5,559,270	3,369,410	1,200,500	410,500	1,758,410
Densities per square mile of available land†					
Manhattan CBD	23,169.3	63,432.2	23,178.9	24,321.7	15,931.6
Rest of core	9,342.4	3,735.2	1,326.5	293.3	2,115.3
Inner ring	1,434.5	897.1	312.8	68.8	515.5
Intermediate ring	333.4	237.9	84.0	15.8	138.2
Outer ring	58.5	27.4	10.6	1.7	15.2
Percentage by ring					
Manhattan CBD	3.5%	15.7%	16.1%	49.4%	7.6%
Rest of core	44.4	29.3	29.2	18.9	31.8
Inner ring	23.5	24.3	23.8	15.3	26.7
Intermediate ring	21.4	25.2	24.9	13.7	28.0
Outer ring	7.2	5.5	6.0	2.7	5.9
Region	100.0	100.0	100.0	100.0	100.0
Percentage of total floor space within ring					
Manhattan CBD	26.7%	73.3%	26.8%	28.1%	18.4%
Rest of core	71.4	28.6	10.2	2.2	16.2
Inner ring	61.5	38.5	13.4	3.0	22.1
Intermediate ring	58.3	41.7	14.7	2.8	24.2
Outer ring	68.1	31.9	12.3	1.9	17.7

Sources: Tri-State Regional Planning Commission *Land Use Inventory*, and Regional Plan Association.
* Includes 12 million square feet underreported in New York City outside the CBD.
† Total area less water, parks, and reservations.

numbers, 12 percent of nonresidential floor space in use in 1963 was in office buildings, 36 percent in factories and warehouses, and 52 percent in all other functions. The latter proportion is nearly identical with that of "all other employment." The discrepancy in the first two categories arises from the fact that office workers, engaged as they are in paper work, require less space per capita than production workers in the goods-handling activities of manufacturing and warehousing.

Because of differences in the occupancy of floor space by employees, the regional distribution of floor space, by ring of development, as shown in Table 4.10 and Figure 4.5, indicates some deviations from the pattern of employment. The Manhattan CBD has only 16 percent of total nonresidential floor space, compared to 27 percent of total employment. The inner and intermediate rings, however, have one-fourth of the nonresidential floor space each, compared to 20 and 17 percent of total employment, respectively. As evident from Tables 4.9 and 4.10, these deviations are explained by the preponderance of office activities in the CBD and manufacturing and warehousing activities in the inner and intermediate rings. Aside from deviations of this type, the overall tendency in the distribution of floor space is the same as that in the distribution of employment: offices are the most centralized activity; goods-handling production and warehousing activities rank second, and all other employment or floor space ranks third, being closely tied to population. These patterns are shown graphically by means of the now familiar density gradients in Figures 4.4 and 4.5. The distribution of office employment, office building employment, and office floor space, compared to total employment and total floor space by county in the Region in 1963–1965 is presented in Table 4.11.

Summarized by ring of development, in absolute numbers, the Manhattan CBD had approximately 800,000 office jobs and 200 million gross square feet of space in office buildings; the core area outside the CBD, including the rest of Manhattan, the boroughs of the Bronx, Brooklyn, and Queens, Hudson County, and the city of Newark, provided 78 million square feet of office buildings for 340,000 office workers; the inner suburban ring had 200,000 office jobs and 63 million square feet of office space; the intermediate, 160,000 office jobs and 56 million square feet of space; and finally the outer ring, 40,000 jobs and 11 million square feet. As a share of each ring of development, office space is obviously most important in the Manhattan CBD, where it accounts for 38 percent of nonresidential floor space; in the other rings, except the outer, it amounts to 7 or 8 percent. Office space as a share of total floor space, shown in Table 4.10, is appropriately lower.

From the figures of office employment and office floor space by ring of development, it would appear that there

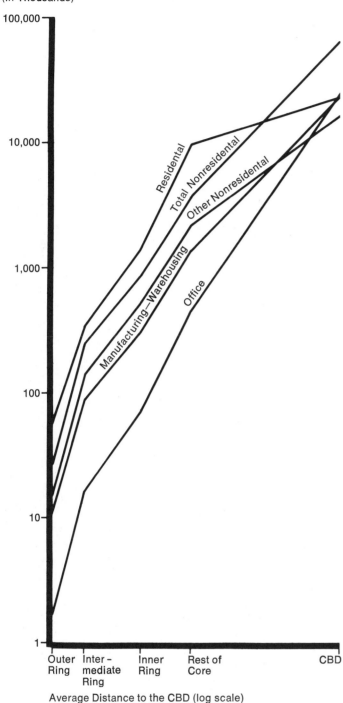

Square Foot Density
per Square Mile
of Available Land
(in Thousands)

Average Distance to the CBD (log scale)

Figure 4.5 Density of floor space by rings of development in the New York Region

Table 4.11. Office Floor Space and Office Employment, Total Non-residential Floor Space, and Total Employment, in the New York Region by County, 1963 and 1965

	1963	1965	1965	1963	1965
	Gross priv. & pub. office fl. space (× 1,000 sq ft)	Total office employ.	Office jobs in office bldgs.†	Gross total nonres. fl. space (× 1,000 sq ft)	Total employ.‡ (× 1,000)
Connecticut	20,600	159,990	62,200	343,092	592.4
Fairfield	11,400	77,050	30,200	159,786	272.3
Litchfield	760	10,440	2,900	19,307	41.9
New Haven	8,440	72,500	29,100	163,999	278.2
New Jersey	87,300	538,190	287,920	1,173,891	2,003.2
Bergen	12,620	79,980	32,100	154,009	275.8
Essex	22,800	126,270	85,760	211,634	428.2
Hudson	8,080	58,180	39,740	182,094	260.9
Hunterdon	360	3,800	1,380	7,742	16.8
Mercer	6,570	37,180	27,220	58,878	130.0
Middlesex	6,620	39,110	16,470	126,950	161.9
Monmouth	5,500	25,640	11,540	76,884	102.2
Morris	4,030	33,630	13,790	58,559	98.4
Ocean	960	8,640	3,640	15,575	33.8
Passaic	5,700	39,700	18,980	103,811	176.7
Somerset	2,340	14,250	4,850	32,992	50.6
Sussex	470	3,510	1,780	6,728	14.6
Union	10,870	63,080	29,210	127,022	229.4
Warren	380	5,220	1,460	11,013	23.9
New York	302,600	1,641,880	1,207,460	1,852,422	5,171.3
New York excl. N.Y.C.	45,620	350,350	148,140	608,855	1,193.8
Dutchess	2,740	22,150	10,440	34,349	76.8
Nassau	16,290	134,770	50,930	198,393	434.5
Orange	1,830	19,530	6,960	30,841	67.0
Putnam	250	2,090	950	3,275	7.6
Rockland	1,700	14,690	5,210	33,857	48.4
Suffolk	10,400	55,060	21,700	128,311	199.6
Sullivan	360	4,750	1,370	8,617	18.7
Ulster	1,080	9,680	4,100	19,031	41.3
Westchester	10,970	87,630	46,480	152,181	299.9
New York City	256,980	1,291,530	1,059,320	1,243,567	3,977.5
Bronx	6,990*	64,750	43,490	114,027	301.0
Brooklyn	16,310*	161,380	101,480	275,721	719.7
Manhattan	208,800	926,430	834,240	648,654	2,406.3
Queens	11,080*	125,420	68,910	173,004	495.5
Richmond	1,800*	13,550	11,200	32,161	55.0
Region	410,500	2,340,060	1,557,580	3,369,405	7,795.6

Sources: Floor space: Regional Plan Association based primarily on the 1963 Tri-State Regional Planning Commission field survey of floor space in commercial offices, banks, professional service buildings, and public/quasi-public office buildings, supplemented by survey data from County Planning Departments and the Sanborn Map series. Employment: Regional Plan Association.

* Figures understated by 12 million square feet in New York City boroughs outside Manhattan. See text.

† Does not include sales jobs in office buildings.

‡ Detail does not add to total because of undistributed regional employment.

One million square feet of office floor space, at a floor-area density, or ratio (FAR), of 20. The 40-story building illustrated here, typical of recent office construction in midtown Manhattan, is 1411 Broadway, on a 1.2 acre site formerly occupied by the Metropolitan Opera. Actually, only about 800,000 square feet are visible in the photograph.

230,000 gross square feet of office floor space, at a floor-area ratio
of about 1. Parking is provided for 750 cars. The 7-story building
illustrated here, typical of medium-density suburban development,
is Park 80 Plaza West One, at the interchange of Interstate 80
and the Garden State Parkway in Saddle Brook, New Jersey.

50,000 square feet of office floor space, at a floor-area ratio of
about 0.5. The 3-story building under construction is typical of
roadside office development in Morris County, New Jersey.

Table 4.12. Per Capita Allocation of Gross Floor Space in the New York Region, 1963

	Square feet of gross fl. space in bldgs.		
	Region	CBD	Rest of Region
Office space per office worker	245	230	260
Residential space per resident	300	360	300
Manufacturing/warehousing space per production worker	495	325	550
Other nonresidential space per other worker	505	215	570
Residential space per worker	730	725	730

Source: Regional Plan Association.

is substantial variation in space allocations per employee. The reason for this discrepancy lies partially in the differing methods of enumerating office floor space within and outside New York City. Outside New York City, the 1963 Tri-State Regional Planning Commission *Land Use Inventory* enumerated virtually all detached office buildings. In New York City, Real Property Assessment records are the only source of information on structure use; they list buildings by structure type, disregarding mixed or changed uses. It appears that the understatement of office floor space in New York City outside the CBD is on the order of 12 million square feet; this figure is included in the aggregates in Table 4.10 but not in the individual borough figures in Table 4.11.

To derive space allocations per employee from two sets of noncomparable data, a number of adjustments are necessary: first, for the difference in dates, 1965 to 1963; second, for underreporting of office space in New York City; third, for the restrictive definition of "office jobs in office buildings." If these adjustments are made, the figures (rounded to the nearest five) shown in Table 4.12 emerge.

It is noteworthy that the most spatially concentrated use—offices—also has the highest "indoor" density of occupancy; manufacturing and other nonresidential uses follow in the same order as they do by our previous measures of concentration; the most decentralized use—housing—also has the highest "indoor" space allocation, if measured per gainfully employed worker, rather than on a per capita basis. Net rentable area in office buildings is generally about 85 percent of gross floor area, so that the 230 square feet of gross area shown here translate into about 196 square feet net, which is larger than the figure for Manhattan from a different source quoted earlier in Chapter 2.

Clear data on office space allocation per worker by ring of development cannot be derived from the figures presented here, but it appears that the Manhattan CBD has a smaller allocation of floor space per worker than the Region as a whole. In the old areas of the core outside the CBD, where there is a dearth of prestige-oriented headquarters, floor space per worker seems to dip down even more, and then rise in the suburban rings. In the suburbs, space allocations are more generous, influenced by cheaper rents and the prominence of local-market activities that seem to consume more extensive amounts of floor space per worker. An inverse relationship between distance from the center and space allocation per person, by contrast, may be true of residential usage. Residential space per resident—as can be deduced in more detail from comparing Tables 4.9 and 4.10—appears to decline as one moves farther toward the periphery: it appears that households living under conditions of high density may be compensating for lack of outdoor space by more indoor space.

The high density of office buildings compared to the land they occupy is sufficiently obvious not to require much elaboration. In the Manhattan CBD, where offices represent some 28 percent of all building floor space, they take up only about 10 percent of the land devoted to building lots—that is, exclusive of streets, sidewalks, parks, and other public uses—which means that on the average they are three times taller than other buildings or, more precisely, have three times the bulk of other buildings. Complete data on land used by offices in the New York Region as a whole is not available, but fragmentary data suggest that, in the suburbs, the contrast is not as crass, and office buildings have just about twice the density of all other structures. In three typical counties of the inner ring—Nassau, Union, and Bergen—offices represent about 3 percent of all building floor space but take up about 2 percent of the developed land, exclusive of streets. The average floor/area ratio, that is, the square feet of building floor space divided by the square feet of lot area, for all buildings in these counties is 0.15, whereas the floor/area ratio of office buildings is about 0.27. In outer counties such as Somerset, Rockland, and Monmouth, where the general densities are lower still (about 0.07), office building densities decline accordingly to floor/area ratios as low as 0.14. Manhattan's office building density, with an average floor/area ratio of 12.5 or so, is almost one hundred times greater. Office buildings completed in Manhattan in 1969 had an average floor/area ratio of about 20, if calculated in terms of gross floor space. (The legal zoning limit in most cases is 18, calculated on the basis of a particular definition of "net" floor space.)

The contrast in building densities reflects an even greater contrast in the prices for land. In outer ring counties, land zoned for industry or commerce and suitable for office parks sells for between 10¢ and 50¢ a square foot, depending on proximity to expressways. Suburban land in inner ring counties, suitable for office development, sells for $1 to $3 per square foot, and in the downtowns of subcenters, for $20 to $30 per square foot. In Manhattan, the price of land for office buildings ranged from about $200 on the periphery of the CBD to $500 at prime sites in the late 1960s.

Subcenters in the New York Region

So far we have viewed the pattern of office location in the New York Region in terms of differences between the Manhattan central business district and the four other rings of development. However, the distribution of offices in each of the other rings is by no means homogeneous; in each of them, offices cluster in a distinct pattern of subcenters. Some of the subcenters are traditional downtowns of smaller cities; some are fairly loose suburban clusters. The pattern of this clustering can be analyzed from Tri-State Regional Planning Commission land-use inventory data, given for each square mile in a square mile grid overlaid on the Region.

To single out from the more than 2,000 square miles of developed land in the Region those square miles that can be characterized as office clusters requires rules which are necessarily somewhat arbitrary. The rules have to take into account both the absolute amount of office space in a given square mile and its relationship to the surrounding area. To begin with, all square miles on the Tri-State grid with more than one-quarter million square feet of office space were mapped; there were 132 of these in 1963. Then, higher concentrations were pinpointed; there were 30 square miles with over 1 million square feet of office space each. Single square miles or groups of adjacent square miles of over a quarter million square feet were outlined as "clusters" if they contained more than 750,000 square feet of office space. In this process, attention was paid to the pattern of peaks and to natural barriers, such as rivers. Not all contiguous square miles of over a quarter million were included as part of a cluster in cases where the presence of office space was largely explainable by a high concentration of residential floor space rather than by the overspill from an adjacent square mile with a high percentage of floor space in office buildings. As a result of this process, 28 office clusters were defined, containing a total of 80 grid square miles. The number of actual square miles of land in these office clusters is somewhat smaller, since many of the square miles on the Tri-State grid contain, in part, bodies of water or parks.

The 28 office clusters are shown on Map 4.1 and the amount of office floor space in each of them in 1963 is listed in Table 4.13. It is apparent that outside the two clusters in the Manhattan CBD, which contained 203 million square feet of floor space, 26 other clusters contained a total of 67 million square feet of office floor space. The remainder, or 141 million square feet, was dispersed. Table 4.13 also gives several measures of concentration for each of the office clusters. It is apparent that office clusters that represent traditional downtowns generally have between 60 to 80 percent of the office floor space concentrated in the highest density square mile within the cluster: midtown and lower Manhattan, Newark, downtown Brooklyn, Paterson-Clifton, White Plains, New Haven, Bridgeport, and Stamford are examples of such clusters. By contrast, the new pattern of loose suburban agglomeration is characterized by the absence of sharp peaks, and clusters such as central Nassau, Elizabeth, central Bergen, and Morristown have only 30 to 40

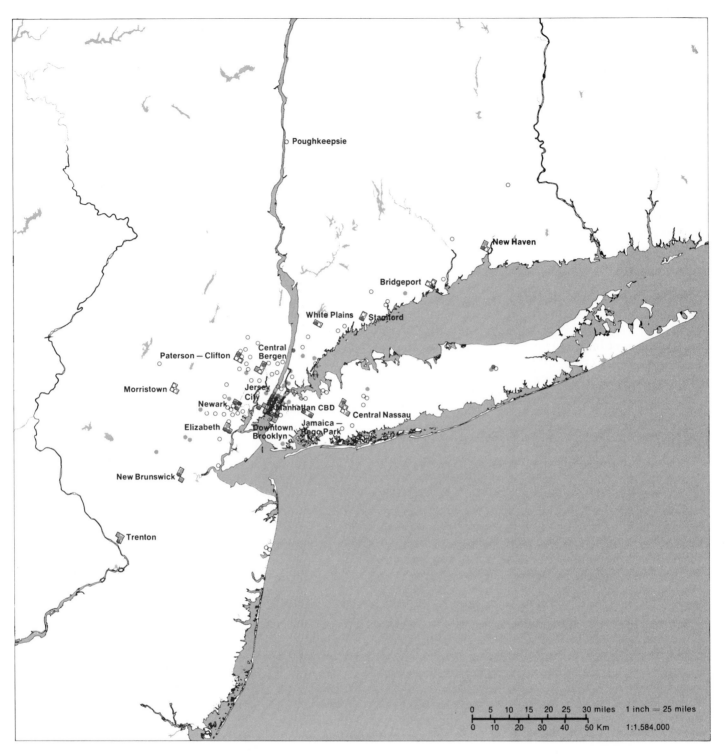

Square Feet of Office Floorspace per Square Mile, 1963:

○   .25—.5 million

●   .5—1 million

●   1.0—2.5 million

●   2.5—5 million

●   5 million and over

◇ Outline of Centers

Map 4.1 Office floor space in the New York Region

Table 4.13. Office Space Distribution in 28 Office Concentrations in the New York Region, 1963

	Office space, in millions of square feet		Measures of concentration		
	Cluster total	Highest sq mile †	% in highest sq mile	No. of grid sq miles in cluster	Offices as % of fl. space in cluster
1. Midtown Manhattan	128.7	85.0	66%	8	29.4%
2. Lower Manhattan	73.9	56.0	76	3	26.1
CBD total	202.6	141.0		11	28.1
CBD as % of ring	100.0%	69.6%			
3. Newark	12.5	8.9	71%	3	17.1%
4. Downtown Brooklyn	7.3	4.9	67	3	9.3
5. Jersey City	2.9	1.5	51	3	5.7
6. Jamaica–Rego Park	2.4	1.2	50	3	5.1
7. Long Island City	1.8	.8	44	3	3.2
8. South Bronx	1.6	.9	56	2	2.7
9. Harlem	1.5	.9	57	2	1.2
10. Union City	.8	.5	62	2	2.7
Non-CBD core clusters	30.8	19.6		21	
Non-CBD core total	77.6 *				
Clusters as % of ring	39.7%	25.3%			
11. Central Nassau	3.7	1.4	38%	5	12.5%
12. Elizabeth	3.1	1.1	35	3	13.8
13. Central Bergen	2.1	.8	38	4	11.8
14. Paterson–Clifton	2.0	1.2	60	3	5.1
15. White Plains	1.4	1.0	71	2	9.1
16. Oranges	1.4	.9	64	2	5.7
17. Plainfield	1.4	.8	57	2	12.1
18. Yonkers	1.0	1.0	100	1	5.3
19. Passaic	.9	.6	66	2	3.4
20. New Rochelle	.9	.5	55	2	7.2
21. Palisades–Ft. Lee	.8	.4	50	2	7.6
Inner ring clusters	18.7	9.7		28	
Inner ring total	62.7				
Clusters as % of ring	29.8%	15.5%			
22. New Brunswick	3.5	1.6	46%	3	17.4%
23. Brookhaven Nat'l Lab.	3.2	.5	16	3	100.0
24. New Haven	3.1	2.2	70	3	7.8
25. Bridgeport	1.8	1.2	66	3	5.1
26. Trenton	3.8	2.0	53	3	n.a.
27. Stamford	1.5	1.2	80	2	9.3
28. Morristown	.8	.3	38	3	10.4
Intermediate ring clusters	17.7	8.6		20	
Intermediate ring total	56.3				
Clusters as % of ring	31.4%	15.3%			
Outer ring total	11.3				
28 clusters, total	269.8			80	
Region	410.5			132 †	

Sources: Tri-State Regional Planning Commission *Land Use Inventory*, and Regional Plan Association.
* Includes 12 million square feet underreported in New York City outside the Manhattan CBD.
† Square miles with over 250,000 square feet of office floor space.

Table 4.14. Office Space in 17 Major Centers in the New York Region, 1963

	Space (× 1 million sq ft)	% of Region
1. Midtown Manhattan	128.7	
2. Lower Manhattan	73.9	
CBD total	202.6	49.4%
3. Newark	12.5	
4. Downtown Brooklyn	7.3	
5. Jersey City	2.9	
6. Jamaica–Rego Park	2.4	
Total, major centers	25.1	6.1
Total, other concentrations	5.7	
Non-CBD core total	77.6*	
7. Central Nassau	3.7	
8. Elizabeth	3.1	
9. Central Bergen	2.1	
10. Paterson–Clifton	2.0	
11. White Plains	1.4	
Total, major centers	12.3	3.0
Total, other concentrations	6.4	
Inner ring total	62.7	
12. New Brunswick	3.5	
13. New Haven	3.1	
14. Bridgeport	1.8	
15. Trenton	3.8	
16. Stamford	1.5	
17. Morristown	.8	
Total, major centers	14.5	3.5
Total, other concentrations	3.2	
Intermediate ring total	56.3	
Outer ring total	11.3	
Region	410.5	100.0
Manhattan CBD	202.6	49.4
15 major subcenters	51.9	12.6
Other concentrations	15.3	3.7
Dispersed	140.7	34.3

Sources: Tri-State Regional Planning Commission *Land Use Inventory*, and Regional Plan Association.
* Includes 12 million square feet underreported in New York City outside the Manhattan CBD.

percent of their floor space in the highest square mile. Of course, these measures are not foolproof indications of peaking, since the incidence of the square mile grid does not necessarily match the pattern of development, and some peaks may be cut in two by the grid. Another measure of concentration, also affected by the incidence of the grid, is the number of square miles in each cluster. For most clusters, this ranges between one and three square miles. Central Nassau County stands out with 5, central Bergen with 4, and the Manhattan CBD takes up 11 grid squares, even though its actual land area is less than 9 square miles. Office floor space as a percentage of total floor space in the cluster ranges from a high of 29 percent in midtown Manhattan to a low that, in most cases, is about 3 percent, and thus not really very distinguishable from the average concentration of office floor space in areas outside Manhattan. In most cases, it is the smaller clusters—those with less than 2 million square feet of office space—that show a preponderance of other uses.

This latter finding leads to the conclusion that not all office clusters, as defined in Table 4.13, are true office centers of regional significance. To single out the major centers from among the 28 clusters listed, the following three rules were applied: (1) the center had to have at least 2 million square feet of office space in 1963; (2) if it had less, it had to exceed the average concentration of office floor space in its ring of development by at least a factor of 3, that is, it had to have in the inner and intermediate rings at least 9 percent of its floor space in office buildings; (3) single-purpose concentrations, such as the Brookhaven National Laboratory, were not considered as office centers. A total of 14 centers outside the CBD qualified under these rules; Bridgeport did not, but was nevertheless included, because of its regional significance, in the list of major centers in Table 4.14.

It is evident from Table 4.14 that the core outside the Manhattan CBD had four centers, namely, Newark, downtown Brooklyn, Jersey City, and Jamaica–Rego Park, totaling 25 million square feet of office floor space, or 32 percent of the floor space in office buildings in the area. The inner ring had five centers—central Nassau, Elizabeth, central Bergen, Paterson, and White Plains, totaling 12 million square feet or 20 percent of the ring total. The intermediate ring had six centers—New Brunswick, New Haven, Bridgeport, Stamford, Trenton, and Morristown—totaling 15 million square feet, and about one-fourth of the ring total. The outer ring had no

Newark (*top*) and Trenton (*bottom*), two of the office centers identified in Tables 4.14 and 5.22, with 14.2 and 4.5 million square feet of office floor space in 1970, respectively. The lesser prominence of highways in downtown Newark in part reflects the fact that only 40 percent of the trips there are made by automobile, as against about 90 percent in Trenton.

centers qualifying for inclusion in either Table 4.13 or 4.14; its major downtown, Poughkeepsie, had 367,000 square feet of office space.

In summary, the 410 million square feet of office floor space in the Region in 1963 were distributed as follows: 49 percent was in the Manhattan CBD, 13 percent was in 15 major subcenters, 4 percent was in 11 minor concentrations, and 34 percent was dispersed. It is now appropriate to see how these proportions changed in the 1963–1970 period, and what changes are implied for the future by the anticipated office growth in the Region. This subject is dealt with in the next chapter.

Chapter 5

**Recent Trends and Future Dimensions
of the Region's Office Activity**

To estimate the future dimensions of a geographically distinct part of the economy such as the New York Region, one should start with the national economy. Having established a benchmark of the nation's future population and employment, one can next trace the changing economic mix of the nation and project it into the future. Then, one can see which shares of various activities in the economic mix the Region has captured so far, assess the changes in these shares, and project them in order to produce a regional total. The same process can be repeated in order to estimate the Region's constituent subareas. While no projection should be equated with a prediction—the future is unknowable—such a process at least makes sure that an estimate for a relatively small geographic area is not out of context with what happens around it, and that the sum of the parts adds up to a whole.

The Region versus the Nation, Projected Trends

OCCUPATIONAL COMPOSITION
Applying the process just described, we first assume that the nation's population in the year 2000 will be slightly in excess of 300 million and total employment, about 118 million. These figures, based on the U.S. Census Series "C" 1965 projection, are widely accepted. Series "C" assumes a declining birth rate and produces lower estimates than those computed for *The Region's Growth* (New York: Regional Plan Association, May 1967). In Chapter 1, Table 1.5 presented the historic trend of an increasing share of white-collar workers and office-type occupations in the economy's total employment. If this long-term trend continues for the next three decades, office workers will increase from about 22 percent of total employment in 1964 to about 31 percent by 2000. After making adjustments for sales workers employed in offices who were omitted from the definition in Chapter 1, one may expect the increase to be from about 24 percent of the total today to about 33.5 percent by 2000.

In absolute numbers, this would mean a nationwide increase from 16.8 million office workers (including sales workers in offices) in 1964 to almost 40 million by 2000, as shown in the last column of Table 5.1. In other words, a 57 percent growth in population would be accompanied by a 136 percent growth in office workers. Further details of this staggering projection, related to the various occupational groupings of white-collar workers in general and office workers in particular, are shown in Table 5.1; their relation to total national employment is indicated in the top part of Table 5.2.

The New York Region has been and still is the pacesetter in the development of the nation's office industry, but will it maintain its leadership into the future? As is the case of other urban economic indicators, one can anticipate an eventual narrowing of the gap between the Region and the nation as smaller urban concentrations experience faster rates of population and employment growth than the larger metropolises. But it is also likely that the Region will continue to be more specialized in office activity than the nation.

As Table 5.3 and Figure 5.1 show, the Region is likely to capture 7.8 million of the nation's 66 million white-collar jobs by the year 2000, and 4.8 million of the nation's 40 million office jobs. In other words, 12 percent of the nation's office workers are still likely to be concentrated in the New York Region 30 years from now. Table 5.3 further summarizes recent trends and future projections by occupational groupings for the Region on a comparable basis with the national breakdown in Table 5.1. Office workers as a percentage of white-collar occupations and of total employment within the New York Region are shown in the bottom part of Table 5.2. It is apparent that office workers (including sales workers in offices) will increase from 31 percent of the Region's total employment in 1964 to 39 percent by the year 2000. The Region's specialization in office work compared to the rest of the nation is thus projected to diminish only slightly.

COMPOSITION BY INDUSTRY

These projections of future office employment are strongly influenced by the industrial composition of the economy. Certain industries, notably finance, government, and services, employ unusually high shares of office-type workers. This has already been shown. Significantly, these three industries are also the fastest growing ones in both the nation and the Region. Thus it is that, apart from all considerations of locational choice among metropolitan areas, a region's future office activity is, to some extent, the product of its present industrial mix.

Of course, the relative weight of office-type occupations in each particular industry is not fixed but also changes over time. Expected changes, by industry, in the New York Region are shown in Table 5.4 for office-type occupations not including sales. It is evident that finance, government, and services are expected to remain the leading office-intensive industries, and even increase their share of office occupations somewhat. More dramatic increases in the share of office-type occupations can be expected in industries for which New York will increasingly become an administrative center rather than a production location; these include, according to Table 5.4, manufacturing and, to a lesser degree, construction.

Applying the expected proportions of office-type occupations by industry, shown in Table 5.4, to the expected total employment by industry in the New York Region (according to revised *Region's Growth* estimates), one can determine the future number of office-type occupations

Table 5.1. Past and Projected Employment in Office-Type Occupations, White-Collar Work, and Office Work for the Nation, 1940–2000 (in thousands)

	Office-type occupation*				White collar total†	Office workers‡				Office workers incl. sales workers§
	Pro.	Mgrl.	Cler.	Total		Pro.	Mgrl.	Cler.	Total	
1940	3,496	4,819	4,488	12,803	15,732	1,007	1,184	4,158	6,349	7,099
1950	4,867	6,646	7,292	18,805	22,580	1,563	1,863	6,657	10,083	11,071
1960	7,280	7,140	9,655	24,075	28,461	2,293	2,574	8,965	13,832	15,165
1964	8,550	7,452	10,667	26,669	31,125	2,796	2,802	9,856	15,454	16,828
1975	12,442	8,631	13,638	34,711	40,026	4,255	3,790	12,615	20,660	22,433
1985	17,767	9,714	17,353	44,834	51,200	6,318	4,823	16,069	27,210	29,486
2000	25,324	11,076	22,239	58,639	66,426	9,522	6,453	20,624	36,599	39,663

Source: Regional Plan Association (based on U.S. Census and National Planning Association data).
Note: Table 5.1 differs from Table 1.5 in that the former represents labor force and the latter total employment.
* The U.S. Census' major occupational classifications which incorporate the detailed skills performed in most office activities.
† The same occupational grouping as that described in the previous footnote, expanded to include sales workers who perform less significant portions of their total work in offices.
‡ Detailed office skills extracted from the category office-type occupations.
§ Detailed office skills extracted from the category office-type occupations and expanded to include the previously unreported portion of sales workers who work in offices.

Table 5.2. Relative Differences in the Nation and the Region Share of Office Jobs in Total Employment, 1940–2000

	Office workers as a share of		Office workers incl. sales workers as a share of	
	Office-type occupations	Total employ.	White-collar occupations	Total employ.
The Nation				
1940	49.59%	13.43%	45.12%	15.01%
1950	53.62	16.87	49.03	18.53
1960	57.45	20.74	53.28	22.74
1964	57.95	21.95	54.05	23.90
1975	59.52	24.62	56.05	26.73
1985	60.69	27.46	57.59	29.75
2000	62.41	30.97	59.71	33.56
The Region				
1940	56.81%	20.43%	51.60%	22.78 %
1950	57.75	23.50	53.18	25.77
1960	60.13	26.87	55.40	29.30
1964	62.41	28.67	57.67	31.32
1975	63.68	30.80	59.37	33.42
1985	64.27	33.24	60.44	35.84
2000	65.31	36.56	61.96	39.20

Source: Regional Plan Association (based on U.S. Census and National Planning Association Data).

Table 5.3. Past and Projected Employment in Office-Type Occupations, White-Collar Work, and Office Work for the New York Region, 1940–2000 (in thousands)

	Office-type occupations*				White collar total †	Office workers ‡				Office workers incl. sales workers §
	Pro.	Mgrl.	Cler.	Total		Pro.	Mgrl.	Cler.	Total	
1940	514.5	554.3	904.5	1,973.3	2,423.1	158.2	210.2	752.6	1,121.0	1,250.2
1950	739.0	777.5	1,196.2	2,712.7	3,229.3	256.5	282.2	1,027.8	1,566.5	1,717.4
1960	1,019.2	752.7	1,505.1	3,277.0	3,878.7	331.0	375.4	1,264.1	1,970.5	2,148.7
1964	1,150.3	760.9	1,640.7	3,551.9	4,198.8	389.6	409.9	1,417.2	2,216.7	2,421.6
1975	1,613.0	784.6	2,014.6	4,412.2	5,134.0	561.8	474.2	1,773.5	2,809.5	3,048.3
1985	2,233.8	794.0	2,458.0	5,485.8	6,291.2	797.4	527.4	2,200.9	3,525.7	3,802.3
2000	3,109.9	726.4	3,047.9	6,884.2	7,781.6	1,150.7	547.6	2,798.0	4,496.3	4,821.3

Source: Regional Plan Association (based on U.S. Census and National Planning Association data).
* The U.S. Census' major occupational classifications which incorporate the detailed skills performed in most office activities.
† The same occupational grouping as that described in the previous footnote, expanded to include sales workers who perform less significant portions of their total work in offices.
‡ Detailed office skills extracted from the category office-type occupations.
§ Detailed office skills extracted from the category office-type occupations and expanded to include the previously unreported portion of sales workers who work in offices.

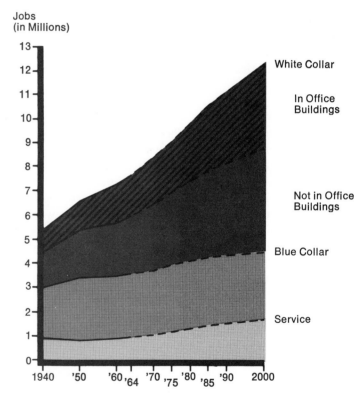

Figure 5.1 New York Region's employment by occupation, 1940–1964–2000

in each industry. Table 5.5 shortcuts this step and proceeds directly to employment in office buildings. As previously shown, office jobs in office buildings currently comprise almost 70 percent of the Region's office employment and about 37 percent of its white-collar jobs. Based on recent trends, these proportions will increase slightly, to about 72 percent and 42 percent, respectively, by the year 2000. What this will mean in absolute numbers for each industry group for 1975, 1985, and 2000 is demonstrated in Table 5.5.

Compared to 1967, office jobs in office buildings in the New York Region will double by 2000, from about 1.7 to about 3.3 million, or from about 1.8 to 3.5 million if sales workers in office buildings are included. The fastest growth will occur in services, where employment in office buildings will triple. Services will become the leading user of office space, with 1 million jobs. The presently leading user of office space—finance, insurance, and real estate—will take second place, with close to 700,000 jobs in office buildings, and government will maintain its third place, with over 600,000 office building jobs. In manufacturing industries and in construction, jobs in office buildings will grow at a rate slightly below the average, and trade and the transportation, communication, and utilities sector are expected to experience even more sluggish rates of growth with regard to jobs in office buildings. The trend in the latter two categories can be explained, in large part, by increasing automation of labor-intensive clerical functions.

One should recall that the New York Region has a decidedly higher concentration of office activity in detached office buildings than the rest of the nation, because of the Region's traditional specialization in finance, corporate headquarters, business services, non-profit organizations, nonlocal government, and other activities whose production, in the main, takes the form of intangible goods—communication, information exchange, and paper work in general. These functions relate to all three classes of office activity—headquarters, middle market, and local. However, over time, office employment will be subjected to different degrees of capital intensity (automation) at each of the three levels, and these changes will affect both the absolute amount of activity in detached office buildings and its locational needs.

COMPOSITION BY CLASS OF ACTIVITY

Over the next three decades, the office industry housed in office buildings in the New York Region is projected to change significantly in composition. As Table 5.6 and Figure 5.2 indicate, headquarters jobs are projected to grow at a staggering rate from about 460 thousand in 1965 to about 1.2 million by 2000 and thus increase their share of the Region's office building employment

Table 5.4. Past and Projected Shares of Office-Type Occupations by Industry for the New York Region, 1960–2000

Industry	1960	1975	1985	2000
Agriculture and mining	13.6%	19.6%	27.3%	34.1%
Construction	19.5	21.0	22.0	23.4
Manufacturing	31.4	36.0	39.1	43.7
Transportation, communications, utilities	40.4	42.8	44.2	46.3
Trade	39.0	38.7	38.4	38.0
Finance, insurance, real estate	73.0	75.2	77.3	80.4
Services	54.4	57.6	60.5	64.9
Government	70.9	73.1	74.2	75.9
Total	44.7	48.4	51.7	56.0

Source: Regional Plan Association (based on U.S. Census and National Planning Association data).

Table 5.5. Present and Projected Office Employment by Industry for the New York Region, 1967–2000 (in thousands)

	1967 office employ.		Projected office employ. in office bldgs.		
	Total workers	In office bldgs.	1975	1985	2000
Agriculture and mining	9.9	7.5	6.3	5.8	6.0
Construction	62.7	57.6	73.9	92.0	109.5
Manufacturing	483.6	247.2	326.4	394.6	430.3
Transportation, communications, utilities	225.8	215.8	227.0	241.5	241.7
Trade	462.2	105.7	113.2	127.5	155.0
Finance, insurance, real estate	430.3	422.6	490.8	585.7	689.3
Services	405.6	332.0	412.8	638.4	1,016.1
Government	324.0	280.8	321.9	421.3	611.9
Total	2,404.1	1,669.2	1,972.3	2,506.8	3,259.8
Total incl. sales		1,812.7	2,134.1	2,696.6	3,487.2

Source: Regional Plan Association.

Table 5.6. Present and Projected Office Building Employment by Class of Activity for the New York Region, 1965–2000

	Total employ. (× 1,000)		Growth, 1965–2000	
	1965	2000	Absolute (× 1,000)	Rate (%)
Headquarters	459.3	1,239.0	779.7	169.8%
Middle market	729.3	1,199.2	469.9	64.4
Local market	369.0	821.6	452.6	122.7
Total	1,557.6	3,259.8	1,702.2	109.3

Source: Regional Plan Association.

Jobs
(in Millions)

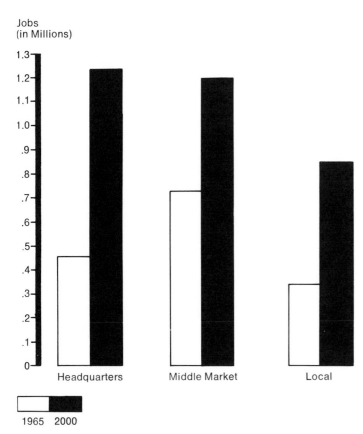

1965   2000

Figure 5.2 Growth in office employment by class of activity in the New York Region, 1965–2000

from 30 to about 38 percent. This projection reflects the demonstrated ability of the Region, over the past decade or so, to attract headquarters-type central administrative jobs.

The next fastest growing segment of the office economy is expected to be local jobs, projected to grow from about 370,000 in 1965 to over 800,000 by 2000, increasing their share of the total from 23 to 25 percent.

The slowest rate of growth is foreseen for middle-market jobs, today the numerically dominant sector of the office economy. They are expected to grow from about 700,000 to a little less than 1.2 million and thus decline in their share of the total from 47 percent to 37 percent. This latter development is attributable to automation, which will reduce the demand for labor in repetitive clerical jobs now very prevalent in the middle-market sector. Let us take a closer look at each of the three sectors.

HEADQUARTERS EMPLOYMENT GROWTH. In Chapter 2, we weighed the Region's competitive placement in the nation and found it to bear all the earmarks of sustaining, long-term growth in headquarters-type office activity. In view of the large share of the nation's increment in central administrative office and auxiliary (CAO&A) jobs that the Region has been capturing during the late 1950s and the 1960s, it is expected that it will gain over 400,000 of the nation's new CAO&A jobs by 2000. Currently in the New York Region, enumerated central administrative office (CAO) employment represents slightly less than half of total headquarters employment. Many of the elite nonmanufacturing headquarters functions that gravitate to New York are excluded from the CAO&A classification. Assuming that these will grow at the same rate as the CAO&A jobs reported by the Census, an increment in headquarters-type jobs of roughly 780 thousand between 1965 and 2000 appears to be in order.

MIDDLE-MARKET EMPLOYMENT GROWTH. Middle-market office employment is a heterogeneous grouping of office activities that is, in part, population-related at a subregional scale and, in part, related to headquarters activity. As a result, the size of the future population and the size of the future headquarters activity are the main determinants of the magnitude of middle-market employment. An important added dimension, however, is future management decisions concerning automation and the relative size of branch offices. At present, middle-market activity is more clerk-intensive than other classes of office employment and has the most room for the employment of automated systems to perform standardized and repetitive clerical tasks. Our assumptions are as follows: over the long run, automation and telecommunications will have, on balance, a concentrating impact on the location of administrative activity either at detached headquarters or at production sites, thereby reducing labor intensity at regional branch offices and at decentralized back offices. Management will move to eliminate duplicate administration and personnel requirements that are needed today to overcome the friction of space both within an urban region and between regions. Integrated computer systems and telecommunication advances will help to direct production, purchasing, sales, and the like from a stronger head office with lowered staff demands in the field. Moreover, firms with large central offices will increasingly service themselves in such administration-related activities as advertising, public relations, and legal work. Thus, some of these functions, now performed by independent firms in the middle-market category, will be absorbed by headquarters offices. It is for these reasons that the growth in middle-market office activity is projected to increase at a lesser rate than previously experienced, resulting in a total increment of about 470,000 jobs.

LOCAL-MARKET EMPLOYMENT GROWTH. Local-market office employment is engaged in services at the community level, and its growth is a function of population growth and increasing consumer income. The small, residence-related offices of local realtors, insurance agents, brokers, and the functions of small units of local government are least susceptible to automation. With a 48 percent increase in population between 1965 and 2000 in the New York Region, from 18.98 million to 28.18 million, and a virtual doubling of per capita income in constant dollars from $3,676 in 1965 to $7,950 in the year 2000, local-market employment in offices is expected to somewhat more than double and add about 450,000 jobs.

OFFICE BUILDING CONSTRUCTION

The estimates and projections we have developed deal with employment and have been formulated on the basis of economic statistics dealing with employment. The question arises, to what extent are the statistics corroborated by physical changes in the urban scene, in the form of buildings, and what do the projections signify in terms of new office buildings?

As has been pointed out on several occasions, there is no national inventory of office buildings and no comprehensive reporting of current additions to or deletions from the office stock by any official agency. However, the F. W. Dodge Division of McGraw-Hill Information Systems Company does collect detailed and rather comprehensive data on construction contracts, by type of building, mostly to fill the needs of the construction industry. Thus, national data more comprehensive than those of U.S. Census current construction statistics are available from this source; specifically, size of projects is listed in square feet of building area, and geographic detail to the county level can be obtained. The data on new con-

Table 5.7. Recent Trends in Office Building Construction in the Region and the Nation, 1957–1969

Year	Construction* (× 1,000 sq ft)			Region as a % of nation
	Nation	Region	Manhattan	
1957	75,899	17,222	12,368	22.7%
1958	70,952	11,645	9,263	16.4
1959	71,070	8,726	5,462	12.3
1960	76,413	12,241	8,939	16.0
1961	75,765	9,578	4,907	12.6
1962	89,431	14,255	9,039	15.9
1963	104,033	9,377	3,074	9.0
1964	95,463	9,302	4,186	9.7
1965	107,862	13,329	5,801	12.4
1966	109,381	13,711	7,263	12.5
1967	121,276	16,690	7,829	13.8
1968	151,656	29,442	11,798	19.4
1969	190,965	41,840	29,728	21.9
Period total	1,340,166	207,358	119,657	15.5

Sources: F. W. Dodge Company and Regional Plan Association.
Note: Manhattan construction reported in this table differs from that in Table 5.18 for the following reasons: F. W. Dodge reports data for the borough as a whole; space is in gross dimensions; the year of reporting is the start of construction; and the series excludes government administration buildings but includes alteration activity.
* Includes new construction, additions, alterations, and conversions in office and bank buildings.

Table 5.8. Estimated Past and Projected Office Building Floor Space in the Nation and the New York Region, 1963–2000

| Year | Floor space (× 1 million gross sq ft) | | | Region as a % of nation | Manhattan CBD as a % of Region |
	Nation	Region	Manhattan CBD		
1963	2,200	411*	203	18.7%	49.4%
1967	2,600	455*	221	17.5	48.6
1975	3,400	594	310	17.5	52.2
1985	5,000	735	340	14.7	46.3
2000	7,000	975	400	13.9	41.0

Sources: Regional Plan Association (based partly on Tri-State Regional Planning Commission's 1963 inventory for the New York Region and trends in public and private office construction reported by F. W. Dodge, as well as other sources).
Notes: The definition of office building floor space in this table differs from Table 5.7 in that government administration buildings as well as private office and banks are included. With the exception of the Manhattan 1975 forecast, projections are based on office employment in office buildings including sales workers in offices. Past changes in the stock of office space in Manhattan and the Region reflect construction of new office buildings less demolition. Projection of the 1975 Manhattan inventory is based upon estimated completion of projects currently authorized or under construction, less a continuation of past rates of demolition (nearly 11 million gross square feet of office space in the CBD, 1957–1970, or ¾ million per annum). As such, the 1975 forecast for the CBD reflects a considerable level of overbuilding which will have to be absorbed in subsequent years. Although no overbuilding is foreseen for the rest of the Region, the CBD surplus affects the total regional forecast.
* Includes correction for the under-reporting of about 12 million square feet in New York City outside the Manhattan CBD.

struction presented in the following discussion were aggregated from detailed tabulations purchased from the F. W. Dodge Division of McGraw-Hill Information Systems Company.

The data, as presented in Table 5.7 and in Tables 5.9 and 5.10 subsequently, refer to all new construction (by year of construction starts) of private office and bank buildings, including alterations to existing buildings and conversions of nonoffice building space to office use. The data do not account for demolition of existing office space, nor are alterations listed separately; thus, the figures shown are greater than the actual net increment to the office stock; however, the figures in Table 5.7 exclude government office buildings; in the New York Region, new construction of government offices, included in Tables 5.9 and 5.10, amounted to 9.25 percent of private office and bank building construction. The omission of government office construction in Table 5.7 balances somewhat the overstatement due to the inclusion of alterations, which may amount to around 12 percent of the total.

The message of Table 5.7 is dramatic. Over the 13-year period, 1957 to 1970, roughly 1.3 billion square feet of new private office space was built or rebuilt in the nation, which is more than half the floor space that existed in the nation at the beginning of the period. The pace of office construction and reconstruction nationwide shows a sharp upward trend—from 73.6 million square feet annually in the first four years of the period, to 91.2 million square feet annually in the next four years, to 136 million in the last five years, or a rise in the rate of growth from about 4 to about 5 percent annually.

Of this nationwide construction, the New York Region, in line with its past share of the nation's office-type jobs, captured 15.5 percent or 207 million square feet, and Manhattan captured almost 9 percent, or about 120 million square feet. The Region's share of the nation seems to have fluctuated considerably over the period, starting with 22 percent in 1957, dropping to a low of 9 percent in 1963, and gradually increasing again to 22 percent in 1969. On the whole, however, apart from the 1963–1964 dip, which may have been caused in part by a slowdown in new construction in the wake of the new 1961 New York City zoning resolution, the statistics on construction confirm the earlier economic findings about the Region's undiminished attractiveness as an office location compared to the rest of the nation.

Combining the data on office employment presented earlier with the data on new office construction, one can make an approximate estimate of both the total national inventory of office floor space and its projected future dimensions. As indicated in Table 5.8 and Figure 5.3, it appears that by the year 2000 the national inventory of office space will more than triple, compared to 1963,

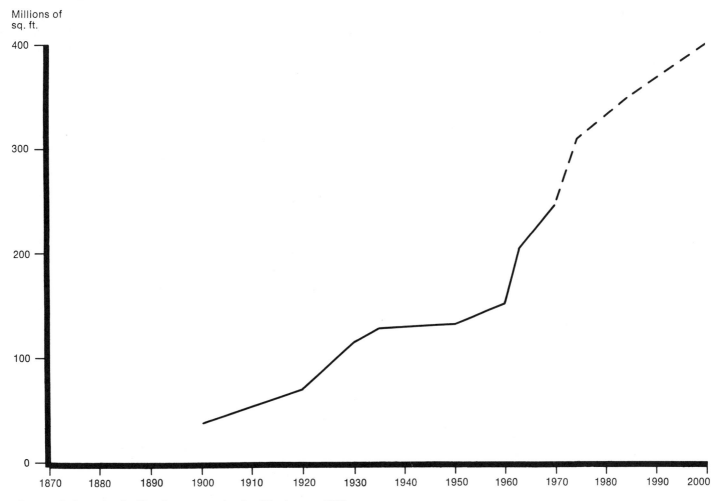

Figure 5.3 Growth of office floor space in the Manhattan CBD,
1900–2000

Table 5.9. Past Stock of Office Floor Space and Recent Trends in Public and Private Office Construction in the New York Region by Ring and Sector of Development, 1963–1970

	Gross pub. & priv. office fl. space (× 1,000 sq ft)		As a % of Region	
	In place 1963	Constr. started 1963–1970	Existing 1963	Started 1963–1970
Manhattan	208,800	74,238.4	50.9%	50.8%
Rest of core	71,360*	9,470.8	17.4	6.5
New York sector	46,380*	5,738.6	11.3	3.9
New Jersey sector	24,980	3,732.2	6.1	2.6
Inner ring	62,720	30,754.4	15.3	21.1
New York sector	27,730	14,420.0	6.7	9.9
New Jersey sector	34,990	16,334.4	8.5	11.2
Intermediate ring	56,310	26,946.2	13.7	18.4
New York sector	12,330	9,239.5	3.0	6.3
New Jersey sector	25,160	9,990.9	6.1	6.8
Connecticut sector	18,820	7,715.8	4.6	5.3
Outer ring	11,310	4,652.3	2.7	3.2
New York sector	7,360	2,579.3	1.8	1.8
New Jersey sector	2,170	1,203.2	.5	.8
Connecticut sector	1,780	869.8	.4	.6
Region	410,500	146,062.1	100.0	100.0

Sources: Floor space in place: Regional Plan Association based primarily on the 1963 Tri-State Regional Planning Commission field survey of floor space in commercial offices, banks, professional service buildings, and public/quasi-public office buildings, supplemented by survey data from County Planning Departments and the Sanborn Map series. Construction started: Regional Plan Association based on construction data from F. W. Dodge Company.
Note: Construction started covers new construction, additions, alterations, and conversions reported, 1963 through 1969, on office, bank, and government administration building projects. Does not include demolitions.
* Includes 12 million underreported square feet in New York City outside the CBD.

and reach about 7 billion square feet. The New York Region will grow from roughly 411 million square feet in 1963 to about 1 billion in 2000, but as a share of the nation, it will decline from about 19 to about 14 percent. The question now arises of where the additional half-billion square feet of office space will locate in the New York Region.

Allocation of Growth within the Region

RECENT GROWTH BY SECTOR AND RING OF DEVELOPMENT
Before answering the question of where offices in the New York Region will—or should—be located in the future, it is useful to recapitulate where they were as of the date of the last inventory and where the most recent increment of new offices located. Both are illustrated in Table 5.9. The surprising message of Table 5.9 is that, to a much greater degree than one might expect, new offices in 1963–1970 located pretty much in the same manner as offices that were in place by 1963. Specifically, one would look in vain for a great wave of decentralization.

To begin with, 50.9 percent of the Region's office space in 1963 was located in Manhattan, and 50.8 percent of the new office space started in 1963–1970 was likewise located in Manhattan. Thus, Manhattan has retained, against formidable odds, its attractiveness for offices vis-à-vis the rest of the Region. No decentralization of office construction—as opposed to employment—took place from Manhattan in the 1960–1970 decade.

Relative decentralization did occur, but in a somewhat different context, namely, from the remainder of the core to the counties of the inner and intermediate rings. Specifically, the rest of the core, namely, the boroughs of the Bronx, Brooklyn, Queens, the county of Hudson, and the city of Newark together accounted for about 17 percent of the office space in the Region in place as of 1963. Between 1963 and 1970, they got only 6.5 percent of the increment in new office space. By contrast, the counties of the inner ring—Westchester, Nassau, Bergen, Essex, and Union—which possessed 15 percent of the Region's office floor space in 1963, obtained 21 percent of the increment, and the counties of the intermediate ring, which had about 14 percent, obtained 18 percent of the increment. The outer ring remained at 3 percent of the total.

The reason for the relative dearth of new office construction in the "gray areas" of the core lies, of course, largely in the dynamics of population change, since so much of the office activity outside Manhattan—whether "middle market" or "local"—is essentially population related. The rest of the core has been stable or declining in population and subjected to the suburban exodus of the middle class, while the suburban counties have ex-

perienced rapid population growth and increasing afflu-
ence. Under these conditions, it may be encouraging that
the rest of the core did get as much as 9.5 million square
feet of new office floor space.

If one compares the 1963 inventory with 1963–1970
construction starts in Table 5.9 by sector within rings
of development, it becomes apparent that offices prefer
those parts of the Region located in the state of New
York. Increases in the percentage of building starts versus existing buildings are the greatest in the New York
State sectors of the inner and intermediate rings (Nassau,
Westchester, Rockland, and Suffolk counties), and even
in New York City outside Manhattan the decline in the
share is not as sharp as it is on the New Jersey side of the
core, where office construction in Newark and Hudson
County was relatively low. After New York State, the
second most attractive sector for offices appears to be
Connecticut, and New Jersey ranks third.

Additional information on the construction starts presented in Table 5.9 is given in Table 5.10. Most useful
is the last column, indicating that in 1966–1970, the
average per square foot cost of office construction was
$41 in Manhattan, $32 in the remainder of the core, and
about $25 in the suburbs. These are construction con-
tract costs that exclude land acquisition. Manhattan had
only 16 percent of the projects reported by the
F. W. Dodge data but accounted for almost 66 percent
of total project value. The column on average square
feet per project merely indicates that the F. W. Dodge
data contain a multiplicity of small conversion, addition,
and alteration projects. For example, the average new
office building in Manhattan completed in 1964–1970
had almost 750,000 gross square feet, compared to the
77,950 shown for project characteristics in Table 5.10.
The three-quarter million square foot average new office
building size, incidentally, represents a substantial increase in comparison with the early 1950s, when the
typical office building size was about 300,000 square feet.

FACTORS INFLUENCING FUTURE LOCATION
The discussion centering on the differences between
office location patterns in the New York Region prior to
1963 and during 1963–1970, supported by Table 5.9,
demonstrated that the present, to a surprising degree, is
not unlike the past. The major difference was the relatively moderate shift from the "gray areas" of the core
to the green areas of the inner and intermediate rings.
How different will the future be?

It appears that—the soaring number of computers in
the country notwithstanding—the slowness with which
technological innovation may be expected to become
operational will make the future distribution more like
than unlike the present, at least until the later years of
the century. Integrated computer systems, for example,

Table 5.10. Characteristics of New Public and Private Office Construction in the New York Region by Ring and Sector of Development, 1966–1970

| | Share of Region | | Project characteristics by area | | |
	Total projects	Total project value	Average square feet	Average cost ($\times$ $1,000)	Average cost per sq ft
Manhattan	16.1%	65.8%	77,950	$3,211.1	$41
Rest of core	11.3	4.2	9,180	289.7	32
New York sector	7.0	2.6	8,100	291.8	36
New Jersey sector	4.3	1.6	10,950	286.3	26
Inner ring	33.3	14.4	13,790	339.9	25
New York sector	12.8	6.7	16,650	410.7	25
New Jersey sector	20.5	7.7	12,000	295.7	25
Intermediate ring	31.4	13.7	13,650	340.5	25
New York sector	7.2	4.3	22,130	468.1	21
New Jersey sector	13.4	5.1	11,200	299.7	27
Connecticut sector	10.8	4.3	11,070	306.7	28
Outer ring	7.9	1.9	7,970	191.1	24
New York sector	4.0	1.1	9,430	219.4	23
New Jersey sector	2.6	.3	4,680	108.3	23
Connecticut sector	1.3	.5	9,960	267.0	27
Region	100.0	100.0	23,060	783.5	34

Source: Regional Plan Association based on construction data from F. W. Dodge Company.
Note: Data cover new construction, additions, alterations, and conversions reported in construction starts, 1963 through 1969, on office, bank, and government administration building projects.

will probably not come into widespread use until after 1980. The lagged effect should sustain present trends in office growth and location. For example, it is estimated that the middle-market sector of office activity will grow rapidly until the mid-1980s, after which the leveling-off in demand will dampen the overall office growth in the Region toward the end of this century.

In the meantime, it is reasonable to expect that the "peeling off" of clerk-intensive and other repetitive or mechanical office functions from Manhattan headquarters may accelerate to some extent, abetted by rising price differentials and by an easier accessibility to a growing clerical labor pool in places farther from Manhattan. Possible locations for these "spinoff" functions include not only the inner and intermediate ring suburbs but also the so-far bypassed remainder of the core —subcenters such as downtown Brooklyn, Newark, and Jamaica. At the same time, the Manhattan CBD should continue upgrading its office functions to a more elite composition with a relatively stronger role for central offices.

A more selective distribution of office activities within the Region in the future will be reinforced by the structure of the regional labor market and the regional transportation systems. In the past, before widespread suburbanization, the CBD functioned as the center of the labor market for all occupation groups; it was easily accessible to all. Today, however, Manhattan is central to the regional labor market taken as a whole, but not equally to the domiciles of all job skills. Higher-income or more-skilled occupation groups exhibit a greater endurance for longer journeys to work (or are more likely to trade off greater travel time and cost for space), while lower-paid, less-skilled white-collar workers travel only relatively short distances. As population densities increase at the Region's periphery, suburban centers become highly accessible to a growing clerical labor force while the prime business center penetrates the more skilled occupational areas with rail lines or express buses, and taps them in a more selective way. Thus, elite growth is channeled to the main center, while subregional labor markets in more routine occupations become oriented to their respective subcenters.

Once over the technology hump, sometime in the mid-1980s, clerical demands in the suburban labor markets should diminish while the center, fortified in its headquarters position, will continue to grow in space provided for central management and professional activity. On an intraregional basis, firms will find less reason to split within the Region (that is, decentralize portions of their head office) and will choose either a central or a suburban location for the entire firm. They will stay within the CBD for reasons of interfirm communication and specialized labor market orientation, while tapping the markets for their products and managing their production through the increased use of telecommunication devices. Undoubtedly, detached sales offices will remain, but their demand for attending staffs will be transferred in part to headquarters offices. Those firms moving out of the CBD will leave because they have a lesser orientation to the overall regional executive and professional labor market, and because the cost of a CBD location will not offset the advantages to be gained from face-to-face contacts with other firms or with supporting services. Moreover, to the extent that the need to spinoff certain functions from the headquarters will remain, the spinoff may increasingly be not just to a White Plains or a Jamaica but perhaps to Denver or Phoenix.

Within the Region, competition to a growing central business district—in terms of sheer numbers—will also come from the growth in population-related office activities, which involves an outward shift in the locational preference of certain industry groups. As we have noted before, the growth in local office functions will be a close second to headquarters growth, judged by the percentage increase, and will add almost half a million new jobs. While the CBD will grow because of the Region's attraction for headquarters and headquarters-serving functions, the environs will grow faster in new office employment mainly because of the vast increases in population which will occur outside the core and provide an abundant market for population-related office functions.

Having made these general observations, we can now turn to translating them into figures. The importance of access to white-collar labor markets was sufficiently emphasized before. Table 5.11 shows the residential location of office workers in the New York Region by county in 1960, and Table 5.12 shows a projected distribution for 2000, where the future population is assumed to be that given in the table. The outward shift in the Region's white-collar labor market becomes apparent from comparing the two tables.

For example, 960,000 office workers resided in New York City in 1960; that number is projected to increase to 1.4 million by 2000, assuming the city's population will remain stable at about 8 million; however, as a share of the Region, office workers residing in New York City will shrink from almost one-half to about one-third. Two-thirds rather than one-half of the Region's office workers in the year 2000 are likely to be residing outside New York City, and more than two-thirds of the Region's population will be located there.

New Jersey, which in 1960 had about 500,000 office workers, will triple their number to 1.5 million (its population will almost double), and the portions of New York State outside New York City, namely, Long Island and the Hudson Valley, will similarly increase their number of resident office workers from about 360,000

Table 5.11. Residential Location of Office Workers by County in the New York Region, 1960

County	Office workers in major occupational groups*				As a percentage of Region			
	Pro., tech.	Mgrs., offics., props.	Cler.	Total	Pro., tech.	Mgrs., offics., props.	Cler.	Total
Connecticut	26,260	29,110	83,270	138,640	7.93%	7.75%	6.59%	7.03%
Fairfield	14,210	16,530	36,870	67,610	4.29	4.40	2.92	3.43
Litchfield	1,840	2,110	5,950	9,900	.56	.56	.47	.50
New Haven	10,210	10,470	40,450	61,130	3.08	2.79	3.20	3.10
New Jersey	94,710	101,220	315,200	511,130	28.62	26.96	24.93	25.94
Bergen	20,350	24,960	54,210	99,520	6.15	6.65	4.29	5.05
Essex	16,640	18,500	62,290	97,430	5.03	4.93	4.93	4.94
Hudson	6,480	6,670	50,290	63,440	1.96	1.78	3.98	3.22
Hunterdon	780	1,050	2,380	4,210	.24	.28	.19	.21
Mercer	4,960	4,080	17,660	26,700	1.50	1.09	1.40	1.36
Middlesex	7,010	6,550	23,340	36,900	2.12	1.74	1.84	1.87
Monmouth	6,010	6,230	15,490	27,730	1.82	1.66	1.22	1.41
Morris	7,910	6,800	14,270	28,980	2.39	1.81	1.13	1.47
Ocean	1,310	2,170	4,280	7,760	.39	.58	.34	.39
Passaic	5,920	6,340	24,010	36,270	1.79	1.69	1.90	1.84
Somerset	3,220	3,010	7,940	14,170	.97	.80	.63	.72
Sussex	880	880	2,290	4,050	.26	.23	.18	.21
Union	12,550	13,120	34,070	59,740	3.79	3.49	2.69	3.03
Warren	690	860	2,680	4,230	.21	.23	.21	.22
New York	210,020	245,120	865,640	1,320,780	63.45	65.29	68.48	67.03
New York excl. N.Y.C.	78,240	93,320	184,850	356,410	23.64	24.86	14.62	18.09
Dutchess	4,630	2,640	7,900	15,170	1.40	.71	.62	.77
Nassau	33,840	43,260	75,950	153,050	10.22	11.52	6.01	7.77
Orange	2,070	3,240	7,950	13,260	.63	.86	.63	.67
Putnam	650	650	1,470	2,770	.20	.17	.12	.14
Rockland	2,320	2,520	6,400	11,240	.70	.67	.50	.57
Suffolk	10,540	9,820	27,260	47,620	3.18	2.62	2.16	2.42
Sullivan	460	1,070	1,790	3,320	.14	.29	.14	.17
Ulster	2,360	2,180	5,350	9,890	.71	.58	.42	.50
Westchester	21,370	27,940	50,780	100,090	6.46	7.44	4.02	5.08
New York City	131,780	151,800	680,790	964,370	39.81	40.43	53.86	48.94
Bronx	17,270	21,030	125,410	163,710	5.22	5.60	9.92	8.31
Brooklyn	32,730	39,950	218,300	290,980	9.89	10.64	17.27	14.77
Manhattan	40,280	42,960	139,670	222,910	12.17	11.44	11.05	11.31
Queens	38,210	44,490	178,890	261,590	11.54	11.85	14.15	13.27
Richmond	3,290	3,370	18,520	25,180	.99	.90	1.47	1.28
Region	330,990	375,450	1,264,110	1,970,550	100.00	100.00	100.00	100.00

Source: Regional Plan Association, based on U.S. Census, *Census of Population: 1960, Detailed Characteristics.*
* See Table 1.8 for the detailed occupational composition of office workers in major groups.

Table 5.12. Estimated Future Residential Location of Office Workers by County in the New York Region, 2000

County	Office workers in major occupational groups*				Total as a % of Region	Total population
	Pro., tech.	Mgrs., offics., props.	Cler.	Total		
Connecticut	117,800	55,400	249,500	422,700	9.40%	2,820,000
Fairfield	67,400	33,200	118,400	219,000	4.87	1,220,000
Litchfield	6,700	3,100	14,500	24,300	.54	300,000
New Haven	43,700	19,100	116,600	179,400	3.99	1,300,000
New Jersey	422,400	200,900	899,200	1,522,500	33.86	9,710,000
Bergen	75,600	39,200	136,400	251,200	5.59	1,350,000
Essex	32,600	15,300	82,300	130,200	2.90	1,120,000
Hudson	14,200	6,200	74,900	95,300	2.12	650,000
Hunterdon	8,600	4,900	22,900	36,400	.81	220,000
Mercer	31,900	11,300	78,300	121,500	2.70	650,000
Middlesex	48,300	19,100	108,000	175,400	3.90	1,150,000
Monmouth	43,400	18,700	74,500	136,600	3.04	1,100,000
Morris	59,300	35,400	102,100	196,800	4.38	960,000
Ocean	12,100	8,400	26,900	47,400	1.05	520,000
Passaic	16,500	7,600	44,900	69,000	1.53	560,000
Somerset	28,200	11,300	47,300	86,800	1.93	450,000
Sussex	9,900	4,100	17,200	31,200	.69	170,000
Union	32,400	14,400	59,200	106,000	2.36	600,000
Warren	9,400	5,000	24,300	38,700	.86	210,000
New York	610,500	291,300	1,649,300	2,551,100	56.74	15,650,000
New York excl. N.Y.C.	352,800	171,500	602,800	1,127,100	25.07	7,650,000
Dutchess	38,400	9,300	44,200	91,900	2.04	550,000
Nassau	87,000	47,300	132,400	266,700	5.93	1,700,000
Orange	17,000	11,200	43,800	72,000	1.60	700,000
Putnam	8,000	3,200	12,400	23,600	.53	140,000
Rockland	16,100	7,400	29,500	53,000	1.18	360,000
Suffolk	77,000	34,300	162,100	273,400	6.08	2,300,000
Sullivan	2,800	2,800	7,500	13,100	.29	100,000
Ulster	17,100	6,700	26,400	50,200	1.12	300,000
Westchester	89,400	49,300	144,500	283,200	6.30	1,500,000
New York City	257,700	119,800	1,046,500	1,424,000	31.67	8,000,000
Bronx	22,700	11,600	140,800	175,100	3.89	1,350,000
Brooklyn	45,700	23,700	263,700	333,100	7.41	2,550,000
Manhattan	74,900	29,400	184,200	288,500	6.42	1,300,000
Queens	92,600	45,600	374,200	512,400	11.40	2,200,000
Richmond	21,800	9,500	83,600	114,900	2.55	600,000
Region	1,150,700	547,600	2,798,000	4,496,300	100.00	28,180,000

Source: Regional Plan Association.

* See Table 1.8 for the detailed occupational composition of office workers in major groups.

to 1.1 million, as their population grows to somewhat more than twice its present size. Office workers in the three Connecticut counties of the Region will increase from about 140,000 to about 420,000.

The projections given in Table 5.12 imply that the increase in office workers as a share of the total population will be the fastest in Connecticut, somewhat slower in New Jersey, and substantially slower in New York State both in and outside the City. Nevertheless, at the end of the projection period, New York City ends up with the highest ratio of office workers to total population (17.8 percent), New Jersey ranks second (15.7 percent), and Connecticut and the remainder of New York State are about equal with slightly under 15 percent. Needless to say, these are illustrative allocations, and the reality will depend on office location itself, on future transportation, and on the resolution of a number of social issues having to do with housing policy, education, and the integration of disadvantaged groups into the white-collar labor force.

Having gained an impression of where office workers might live in the future, we can now proceed to see where their jobs may be located. Table 5.13 allocates projected office jobs to counties of the New York Region according to the three classes of office activity—headquarters, middle market, and local. The headquarters allocation is based on recent trends in the location of CAO&A employment within the Region. The data for four major industries (manufacturing, retail, wholesale, and services), available from the Census *County Business Patterns,* were charted for the years 1959 through 1967 on the basis of county groupings by ring of development, as a share of the Region's total. Trend lines in the share of the Region's total CAO&A employment by ring were then extrapolated to the year 2000 and converted to central office (CAO) allocations on the basis of the known relationship between the two classifications that existed in 1963. As a result of this approach, changes in the locational preferences of specific industries over time were integrated into the projection. For instance, manufacturing CAO&A shifts from the central business district to inner and intermediate ring locations were extended forward in time. Manufacturing CAO employment in the CBD is thus projected to decline from 72.5 percent of the Region's total to 43 percent between 1963 and 2000. The services CAO employment, by contrast, well over 80 percent of which is presently in the CBD, is projected to maintain this share. The other CAO&A employment, which represents less than 10 percent of the forecast central office jobs, was projected as a whole based on the combined distribution of such minimally reported industries as mining, transportation, communications, and others. Headquarters employment that is not reported in the multiestablish-

Table 5.13. Projection of Headquarters, Middle Market, and Local Office Employment by County in the New York Region, 2000

	Jobs in office buildings					As a percentage of Region			
	Hdqrs.	Middle market	Local market	Total	Total incl. sales	Hdqrs.	Middle market	Local market	Total incl sales
Connecticut	84,430	55,000	81,980	221,410	229,870	6.82%	4.59%	9.98%	6.59%
Fairfield	54,450	26,900	36,230	117,580	122,070	4.40	2.24	4.41	3.50
Litchfield	1,100	1,600	8,310	11,010	11,430	.09	.14	1.01	.33
New Haven	28,880	26,500	37,440	92,820	96,370	2.33	2.21	4.56	2.76
New Jersey	253,550	253,440	281,860	788,850	819,010	20.46	21.13	34.30	23.49
Bergen	42,110	19,500	40,910	102,520	106,650	3.40	1.63	4.98	3.06
Essex	37,590	76,850	32,480	146,920	151,770	3.03	6.41	3.95	4.35
Hudson	13,410	22,660	17,550	53,620	55,670	1.08	1.89	2.14	1.60
Hunterdon	—	1,640	6,030	7,670	7,970	—	.14	.73	.23
Mercer	21,800	40,960	18,660	81,420	84,530	1.76	3.42	2.27	2.42
Middlesex	28,530	17,480	33,810	79,820	83,080	2.30	1.46	4.11	2.38
Monmouth	21,490	9,160	32,120	62,770	65,260	1.74	.76	3.91	1.87
Morris	34,730	12,650	28,800	76,180	79,210	2.80	1.05	3.51	2.27
Ocean	—	3,900	14,140	18,040	18,730	—	.32	1.72	.54
Passaic	18,070	21,230	15,960	55,260	57,370	1.46	1.77	1.94	1.65
Somerset	10,610	10,350	13,410	34,370	35,830	.86	.86	1.63	1.03
Sussex	900	1,410	4,510	6,820	7,080	.07	.12	.55	.20
Union	21,680	13,690	18,060	53,430	55,470	1.75	1.14	2.20	1.59
Warren	2,630	1,960	5,420	10,010	10,390	.21	.16	.66	.30
New York	901,030	890,720	457,770	2,249,520	2,438,320	72.72	74.28	55.72	69.92
New York excl. N.Y.C.	177,660	107,990	226,390	512,040	531,620	14.34	9.01	27.56	15.24
Dutchess	27,390	15,610	15,840	58,840	61,090	2.21	1.30	1.93	1.75
Nassau	28,450	30,100	52,700	111,250	115,500	2.30	2.51	6.41	3.31
Orange	9,210	7,600	18,830	35,640	37,000	.74	.63	2.29	1.06
Putnam	4,290	1,770	4,000	10,060	10,450	.35	.15	.49	.30
Rockland	18,180	5,960	10,760	34,900	36,240	1.47	.50	1.31	1.04
Suffolk	4,340	13,880	67,390	85,610	88,880	.35	1.16	8.20	2.55
Sullivan	—	840	2,630	3,470	3,600	—	.07	.32	.10
Ulster	5,450	4,730	8,190	18,370	19,070	.44	.40	1.00	.55
Westchester	80,350	27,500	46,050	153,900	159,790	6.48	2.29	5.61	4.58
New York City	723,370	782,730	231,380	1,737,480	1,906,700	58.38	65.27	28.16	54.68
Bronx	6,090	24,130	33,530	63,750	65,400	.49	2.01	4.08	1.88
Brooklyn	9,080	83,650	66,120	158,850	172,770	.73	6.98	8.05	4.95
Manhattan	698,770	594,800	55,780	1,349,350	1,498,350	56.40	49.60	6.79	42.97
Queens	8,250	69,230	59,430	136,910	140,860	.67	5.77	7.23	4.04
Richmond	1,180	10,920	16,520	28,620	29,320	.09	.91	2.01	.84
Region	1,239,010	1,199,160	821,610	3,259,780	3,487,200	100.00	100.00	100.00	100.00

Source: Regional Plan Association.
Notes: Detail may not add to totals because of rounding.
See text for assumptions underlying projections. Because of the nature of the projection technique, future estimates of headquarters and middle-market employment by county are interchangeable to a degree between counties within the same labor market area.

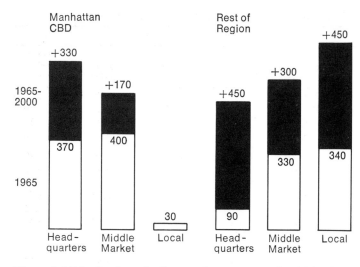

Figure 5.4 Distribution of office employment growth within the New York Region, 1965–2000

ment CAO category by the Census was projected by ring of development assuming a somewhat weaker decentralization tendency. This employment has, in the past, retained a greater degree of preference for central location due in part to its more specialized character and smaller firm size. Although this preference is expected to weaken over time, the remaining headquarters employment is not expected to achieve the degree of independence from interfirm transactions that will undoubtedly characterize the larger, more autonomous headquarters establishments. Total headquarters employment control figures by ring of development having been established, they were further allocated to counties, taking into account such factors as the CAO distribution by county, the projected office workers by place of residence, the availability of vacant land, and the presence of office subcenters.

The allocation of local office employment is based on the assumption that 70 percent of the forecast growth is attributable to real increases in spending power per capita and 30 percent to population increases in the Region; this assumption, in turn, reflects the relationship between the forecast growth in local employment and the forecast growth in income and population. Thus, the perspectives for the growth of local office employment can be considered a function of population increases within a county, and of the relative position of the county in the Region's income profile. Local office jobs were therefore projected by ring and by county on the basis of population growth and an area's disparity from the Region's average income at present; there was no way to take into account future changes in the relative income position of individual counties.

In the allocation of middle-market office jobs, a number of factors had to be taken into account: first, middle-market jobs are staffed largely by office personnel who live within a relatively short commuting distance from work; second, middle-market office jobs in the context of this study serve population concentrations of a metropolitan scale, on the order of 1 million or more; third, middle-market jobs require a certain ease of communication with headquarters activities, particularly the less autonomous headquarters establishments. An allocation of middle-market employment thus initially required a projection of the extent of Manhattan's future office commuting area. Having established a profile of how deeply into the suburban labor market Manhattan's future office economy would reach, the residual office force in the suburban areas was then matched with their own demand for office personnel in headquarters, local, and nonoffice buildings. The projections of middle-market employment do not, however, bear a one-to-one relationship with labor availability at the county level; the distribution is skewed in two directions: to counties in which a large amount of headquarters activity requires a commensurate amount of middle-market activity and to counties which perform residence-related office functions at the subregional, or metropolitan, scale.

The county allocation, presented in Table 5.13, is summarized by ring of development in Table 5.14. The Manhattan CBD still receives the lion's share of the increment in headquarters jobs, 330,000 or 42 percent of the total. The next largest share, 233,000 or almost 30 percent, goes to the intermediate ring, followed by 134,-000 or 17 percent for the inner ring. The old areas of the rest of the core and the sparsely populated areas of the outer ring receive, in line with the 1959–1967 experience, only very small shares of the new headquarters employment.

The picture is quite different for middle-market employment. The Manhattan CBD, in line with the hypothesis about the spinoff of middle-market functions from the center, receives only 169,000 middle-market office jobs, or 36 percent of the increment. Much of the spinoff goes into the remainder of the core, with its subcenters such as Newark, downtown Brooklyn, and Jamaica; it receives the next largest increment in middle-market jobs, namely 133,000 or 28 percent of the total. The intermediate ring, with its subregional, or metropolitan-scale functions, receives about 87,000, or 18 percent; the rest is shared about equally between the inner and outer rings.

Finally, with regard to local office employment, the intermediate ring, which will have the highest absolute increase in population and has a relatively high standing on the income scale, captures almost half the increment in that office category. Almost another 40 percent is distributed between the inner and the outer rings.

The summary of the office employment in office buildings projection by county for the year 2000 is given in Table 5.15, which also contains a projection for 1985 and estimates of employment in office buildings for 1959 and 1967 for comparison. The fastest growth in office building employment—more than a threefold increase —is expected in the Connecticut sector of the Region, with Fairfield County experiencing the greatest increase both absolutely and relatively.

The next fastest growing sector—with roughly a threefold increase between 1967 and 2000—is expected to be the portion of the Region in New York State outside New York City. Of the counties that presently have more than 10,000 office jobs, Dutchess, Suffolk, and Westchester stand out with above-average growth rates. Nassau, which between 1959 and 1967 increased its office building employment by 57 percent, is expected to grow at a more moderate rate over the following three decades.

Rockland, on the other hand, which in 1967 had some 6,000 office building jobs, is expected to multiply them almost six times.

The counties of the New Jersey sector of the Region are expected to increase their office building employment 2.5 times on the average. Of those that presently have more than 10,000 office building jobs, the fastest growing ones are expected to be, quite plausibly, Monmouth, Morris, and Middlesex, all multiplying their office building employment four to five times. Bergen, which increased its office building employment by 43 percent between 1959 and 1967, is expected to continue its growth at roughly the same rate. Passaic, which grew by 37 percent between 1959 and 1967, is expected to continue growth at a rate above the state average, but below that of the neighboring Bergen and Morris counties. The more built-up counties, such as Essex, Union, and Hudson, are projected to grow at a below-average rate.

New York City, as a whole, is expected to increase its office building employment 1.5 times, with Queens growing somewhat above the average, and the Bronx, somewhat below. A projected 1.5-fold increase in office building employment in Manhattan means that in the borough, as a whole, the 889,000 office jobs in office buildings (not counting sales jobs in offices) in 1967 would increase to 1,350,000 in the year 2000. The increment of 460,000 office jobs in Manhattan over 33 years represents, of course, a rather staggering projection, substantially in excess of previous estimates. If sales workers in office buildings are included, as they are in the summary Table 5.16, then the total increase in office building jobs in the central business district of Manhattan alone amounts to 492,000 jobs between 1967 and 2000. The implications of this growth for the Manhattan CBD deserve a separate discussion.

THE FUTURE OF THE MANHATTAN
CENTRAL BUSINESS DISTRICT

The prospective addition of 490,000 office jobs to the Manhattan central business district between 1967 and 2000 by no means represents a net increment. To what extent total employment in the CBD will increase depends on what happens to the two major nonoffice employment categories, namely production-oriented jobs in manufacturing and wholesaling, and "other" jobs, a category that includes retail, service, and institutional workers, and a variety of miscellaneous jobs, some of them linked to the presence of office workers, some linked to the resident population, some independent of either of these.

The out-migration of blue-collar, production-oriented jobs from the Manhattan CBD to outer parts of the Re-

Table 5.14. Change in Office Employment by Class of Activity and Ring of Development, 1965–2000

	1965			2000			Absolute Change		
	Hdqrs.	Middle market	Local market	Hdqrs.	Middle market	Local market	Hdqrs.	Middle market	Local market
Manhattan CBD	368,090	404,420	31,910	698,770	573,350	27,880	330,680	168,930	−4,030
Rest of core	27,860	148,590	166,080	61,950	281,280	218,820	34,090	132,690	52,740
Inner ring	29,580	87,550	86,800	163,690	131,950	186,510	134,110	44,400	99,710
Intermediate ring	28,670	75,600	59,350	261,280	162,230	283,720	232,610	86,630	224,370
Outer ring	5,110	13,100	24,870	53,320	50,350	104,680	48,210	37,250	79,810
Region	459,310	729,260	369,010	1,239,010	1,199,160	821,610	779,700	469,900	452,600

Source: Regional Plan Association.

gion has been a familiar phenomenon since about 1947, when total CBD employment apparently reached a peak. Between 1956 and 1959 alone, goods-handling jobs in the Manhattan CBD declined from 750,000 to 650,000. Since 1959, the rate of decline has slowed down considerably, especially, it appears, in recent years. The 1967 estimate of production-oriented jobs in the CBD, the latest one available, is 595,000. Should the 1959–1967 rate of decline in blue-collar jobs—some 8.5 percent every eight years—continue, about 415,000 such jobs would be left in the CBD in 2000. What is the likelihood that this rather moderate rate of decline will continue? Or is it likely to accelerate? The main argument against its acceleration is the availability of a huge pool of low-skilled labor in New York City within reach of the CBD, a pool that is likely to melt only gradually under the impact of skill upgrading and out-migration to suburban areas, closer to the future factory jobs. The pursuit of policies by the City of New York designed to prevent a precipitous loss of low-skilled jobs to obviate increases in unemployment seems likely. On the other hand, the increasing obsolescence of much of the CBD factory loft space, much of which will be over 100 years old in the coming decades, and the competition from more lucrative uses, not only offices, but also high-priced residence buildings and institutions, argues for an accelerated decline. The existence of much of the present goods-handling activity in the CBD is very precarious from a purely economic standpoint, and quite vulnerable to replacement by other uses. Thus, a sharp drop in production-oriented jobs in the CBD to as low as 250,000 toward the end of the forecast period is by no means excluded.

Precipitous variations in the level of the "other" employment appear less likely. That part of it which consists of retail and consumer services catering to the office worker is likely to increase roughly in proportion to the office growth. Institutional employment is likely to increase. On the other hand, the part related to the resident population is likely to remain stable, reflecting the crosscurrents of a declining resident population but increasing per capita income. The part unrelated to either offices, institutions or the resident population, and present in the CBD through historical inertia, may well follow the pattern of manufacturing employment. Increases in productivity may also cut into the service jobs of the "other" category. On balance, stability in the "other" employment, put at 660,000 in 1967, appears to be a rather probable first assumption, though an increase to the level of about 825,000 jobs is not unlikely. The latter figure represents a 25 percent increase, or roughly half the rate apparent in the 1956–1967 trend.

The combination of either the higher goods-handling projection with the lower "other" projection, or vice versa, produces a total nonoffice employment component

Table 5.15. Past and Projected Office Employment in Office Buildings by County in the New York Region, 1959–2000

	1959	1967	1985	2000
Connecticut	51,570	68,790	142,990	221,410
Fairfield	23,370	34,210	74,400	117,580
Litchfield	2,620	3,180	6,460	11,010
New Haven	25,580	31,400	62,130	92,820
New Jersey	240,580	311,670	521,880	788,850
Bergen	25,100	36,090	69,950	102,520
Essex	74,700	92,580	119,470	146,920
Hudson	37,790	40,950	46,870	53,620
Hunterdon	1,260	1,400	3,400	7,670
Mercer	21,070	29,760	47,690	81,420
Middlesex	13,520	18,080	45,590	79,820
Monmouth	9,240	12,700	36,090	62,770
Morris	9,330	16,070	41,870	76,180
Ocean	2,930	4,100	9,410	18,040
Passaic	14,540	20,020	33,810	55,260
Somerset	4,310	5,130	17,670	34,370
Sussex	1,390	1,900	3,550	6,820
Union	24,160	31,230	41,340	53,430
Warren	1,240	1,660	5,170	10,010
New York	1,125,370	1,288,760	1,841,920	2,249,520
New York excl. N.Y.C.	113,740	163,360	328,520	512,040
Dutchess	9,550	12,890	30,400	58,840
Nassau	36,070	56,840	80,980	111,250
Orange	6,330	7,380	17,720	35,640
Putnam	910	1,030	5,840	10,060
Rockland	3,840	6,100	20,760	34,900
Suffolk	17,080	24,350	64,190	85,610
Sullivan	1,160	1,430	2,210	3,470
Ulster	4,020	4,300	10,310	18,370
Westchester	34,780	49,040	96,110	153,900
New York City	1,011,630	1,125,400	1,513,400	1,737,480
Bronx	42,220	45,160	55,180	63,750
Kings	99,900	104,090	130,550	158,850
Manhattan	792,080	889,490	1,203,450	1,349,350
Queens	66,410	74,070	107,500	136,910
Richmond	11,020	12,590	16,720	28,620
Region	1,417,520	1,669,220	2,506,790	3,259,780
Region incl. sales	1,527,900	1,812,700	2,696,600	3,487,200

Source: Regional Plan Association.
Notes: County data do not include past and projected sales workers in office buildings for consistency with earlier published series (*The Region's Growth*) and the 1965 benchmark data included in this study. For purposes of projecting space requirements in the suburban counties of the Region, this omission of sales workers in office buildings is of small significance. Detached sales workers in office buildings outside the core of the Region are projected to increase by fewer than 20,000 jobs, 1967–2000, accounting for only 2% more than the increment projected in this table. The majority of past and projected sales workers, who are detached from production, store, or other nonoffice sites, are located in the Manhattan CBD. (See Table 5.16.) However, their number in the CBD is equivalent in occupancy requirements to the amount of converted office space located in loft and residential structures in Manhattan. Because of the inventory criteria used in tabulating central city office building square footage, this converted space was not included and represents a 9% underreporting of CBD office square footage. The projection of total floor space in the Manhattan CBD and the Region, contained in Table 5.8, is based on a full occupancy of total office workers (including sales) in detached office buildings.

Table 5.16. Past and Projected Office Employment in Office Buildings by Ring of Development in the New York Region, 1959–2000 (thousands of jobs)

	Total excl. sales				Total incl. sales				As a % of Region	
	1959	1967	1985	2000	1959	1967	1985	2000	1967	2000
Manhattan CBD	764.6	857.2	1,166.8	1,300.0	838.7	949.0	1,281.8	1,441.3	52.4%	41.3%
Rest of core	325.3	358.5	457.8	562.1	339.0	376.0	480.3	595.2	20.7	17.1
Inner ring	160.2	224.2	337.9	482.2	171.0	240.7	357.6	499.6	13.3	14.3
Intermediate ring	129.7	181.0	431.0	707.2	138.9	194.9	456.9	734.8	10.7	21.1
Outer ring	37.7	48.4	113.3	208.4	40.4	52.1	120.1	216.3	2.9	6.2
Region	1,417.5	1,669.2	2,506.8	3,259.8	1,527.9	1,812.7	2,696.6	3,487.2	100.0	100.0

Source: Regional Plan Association.
Notes: See Note on Table 5.15. Detail may not add to totals because of rounding.

of 1,075,000 jobs, ± 165,000, should low coincide with
low, or high with high, combinations which appear less
likely. The assumption that production-oriented jobs
and "other" jobs are somewhat interchangeable seems
more reasonable. Thus, adding the nonoffice component
to the projected office jobs, total CBD employment in
the order of 2,515,000 in 2000 seems likely; this is shown,
in the context of recent experience, in Table 5.17.

One should note that below the "total employment"
line, Table 5.17 contains an additional line entitled
"total workers." The two concepts are by no means
synonymous. "Employment" as discussed up to now
represents jobs held, as reported in various sources of
economic statistics; in some cases, two jobs may be held
by the same person; furthermore, the possibility exists
that some jobs are reported as being located in Manhattan because that is the address of an establishment,
which might actually have some workers on the job elsewhere. Hence, the actual number of workers at work in
the course of a week in the Manhattan CBD is smaller
than the number of jobs reported. So far, the only source
of data on workers, rather than jobs, is the 1960 Census.
The figure of 1,860,000 workers, shown under 1959, is
based on 1960 Census journey-to-work data, available
for Manhattan as a whole and adjusted for the central
business district by Regional Plan Association. The
number of "workers" for the other years is derived by
applying the 1959–1960 ratio of workers-to-total-em-
ployment to the total employment estimate for these
years. Thus, in terms of actual workers, the projected
1967–2000 increment is only 280,000 above the estimated 2 million base.

To introduce a further caveat, even the figure of "total
workers" should not be used for some purposes, such as
estimating the total daytime population of the central
business district on a typical business day, without further adjustments. Data on 1965 travel to and from the
Manhattan CBD by all modes, for each hour of the day,
indicate that while 3,364,000 inbound and an equal
number of outbound trips occurred, the peak net accu-
mulation of nonresidents in the CBD was only 1,563,000
at 2:00 P.M. Adding to these the 557,000 residents (1960
Census data), the peak daytime population of the Manhattan CBD on a typical weekday in 1965 appears to
have been only 2,120,000. Considering the fact that 290,-
000 of the CBD residents did not work, only 1,830,000
persons actually present in the CBD at 2:00 P.M. on a
typical business day in 1965 are left to account for both
workers and other visitors, such as shoppers, business
callers, nonresident students, or tourists. This figure can
be reconciled with figures of "total workers" given for
1959 to 1967 in the bottom line of Table 5.17 if one assumes that some 10 percent of the workers, working
during any week, are not physically present in the CBD

Table 5.17. Past and Projected Changes in the Manhattan CBD's Total Employment, 1956–2000 (in thousands)

	1956	1959	1967	2000
Office	815	840	950	1,440
In office buildings	745	765	860	1,440
In converted office space	70	75	90	—
Production	750	650	595	415–250
Other	575	565	660	660–825
Total employment	2,140	2,055	2,205	2,515 (±165)
Total workers	1,930	1,860	2,000	2,280 (±150)

Source: Regional Plan Association.

Table 5.18. Office Building Completions in Manhattan Central Business District, 1950–1973

Key	Address	Bldg. name	Stories	Rentable sq ft (× 1,000)	Year	Average size of bldg. (× 1,000 sq ft)	Total sq ft (× 1,000)
Part I: Midtown Manhattan							
1	575 Madison Avenue		25	350			
2	1740 Broadway	Mutual Life Ins. Co.	25	414			
3	640 Fifth Avenue	Crowell-Collier	18	200			
4	488 Madison Avenue	Look	23	351			
5	First Avenue, 42nd Street	United Nations	39	500			
6	100 Park Avenue		36	630			
7	1407 Broadway		42	700			
8	12 East 48th Street	Carol Management Corp.	7	12			
9	220 West 58th Street	United Jewish Appeal	6	70			
					1950	358.6	3,227
10	390 Park Avenue	Lever House	22	235			
11	55 East 34th Street		6	42			
12	600 Fifth Avenue	Sinclair Oil	26	285			
13	655 Madison Avenue		24	167			
14	55 East 52nd Street	CBS Radio	7	34			
					1951	152.6	763
15	260 Madison Avenue		21	414			
16	161 East 42nd Street	Chrysler Building East	32	419			
17	1460 Broadway	Stevens	16	162			
					1952	331.7	995
18	1120 Avenue of Americas	Hippodrome	5	108			
19	380 Madison Avenue		25	665			
20	345 East 46th Street	Carnegie Endowment	11	115			
					1953	296.0	888
21	579 Fifth Avenue		16	110			
22	589 Fifth Avenue		17	135			
23	261 Madison Avenue	American Machine & Foundry	27	299			
24	99 Park Avenue	National Distillers	25	446			
25	720 Fifth Avenue	Sabena Airlines	15	91			
26	477 Madison Avenue		23	245			
27	430 Park Avenue		18	206			
28	130 East 59th Street	Fed. of Jewish Philanthropy	17	189			
29	112 West 34th Street	Kratter	26	525			
30	510 Fifth Avenue	Manufacturers Trust	5	53			
					1954	229.9	2,299
31	555 Fifth Avenue	Amoco	19	195			
32	300 Park Avenue	Colgate-Palmolive	25	555			
33	460 Park Avenue	Davies	22	244			
34	1430 Broadway		22	320			
35	65 East 52nd Street	Hadassah	4	30			
					1955	268.8	1,344
36	10 Columbus Circle	Coliseum Tower	26	531			
37	60 East 56th Street		12	51			
38	3 East 54th Street		19	175			
39	545 Madison Avenue	Douras	17	99			
40	150 East 42nd Street	Socony Mobil	42	1,300			
41	711 Third Avenue	Grand Central	19	403			

Key	Address	Bldg. name	Stories	Rentable sq ft (× 1,000)	Year	Average size of bldg. (× 1,000 sq ft)	Total sq ft (× 1,000)
42	485 Lexington Avenue		30	680			
43	415 Madison Avenue		24	200			
44	625 Madison Avenue	Standard Brands	17	436			
					1956	430.6	3,875
18A	1120 Avenue of Americas	Hippodrome (addition)	3	132			
45	530 Fifth Avenue	Bank of New York	26	415			
46	800 Second Avenue		18	240			
47	666 Fifth Avenue	Tishman	38	1,080			
48	635 Madison Avenue	Vision	19	130			
49	375 Park Avenue	Seagram	38	618			
50	400 Park Avenue		21	200			
51	405 Park Avenue		16	125			
52	425 Park Avenue		31	480			
53	830 Third Avenue	Girl Scouts	13	130			
54	48 East 52nd Street		7	23			
55	650 Madison Avenue	CIT Finance Co.	8	266			
					1957	319.9	3,839
56	48 East 50th Street	Bachrach	5	9			
57	1045 Avenue of Americas	Deering Milliken	8	100			
58	575 Lexington Avenue	Grolier	34	510			
59	660 Madison Avenue	Getty	22	400			
60	680 Fifth Avenue	Mutual Benefit	26	180			
61	111 West 40th Street	Union Dime	34	523			
62	20 East 46th Street		15	75			
63	200 East 42nd Street	Lorillard	28	315			
64	750 Third Avenue		34	630			
65	630 Third Avenue	Belco Petroleum	22	220			
66	360 Lexington Avenue		24	184			
67	355 Lexington Avenue		22	195			
68	546 Fifth Avenue	Seamen's Bank	6	60			
					1958	261.6	3,401
69	730 Third Avenue	General Telephone	27	340			
70	529 Fifth Avenue	Banker's Trust	20	225			
71	230 East 42nd Street	Daily News	18	340			
72	144 East 44th Street	Frederic R. Harris	7	50			
73	1271 Avenue of Americas	Time-Life	48	1,550			
74	717 Fifth Avenue	Corning Glass	28	380			
75	532 Madison Avenue		7	12			
76	410 Park Avenue		21	210			
77	500 Park Avenue	Pepsi-Cola	11	95			
					1959	355.8	3,202
78	130 West 34th Street		16	200			
79	270 Park Avenue	Union Carbide	52	1,150			
80	320 Park Avenue	IT&T	33	526			
81	350 Park Avenue	Manufacturers Hanover Trust	30	465			
82	399 Park Avenue	First National City Bank	43	1,250			
					1960	718.2	3,591
83	522 Fifth Avenue	Morgan Guaranty Trust	23	420			

Table 5.18. (continued)

Key	Address	Bldg. name	Stories	Rentable sq ft (× 1,000)	Year	Average size of bldg. (× 1,000 sq ft)	Total sq ft (× 1,000)
84	633 Third Avenue	Continental Can	41	800			
85	733 Third Avenue	Diamond National	24	307			
86	685 Third Avenue	American Home Products	25	210			
87	850 Third Avenue	Western Publishing	20	431			
88	235 East 42nd Street	Pfizer	33	600			
89	555 Madison Avenue		32	340			
90	770 Lexington Avenue		18	135			
91	771 First Avenue	Herbert Hoover	5	17			
92	803 U.N. Plaza	U.S. Mission to U.N.	12	48			
93	845 U.N. Plaza	United Engineering Center	20	180			
94	1285 Avenue of Americas	Equitable Life	42	1,300			
					1961	399.0	4,788
95	201 Park Avenue South	Guardian Life (annex)	4	89			
96	1290 Avenue of Americas	Sperry-Rand	43	1,700			
97	215 Lexington Avenue	National Furniture Mart	21	170			
98	280 Park Avenue	Banker's Trust	30	321			
99	1180 Avenue of Americas	Phoenix	22	298			
18B	1120 Avenue of Americas	Hippodrome (addition)	13	218			
					1962	466.0	2,796
100	330 Madison Avenue	Sperry and Hutchinson	40	665			
101	200 Park Avenue	Pan Am	59	2,400			
102	605 Third Avenue	Burroughs	43	800			
103	757 Third Avenue	Harcourt, Brace, Jovanovich	27	384			
104	777 Third Avenue	U.S. Plywood	38	488			
105	820 Second Avenue		19	150			
106	300 East 42nd Street		17	177			
107	104 West 40th Street	Spring Mills	21	153			
108	845 Third Avenue		21	303			
109	135 West 50th Street	American Management Assn.	23	700			
110	815 Second Avenue	Episcopal Church Center	11	113			
111	777 U.N. Plaza	Church Center for U.N.	12	70			
112	288 East 56th Street	New York Telephone Co.	4	60			
113	809 U.N. Plaza	Inst. of International Education	13	70			
					1963	466.6	6,533
114	880 Third Avenue		18	115			
115	979 Third Avenue	Decorator and Design	17	327			
116	641 Lexington Avenue	Saturday Evening Post	33	400			
117	90 Park Avenue	Sterling Drug	41	768			
118	277 Park Avenue	Chemical Bank	50	1,500			
119	1212 Avenue of Americas		24	250			
120	1301 Avenue of Americas	J. C. Penney	46	1,300			
121	304 West 58th Street		8	70			
122	412 Madison Avenue	Franklin National Bank	7	46			
123	205 Lexington Avenue	Home Furnishing Mart	18	112			
					1964	488.8	4,888
124	592 Fifth Avenue	Trade Bank & Trust Co.	11	57			
125	1300 Avenue of Americas	CBS	38	722			

Key	Address	Bldg. name	Stories	Rentable sq ft (× 1,000)	Year	Average size of bldg. (× 1,000 sq ft)	Total sq ft (× 1,000)
126	1330 Avenue of Americas	ABC	40	350			
127	600 Madison Avenue		25	283			
128	201 East 42nd Street		31	250			
129	866 U.N. Plaza		6	300			
130	1855 Broadway		12	76			
					1965	291.1	2,038
131	866 Third Avenue	Crowell, Collier, Macmillan	31	400			
132	1350 Avenue of Americas	MGM	33	400			
					1966	400.0	800
133	245 Park Avenue	American Brands	47	1,400			
					1967	1,400.0	1,400
134	299 Park Avenue	Westvaco	42	900			
135	235 East 37th Street	New York Telephone Co.	24	478			
136	2 Penn Plaza	Madison Square Garden	29	1,300			
137	437 Madison Avenue	ITT Americas	40	640			
138	321 East 42nd Street	Ford Foundation	12	250			
					1968	713.6	3,568
139	345 Park Avenue	Bristol Meyers	44	1,400			
140	765 Fifth Avenue	General Motors	50	1,580			
141	33 East 48th Street	Banker's Trust (annex)	41	763			
142	110 East 59th Street		38	400			
143	1250 Broadway		40	600			
144	1700 Broadway		41	527			
145	909 Third Avenue	FDR Post Office	32	687			
146	1133 Avenue of Americas	Interchemical	44	730			
147	5 East 42nd Street	Emigrant Savings	27	275			
148	1411 Broadway		40	1,000			
149	1345 Avenue of Americas	Burlington House	50	1,800			
150	964 Third Avenue (150 E. 58th Street)		39	433			
151	825 Third Avenue	Random House	40	500			
					1969	822.7	10,695
152	15 Columbus Circle	Gulf-Western	44	540			
153	919 Third Avenue		47	1,152			
154	888 Seventh Avenue		42	720			
155	1185 Avenue of Americas	Stevens Tower	42	850			
156	810 Seventh Avenue		39	600			
157	475 Park Avenue South		34	365			
158	540 Madison Avenue	Finland House	37	250			
159	645 Madison Avenue		22	140			
					1970	577.1	4,617
160	1301 Avenue of Americas	J. C. Penney (annex)	13	225			
161	866 Second Avenue		15	100			
162	600 Third Avenue		42	475			
163	1370 Avenue of Americas	Capitol Industries	32	300			
164	1 Astor Plaza (1515 Broadway)	W. T. Grant	53	1,148			
165	950 Third Avenue	Greenwich Savings Bank	34	330			
166	450 Park Avenue	Franklin National Bank	31	300			

Table 5.18. (continued)

Key	Address	Bldg. name	Stories	Rentable sq ft (× 1,000)	Year	Average size of bldg. (× 1,000 sq ft)	Total sq ft (× 1,000)
167	1251 Avenue of Americas	Esso	54	2,100			
168	1633 Broadway	Uris Building	50	2,050			
169	10 East 53rd Street		37	330			
170	555 West 57th Street	Ford Motor Company	20	500			
171	1 Lincoln Plaza		43	252			
					1971	675.8	8,110
172	800 Third Avenue		41	511			
173	489 Fifth Avenue		34	139			
174	1114 Avenue of Americas		50	1,250			
175	1 Madison Square Plaza		42	500			
176	622 Third Avenue		38	867			
177	1095 Avenue of Americas	New York Telephone Co.	40	1,200			
178	1221 Avenue of Americas	McGraw-Hill	51	2,200			
179	9 West 57th Street	Solow Building	50	1,500			
180	40 West 57th Street	Lefrak Building	33	648			
181	1 Penn Plaza	Bowery Savings Bank	57	2,300			
					estimated completion 1972	1,111.5	11,115
182	1166 Avenue of Americas		44	1,430			
183	1205 Avenue of Americas	Time/Celanese	45	1,800			
184	1 Dag Hammarskjöld Plaza		50	665			
185	747 Third Avenue		38	350			
186	1500 Broadway		43	480			
187	645 Fifth Avenue	Olympic Tower	43	500			
					estimated completion 1973	870.8	5,225

Part II: Downtown Manhattan

Key	Address	Bldg. name	Stories	Rentable sq ft (× 1,000)	Year	Average size of bldg. (× 1,000 sq ft)	Total sq ft (× 1,000)
1	250 Church Street	Department of Welfare	15	206			
					1950	206.0	206
2	161 William Street		21	140			
3	99 Church Street	Dun and Bradstreet	11	289			
					1951	214.5	429
—	—	—	—	—	1952	—	—
—	—	—	—	—	1953	—	—
—	—	—	—	—	1954	—	—
4	199 Church Street	State Insurance Fund	15	210			
5	30 Wall Street	Seamen's Bank	12	100			
6	156 William Street		12	193			
					1955	167.7	503
—	—	—	—	—	1956	—	—
7	20 Broad Street		27	414			
8	79 Pine Street	New York Coffee and Sugar Exchange	12	120			
9	72 Wall Street		15	105			
10	19 Rector Street		11	56			
11	123 William Street		26	410			
					1957	221.0	1,105

Key	Address	Bldg. name	Stories	Rentable sq ft (× 1,000)	Year	Average size of bldg. (× 1,000 sq ft)	Total sq ft (× 1,000)
12	100 Church Street		20	925			
13	110 William Street		22	475			
					1958	700.0	1,400
14	2 Broadway		33	1,300			
15	45 Wall Street	Atlantic	27	375			
16	83 Maiden Lane		13	120			
17	125 Maiden Lane	U.S. Life	16	260			
13A	110 William Street		9	200			
18	155 William Street		6	40			
19	30 West Broadway		15	300			
					1959	370.7	2,595
20	80 Pine Street		38	900			
					1960	900.0	900
21	66 Beaver Street		24	250			
22	1 Chase Manhattan Plaza	Chase Manhattan Bank	60	1,820			
23	222 Broadway	Western Electric	31	525			
					1961	865.0	2,595
24	60 Broad Street		39	850			
25	1 Whitehall Street		21	300			
					1962	575.0	1,150
26	250 Broadway		30	515			
27	100 Broad Street	New York Clearing House	3	21			
28	120 Church Street	Internal Revenue	21	376			
					1963	304.0	912
29	130 Pearl Street	Franklin National Bank	13	110			
					1964	110.0	110
30	1 Wall Street	Irving Trust Co.	30	366			
31	110 Wall Street		27	250			
32	59 Maiden Lane	Home Insurance	44	1,000			
					1965	538.7	1,616
33	140 Broadway	Marine Midland Trust	52	1,000			
					1966	1,000.0	1,000
34	55 Broad Street		30	320			
35	110 Church Street	Merck, Sharp & Dohme	16	136			
36	90 William Street		15	148			
					1967	201.3	604
37	111 Wall Street	First National City Bank	24	879			
38	4 New York Plaza (115 Broad Street)	Manufacturers Hanover Trust	22	850			
39	26 Federal Plaza	Federal Building	41	1,200			
40	15 State Street	Seamen's Church Institute	23	400			
					1968	832.3	3,329
41	1 New York Plaza	Chase Manhattan	50	2,200			
42	100 Gold Street	Tishman Downtown Center	9	630			

Table 5.18. (continued)

Key	Address	Bldg. name	Stories	Rentable sq ft (× 1,000)	Year	Average size of bldg. (× 1,000 sq ft)	Total sq ft (× 1,000)
43	90 Washington Street	The Bank of New York	25	381			
					1969	1,070.3	3,211
44	Battery Park Plaza (24 Whitehall Street)		35	750			
45	77 Water Street	Walston & Company	26	510			
46	2 New York Plaza		40	1,100			
47	160 Water Street		24	430			
48	100 Wall Street (replaces 1953 structure not included)		28	410			
49	95 Wall Street		23	430			
50	17 Battery Place North		20	350			
					1970	568.6	3,980
51	1 State Street Plaza		32	747			
52	130 John Street		25	425			
53	127 John Street		32	510			
54	40 Rector Street		15	75			
55	1 Liberty Plaza	U.S. Steel	50	1,500			
56	Church Street	World Trade Center (part)	110	4,600			
					1971	1,309.5	7,857
57	221 Church Street	New York Telephone Switching Center	29	800			
58	10 Hanover Square		22	457			
59	88 Pine Street	Orient Overseas	31	525			
60	22 Cortlandt Street		35	600			
61	Park Row	Police Administration Building	15	750			
56A	Church Street	World Trade Center (part)	110	3,000			
					estimated completion 1972	1,022.0	6,132
62	55 Water Street	Chemical Bank	53	3,300			
56B	Church Street	World Trade Center (part)	110	1,400			
					estimated completion 1973	2,350.0	4,700

Table 5.18. (continued)

Year	Midtown		Downtown		Total central business district	
	No. of bldgs.	Rentable sq ft (× 1,000)	No. of bldgs.	Rentable sq ft (× 1,000)	No. of bldgs.	Rentable sq ft (× 1,000)
Part III: Summary						
1950	9	3,227	1	206	10	3,433
1951	5	763	2	429	7	1,192
1952	3	995	—	—	3	995
1953	3	888	—	—	3	888
1954	10	2,299	—	—	10	2,299
1955	5	1,344	3	503	8	1,847
1956	9	3,875	—	—	9	3,875
1957	11	3,839	5	1,105	16	4,944
1958	13	3,401	2	1,400	15	4,801
1959	9	3,202	6	2,595	15	5,797
1960	5	3,591	1	900	6	4,491
1961	12	4,788	3	2,595	15	7,383
1962	5	2,796	2	1,150	7	3,946
1963	14	6,533	3	912	17	7,445
1964	10	4,888	1	110	11	4,998
1965	7	2,038	3	1,616	10	3,654
1966	2	800	1	1,000	3	1,800
1967	1	1,400	3	604	4	2,004
1968	5	3,568	4	3,329	9	6,897
1969	13	10,695	3	3,211	16	13,906
1970	8	4,617	7	3,980	15	8,597
1971	12	8,110	6	7,857	18	15,967
1972 (estimated)	10	11,115	5	6,132	15	17,247
1973 (estimated)	6	5,225	1	4,700	7	9,925

Sources: Regional Plan Association, based primarily on building completion records of James Felt and Company, and *The New York Times.*
Note: Since going to press, the expected completion date of the Olympic Tower in midtown Manhattan (No. 187) moved beyond 1973; on the other hand, 1973 completion of the Bankers Trust Building of 1.2 million square feet at 140 Liberty Street in downtown Manhattan (No. 63 on Map 5.2, but omitted from Table 5.18) is likely. In addition, a small office building above 60th Street in midtown Manhattan (The American Bible Society) was omitted from the tabular summary, but located on Map 5.1. On balance, these minor adjustments result in an underreporting of 820,000 square feet.

at 2:00 P.M. on any one typical business day for a variety of reasons, such as being out of the CBD on business, on vacation, or because of absenteeism, or working on a night shift. Subtracting about 10 percent from the number of "total workers" brings the number of workers contributing to the peak daytime population to some 1,740,000, a figure nearly comparable to the 1963 Tri-State Regional Planning Commission data on work trips to the central business district. On that basis, the number of workers contributing to the peak daytime population of the CBD in 2000 would be on the order of 2 million.

Having reviewed the relationship of the projected future office workers to the total employment picture in the Manhattan CBD, we can now turn to the subject of office space requirements for the projected office force. Table 5.18, Figures 5.5 and 5.6, and Maps 5.1 and 5.2 present an inventory of new office building completions in the Manhattan CBD from 1950 to 1973—a record of the celebrated building boom, based primarily on data from James Felt & Co. and *The New York Times,* and on field checks. According to this table, some 110,000,000 net rentable square feet of office space in 227 buildings were put in place in the Manhattan CBD over the 22-year period ending in 1971. Figures 5.5 and 5.6 show how the pace of office building completions accelerated, with an average of 9.5 million net square feet a year built in the last five-year period, 1967–1972, compared to 1.8 million in the first five-year period, 1950–1955; how the average size of buildings increased from some 250,000 net square feet in the former period to almost 765,000 in the latter; and how the boom expanded to engulf downtown Manhattan. Whereas in the first decade, only 21 percent of the new construction was located downtown, downtown's share in the last 12 years expanded to 34 percent. More geographic detail is given in Maps 5.1 and 5.2. It is evident from Map 5.1, for example, that construction in midtown started in a fairly tight ring around Grand Central Terminal and along Park Avenue in the 1950s, and that it later expanded in a wider circle, shifting at the same time from the East to the West Side.

In comparing the figures on new buildings completed in Table 5.18 with figures on office building employment growth in Table 5.17, it quickly becomes apparent that the two are not directly related. Thus, while 53 million net square feet (corresponding to about 63 million gross square feet) of new office space were completed between 1956 and 1967, the increase in office building employment over the same period, as shown in Table 5.17, amounted to only 115,000 jobs. The reasons for this lie in the replacement of obsolete building stock and in the expanding allocation of space per office worker. It appears that the allocation of gross square footage per worker increased from 208 square feet in 1956 to about 240 square feet in 1967. This expansion alone consumed

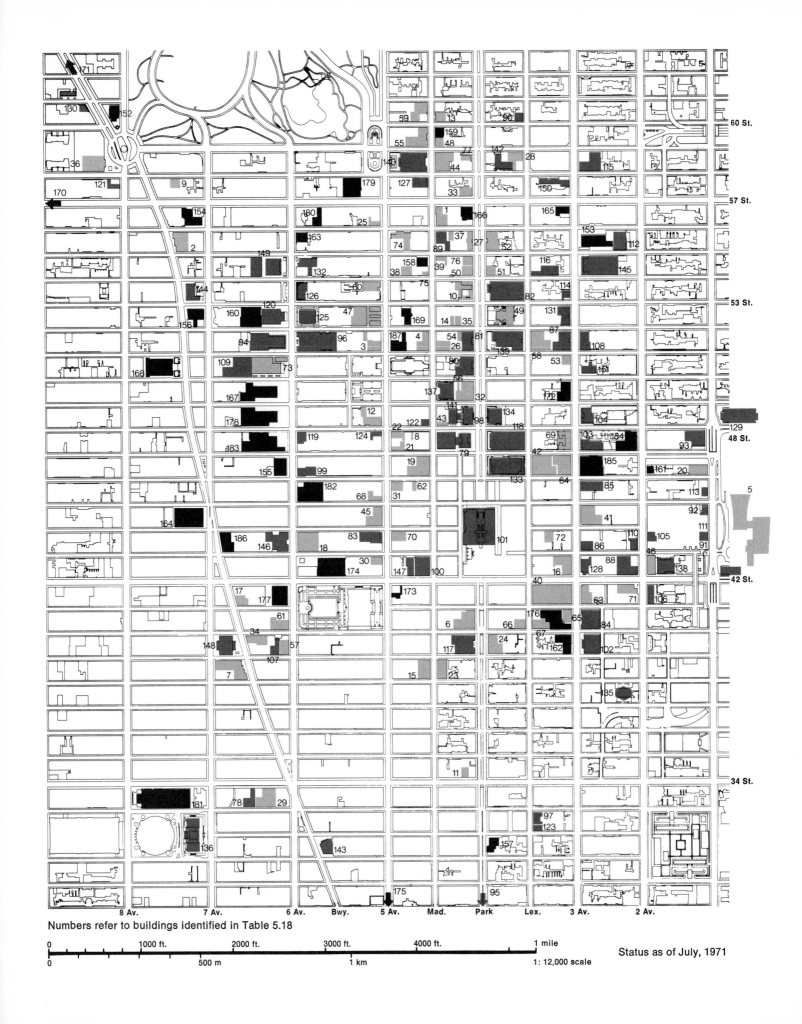

Numbers refer to buildings identified in Table 5.18

0	1000 ft.	2000 ft.	3000 ft.	4000 ft.		1 mile
0		500 m		1 km		

Status as of July, 1971

1: 12,000 scale

about 38 percent of the newly built office space. It further appears that demolitions and the vacating of obsolete office space (as well as nominal vacancies in new structures) took about 11 million square feet out of occupancy and off the market during the same period. Thus, only some 44 percent of the new building space erected served to accommodate the growth in office building employment. The calculation of these proportions is shown in Table 5.19.

The methodology employed in Table 5.19 can be used to project future Manhattan CBD construction needs, which will clearly exceed either the requirements of the projected increment in office employment or the net increment in office floor space. To do that, certain assumptions are necessary. The first has to do with the future expansion of space allocation per worker. It is assumed that space per worker will reach 248.5 square feet in 1972 and 276 square feet by 2000, if past trends are projected at a regularly declining rate. An estimate of future replacement is more tenuous; it is assumed that twice the prevailing rate of demolition, or 1.5 million square feet annually, will occur across the forecast period. This acceleration of replacement, which will be numerically equivalent to the removal of 70 percent of all pre-1925 office space, will result from several factors. Increased emphasis will be placed on leasing of prestige office quarters to a growing headquarters sector; probable vacancies will occur in older office stock as a result of outmoded internal arrangements; and some old—and newer—buildings will realize that the locations they occupy within the CBD are of more value than the densities to which they are developed.[1] It is also assumed that the rate of alterations in the future will reflect the present level, rather than the past, and that the allowance for vacancies will be in the order of 5 percent. The projected volume of future construction, based on these assumptions, is shown in Table 5.20 and Figure 5.7.

1. This does not imply that most pre-1925 office space, including the historically valuable buildings, will or should be replaced over the future of the CBD. A demand exists for cheaper, and older, stock by small or newly established firms that cannot afford the higher rents of new accommodations. Most older buildings can charge substantially lower rents—on the order of $4 to $5 per square foot—because the costs they incur through operation are largely those of building taxation and maintenance. For office buildings recently completed, the break-even point is more in the order of $10 per square foot, excluding an operating profit of $1 per foot but covering the following cost items: $4.50 to build and finance, $1.35 to maintain, $2.25 for taxes, and $1.75 for land.

Map 5.1 Office construction in midtown Manhattan, 1950–1973

1950-59

1960-69

1970-73

Table 5.19. The Use of New Office Building Construction in the Manhattan CBD, 1956–1967

	Thousands of gross sq ft	% of total
Estimated total new construction starts, 1954–1964	70,585	
Of this, alterations (11.4%)	−8,075	
New buildings completed, 1956–1966	62,510	100.0%
Increasing space per worker 745,000 × 208 (1956 standard) = 154,960 745,000 × 240 (1967 standard) = 178,800 Difference	23,840	38.1
Added employment, 1956–1967 115,000 × 240 (1967 standard)	27,600	44.2
Replacement (including vacancy)	11,070	17.7

Source: Regional Plan Association.
Note: Start of construction precedes completion, as shown, by two years.

Table 5.20. Projected Office Construction in the Manhattan CBD, 1967–1972, 1972–2000 (thousands of gross square feet)

	1967–1972	1972–2000
Estimated total new construction	65,130	197,340
Of this, alterations (assume 14%)	−9,400	−28,420
Total, new buildings	55,730	168,920
Increasing space per worker	7,310	28,660
Added employment	22,960	110,260
Replacement	25,460	30,000
Demolition and vacancy	5,460	50,000
Overbuilding	20,000	−20,000

Source: Regional Plan Association.
Notes: Total new buildings constructed, 1967–1972, corresponds to the gross square footage of net rentable completions recorded for 1967 through 1971 in Table 5.18. Estimated total new construction, 1967–1972, corresponds to F. W. Dodge Company construction starts, 1965 through 1969.

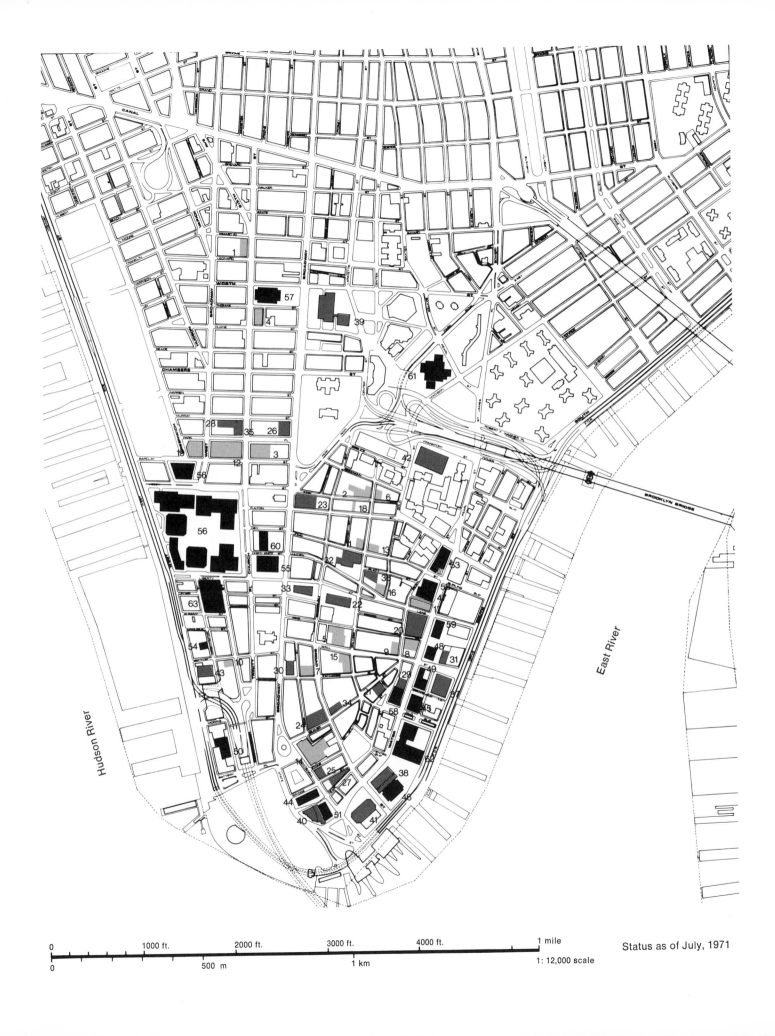

Hudson River

East River

BROOKLYN BRIDGE

Status as of July, 1971

1: 12,000 scale

| 0 | 1000 ft. | 2000 ft. | 3000 ft. | 4000 ft. | 1 mile |
| 0 | 500 m | 1 km | | | |

It appears from Table 5.20 that, to accommodate the projected increase of somewhat under half a million new office workers by the year 2000, and to achieve a total inventory of about 400 million gross square feet of office floor space in the Manhattan CBD by the year 2000, the construction of almost 170 million square feet in new buildings would be required; over a 28-year period, from 1972 to 2000, this would average some 6 million gross square feet a year, a rate considerably lower than the all-time high of 11 million gross square feet annually, registered in 1967 through 1971, but slightly in excess of the previous level of building, 1956–1967. This assumes that the 170 million square feet of post-1972 new construction would be divided as follows: 65 percent would accommodate the projected increase in office jobs, about 17 percent would take care of further, but diminishing, increases in space allocation per worker, and 18 percent would be for replacement of obsolete office buildings or of obsolete office space in nonoffice buildings. The downturn in the rate of forecast construction is related to the latter factor which represents a considerable amount of overbuilding in the recent period. An estimated 20 million gross square feet, categorized in Table 5.20 as replacement for the period 1967–1972, is in actuality surplus stock that will have to be absorbed in forthcoming years.[2]

If we assume that the roughly 140 million square feet of buildings which are to be added to the total inventory in 1972–2000 (that is, not counting replacement) are built at a floor/area ratio of 20 (based on gross square feet, which corresponds to a net floor/area ratio of about 18), the total land requirement of all this new construction would come to 7 million square feet of land, or 160 acres, or 44 fairly typical, 200 × 800 foot city blocks. Were allowable densities to be raised to a floor/area ratio of 30, the land requirement would be accordingly reduced by one-third. Though the requirement of 110 to 160 acres of land in the CBD appears large, it represents only 2 to 3 percent of the land area of Manhattan south of 60th Street.

If we assume that the distribution of expected increases in office building floor space in Manhattan emulates that

2. Aside from the overbuilding of stock in the 1967–1972 period, which has resulted in considerable vacancies in newly constructed buildings at present and can be considered to have fulfilled the requirement for replacement into the early 1980s, the heavy volume of estimated completions for 1972 and 1973, expressed in gross square footage, would represent five years of the forecasted 1972–2000 annual increment. Unless there is an unforeseen acceleration of office employment growth in the CBD over the decade of the 1970s, it is apparent that the market will not support much new construction until the later part of the decade.

Map 5.2 Office construction in downtown Manhattan, 1950–1973

▨ 1950-59   ▧ 1960-69   ■ 1970-73

of recent completions, 1957 to 1973, then 35 percent of new growth can be expected to locate in downtown Manhattan. This would affect the existing 1970 office stock in the following manner, by the year 2000: midtown Manhattan would increase from 161 million gross square feet to 260, and downtown Manhattan would increase from 86 to 140. This, of course, does not represent actual construction over the period, but merely net additions to office stock. Needless to say, the final distribution will depend to a great extent on market forces and public policy influencing the pattern of land values. Without a concerted effort to develop large assemblages of parcels in an integrated cluster of office space, as was illustrated by the "Access Tree" principles of *Urban Design Manhattan* (A Report of the Second Regional Plan, New York, April 1969), much of the new office construction will take place on scattered sites, randomly replacing uses with a poor economic return on location.

A recent study by the New York City Planning Commission indicates what land uses were replaced by Manhattan office building construction over the period 1963–1971. It appears that 41 percent of floor space demolished was old offices; other commercial uses represented 26 percent. However, manufacturing and warehousing space, accommodating some 8,500 jobs, and residential square footage, adequate to house 5,400 households, were also lost during that period by the construction of office buildings. The impending addition of office buildings, authorized or in planning stage as of 1971, will again take the highest share of space out of office and commercial usage, 51 percent of total, although 5,300 blue-collar jobs and 2,000 dwelling units can be expected to be displaced if all projects are completed. Of course, it should be remembered that these figures add up to only 1 percent of Manhattan's 1960 housing stock and 2 percent of its production-oriented jobs.

Having reviewed the building and the land requirements of the projected CBD office employment, we can take a brief look at its transportation requirements. As previously noted, the total *workers* coming to work in the Manhattan CBD in the course of a typical week (including both office workers and others) are projected to increase from 1,860,000 in 1960 to 2,220,000 in 2000, for an increment of 360,000, or about 20 percent, over the 40-year period. Committed rail and rapid transit improvements by the Metropolitan Transportation Authority and the Port of New York Authority over the 1970–1985 period foresee an increase in rail capacity to and from the Manhattan CBD from 50 to 58 tracks, a 16 percent expansion over half the forecast period. While about 40 percent of this new capacity would be used to relieve existing overcrowding on subways, and not to bring in new passengers, it should be also kept in mind that the existing 10 tracks of suburban railroads into

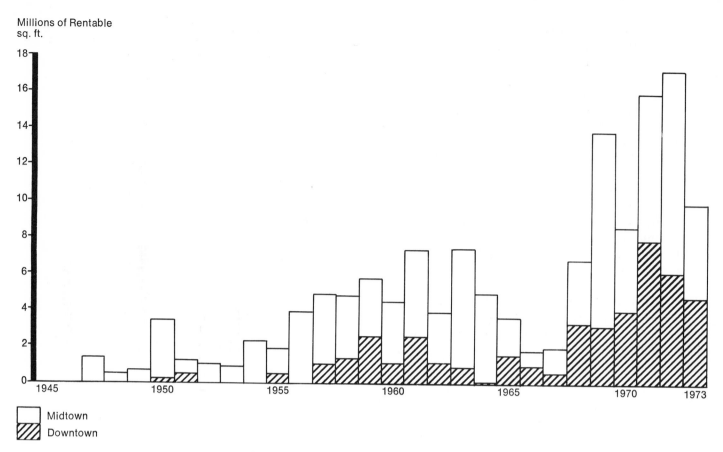

Figure 5.5 Annual completion of office space in the Manhattan CBD, 1945–1973

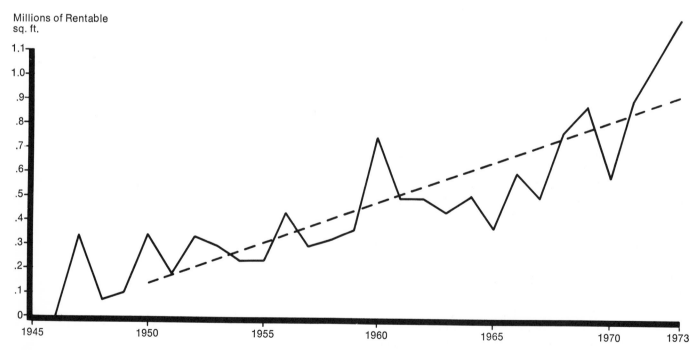

Figure 5.6 Average size of office buildings completed in the Manhattan CBD, 1945–1973

Manhattan are not used to their full potential; improvements in rolling stock, signaling, and track and station layout can increase their carrying capacity very substantially. On balance, it appears that committed construction programs, in conjunction with an extensive upgrading of existing suburban rail lines, can keep up with the projected employment increase through 1985 and provide, at that time, better standards of service than those which existed in 1960. New programs will be required for the post-1985 period.

The shape of future transit programs and, in fact, the effectiveness of existing ones, will be fundamentally affected by where the future Manhattan workers will live. A rigorous allocation of future residences and detailed travel assignment are, quite obviously, beyond the scope of this study. However, the estimated future residential distribution of office workers within the Region, presented earlier in Table 5.12, and the distribution of future office jobs by county, shown in Table 5.15, make it possible to indicate very roughly where the future Manhattan office workers might be coming from (Table 5.21 and Map 5.3).

The continuation of current trends in the population redistribution within the New York Region and the rate of educational attainment among the unskilled population of New York City suggest a staggering increase in office commuting to Manhattan from outside New York City, which implies that by the end of the century the commuter railroad and suburban bus capacity will need to be more than doubled, while the city subways decline in use. Two questions arise in this respect. The first is whether large-scale reconstruction of obsolete residential areas within New York City for office workers and their families would not be a more rational alternative to importing half a million office workers from long distances in the year 2000. This policy would hinge on new intraurban transportation technology—such as Gravity Vacuum Tubes (GVT)—that would make redeveloped residential areas in the boroughs outside Manhattan truly convenient (within 15 to 20 minutes) to Manhattan office workers. The second socially significant question is whether investment in educational training to accelerate the acquisition of white-collar skills among the city's residents should not take precedence over other concerns.

THE FUTURE OF 15 MAJOR SUBCENTERS
IN THE NEW YORK REGION

In the discussion of the distribution of office space within the New York Region at the end of Chapter 4, it was pointed out that 15 major subcenters in the Region, mostly the downtowns of smaller cities, contained some 50 million square feet of office space in 1963, about one-quarter of Manhattan's total. Second Regional Plan policies put major emphasis on expanding many of these

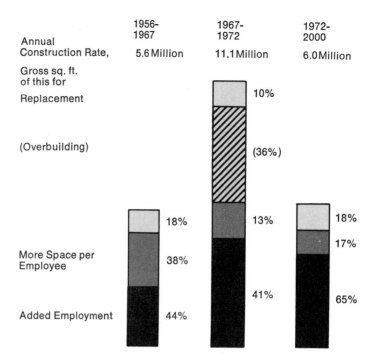

Figure 5.7 Past and projected office construction demand in Manhattan

Table 5.21. Origins of Manhattan CBD Commuters, 1960, and Estimated Origins of Manhattan CBD Office Workers, 1960 and 2000

| Place of residence | All workers, 1960 | | Estimated office workers | | | |
| | | | 1960 | | 2000 | |
	Number (× 1,000)	%	Number (× 1,000)	%	Number (× 1,000)	%
Within CBD	245	13%	100	11%	130	9%
New York City outside CBD	1,271	68	560	64	740	51
Outside New York City	342	19	220	25	570	40
Total	1,858	100	880	100	1,440	100

Sources: All workers: U.S. Census, *Journey to Work: 1960*; Office Workers: Regional Plan Association.

subcenters as an antidote to both urban sprawl and an overconcentration in Manhattan. What is the potential market for new office jobs and the construction of new office space in these subcenters?

Table 5.22 presents the recent experience in office construction for the 15 subcenters and gives two projections for the year 2000 (Map 5.4), one assuming that policies on concentrating office construction in the subcenters will meet with a large measure of success, another assuming that the 1963–1970 trend will continue. First, a look at recent experience.

The four subcenters in the Region's core—Newark, downtown Brooklyn, Jamaica–Rego Park and Jersey City—built 5 million square feet of new office space over the recent 7-year period, in addition to the 25 million in place in 1963, for an increase of 21 percent, compared to the Region's average of 35 percent. Clearly, they have lagged substantially behind the Region's growth. However, a greater degree of concentration in the four centers, compared to the rest of the core area, could be observed. Whereas in 1963 the four centers accounted for 32 percent of the ring's office space, 54 percent of the new construction went into the centers. This can be explained by the fact that most of the dispersed office space in the core went up in the past together with residential construction; today's new office buildings are generally not inserted into the almost fully built-up residential fabric but gravitate toward the centers.

The five subcenters of the inner ring—central Nassau, Elizabeth, central Bergen, Paterson, and White Plains—built close to 3 million square feet of office space over the 7-year period, in addition to the 12 million existing in 1963, for an increase of about 23 percent, slightly larger than that of the core centers but also below the Region's average. However, in contrast to the core, the tendency in the inner ring suburbs was for greater dispersal, not for greater concentration. Whereas almost 20 percent of the existing space was in centers, only 9 percent of the recently built space went there. White Plains stands out as the single major success story among the inner ring centers—about half their growth is attributable to it. White Plains doubled its office space during the 7-year period, and captured more than 20 percent of Westchester County's new office growth.

The six subcenters of the intermediate ring—New Brunswick, New Haven, Bridgeport, Trenton, Stamford, and Morristown—built 3.4 million square feet of new office space between 1963 and 1970, in addition to the 14.5 million that existed at the beginning of the period. This is a rate of growth identical with that of the inner ring centers; the tendency for concentration was only slightly higher than in the inner ring—12.6 percent of

Map 5.3 Estimated office commuting to Manhattan, 1960

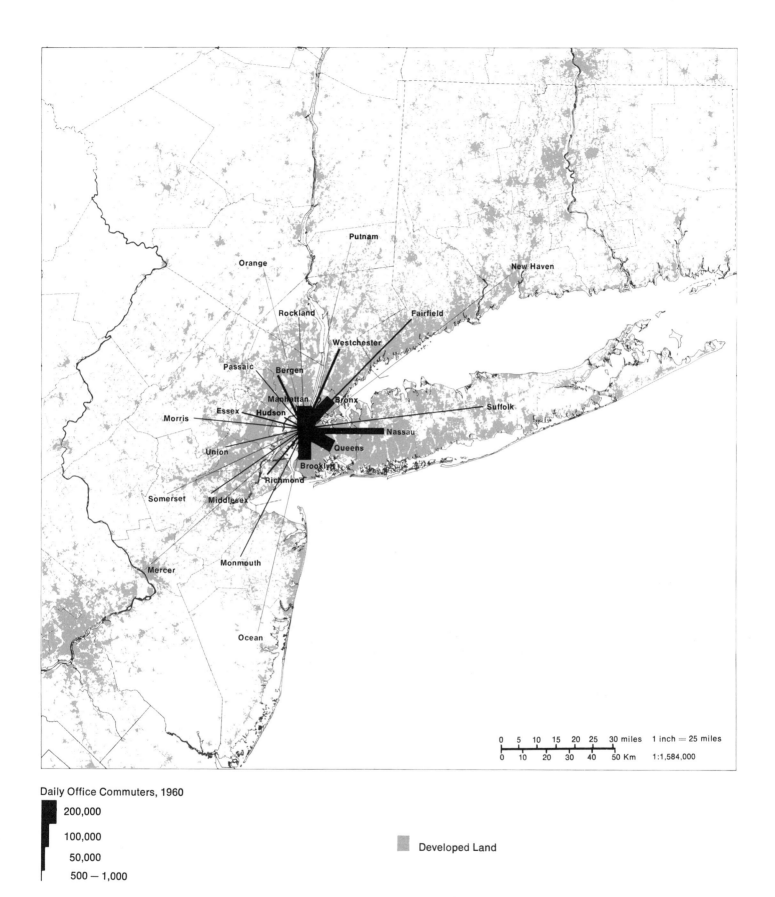

Daily Office Commuters, 1960

200,000

100,000

50,000

500 — 1,000

Developed Land

Table 5.22. Past and Projected Office Building Employment and Office Floor Space in the Major Subcenters in the New York Region, 1963–2000

	Office jobs in office bldgs., 1965	Office fl. space, 1963 (× 1 million sq ft)	Recent office constr., 1963–1970 (× 1,000 sq ft)	Office jobs in office bldgs., 2000	Office fl. space, 2000 (× 1 million sq ft)	New office space increment, 1970–2000 (× 1 million sq ft)	
						Projected	1963–1970 Trend
1. Newark	47,250	12.5	1,671	85,550	23.6	9.4	7.2
2. Downtown Brooklyn	34,750	7.3	2,152	80,840	19.4	9.9	9.2
3. Jersey City	11,550	2.9	288	32,410	8.9	5.7	1.2
4. Jamaica–Rego Park	9,070	2.4	1,046	61,130	14.7	11.3	4.5
Total, major centers	102,620	25.1	5,157	259,930	66.6	36.3	22.1
Total, other concentrations	25,810	5.7	n.a.	42,800	10.3		
Non-CBD Core total	358,920	77.6	9,471	595,150	142.8		
Clusters as % of Ring	35.8%	39.7%	54.5%	50.9%	53.9%		
5. Central Nassau	14,285	3.7	(492)	46,230	13.9	9.7	2.1
6. Elizabeth	8,050	3.1	117	18,460	5.5	2.3	.5
7. Central Bergen	6,860	2.1	509	35,880	10.8	8.2	2.2
8. Paterson–Clifton	7,770	2.0	224	32,660	9.8	7.6	1.0
9. White Plains	5,390	1.4	1,533	48,420	14.5	11.6	6.6
Total, major centers	42,355	12.3	2,875	181,650	54.5	39.4	12.4
Total, other concentrations	20,915	6.4	n.a.	47,820	14.3		
Inner Ring total	218,500	62.7	30,754	499,630	149.9		
Clusters as % of Ring	29.0%	29.8%	9.3%	45.9%	45.9%		
10. New Brunswick	9,230	3.5	325	30,620	9.2	5.4	1.4
11. New Haven	11,640	3.1	1,011	39,960	12.0	7.9	4.3
12. Bridgeport	5,120	1.8	484	33,840	10.2	7.9	2.1
13. Trenton	14,520	3.8	725	41,080	12.3	7.8	3.1
14. Stamford	3,970	1.5	438	23,100	6.9	5.0	1.9
15. Morristown	2,920	.8	413	32,540	9.8	8.6	1.8
Total, major centers	47,400	14.5	3,396	201,140	60.4	42.5	14.6
Total, other concentrations*	7,270	3.2	n.a.	40,000	12.0		
Intermediate Ring Total	175,700	56.3	26,946	734,830	220.4		
Clusters as % of Ring	31.1%	31.4%	12.6%	32.8%	32.8%		
Outer Ring total †	46,240	11.3	4,652	216,310	64.9		

Source: Regional Plan Association.
Notes: Centers represent square mile aggregates and do not correspond with municipalities. The office space constructed, 1963–1970, includes square footage in additions, alterations, and conversions, as well as new buildings. The office space increment, 1970–2000, represents only space required for office employment growth and does not include construction or space for replacement purposes or alterations and conversions of existing square footage. All space figures are gross. ( ) are estimated.
* By the year 2000, several other counties in the Intermediate Ring could support office centers of several million square feet of office space. They have not been included in the inventory of past development but have been projected for the course of future development.
† By the year 2000, Poughkeepsie with 360,000 sq ft in 1963 could become an Outer Ring metropolitan office center containing nearly 3 million square feet of office space.

the new construction in the ring went into the centers, compared to 26 percent of the ring's existing floor space which was concentrated in the centers in 1963.

In sum, almost all the subcenters outside Manhattan have lagged behind the Region's growth in office space over the 1963–1970 period, having experienced an average growth of 23 percent, compared to the Region's average of 35 percent. While 13 percent of the Region's office floor space was located in the 15 subcenters in 1963, only 8 percent of the new construction went there in 1963–1970. And, while there was considerable concentration of new construction in the core centers compared to the distribution of floor space prior to 1963, the tendency in the inner and intermediate rings was toward greater dispersal. Among the centers that grew at an above-average rate was White Plains (more than a doubling); Jamaica (a 40 percent increase, much of it actually occurring in Rego Park); New Haven (32 percent increase, a considerable part of which was in fact replacement of old buildings); downtown Brooklyn (29 percent); Stamford (29 percent); and Bridgeport (27 percent). It is notable that the large increases are mostly associated with downtowns that have ambitious publicly aided urban renewal schemes. It seems that only massive public intervention, on the scale of a large downtown urban renewal project, can overcome the problems of circulation, environmental amenity, and inflated land costs that discourage spontaneous private office investment in the smaller downtowns of the Region.

Having reviewed the recent experience, we can now turn to projections. If new office construction in the 15 subcenters continues at the average annual increments recorded for 1963–1970, the centers will capture almost 50 million square feet of new office construction by the year 2000. This variant—the "trend variant"—is shown in the last column of Table 5.22. However, if policies are pursued to concentrate the suburban office growth in centers—the "policy variant"—about 120 million square feet could be located in the 15 centers. Columns 4, 5, and 6 in Table 5.22 are predicated upon the policy variant. The trend variant would imply an average increase of 75 percent for the 15 centers taken together, and the policy variant would imply a 180 percent increase. In the "trend" case roughly 10 percent, and in the "policy" case roughly 25 percent of the Region's increment of office space over the 1970–2000 period would be located in the 15 centers. In addition, the potential exists for about three new centers of some 3 million square feet each—the present size of White Plains—in such counties of the intermediate ring as Suffolk, Monmouth, and Somerset, and for the growth of Poughkeepsie in the outer ring to the scale of a true metropolitan center with 3 or more million square feet of office space.

The policy variant is predicated on the assumption that, in each county in which a center is located, generally between 40 and 50 percent of the growth in headquarters office jobs, about 60 percent of the middle-market jobs, and about 20 percent of the local jobs would be induced to locate in the center. These proportions vary somewhat depending on particular circumstances; the proportion of office jobs assigned to the center in any particular county can be ascertained by comparing the figures in column 4 of Table 5.22 with those in column 4 in Table 5.15. The proportions are generally similar to those that prevailed in the mid-1960s and, in some cases, are slightly higher. The intent was to illustrate a realistic alternative, one that does not deviate too far from current experience. In terms of the county's total office building employment assigned to its center in 2000 under the policy variant, the shares range from roughly 60 percent for Essex, Hudson, and Passaic, to between 40 and 50 percent for Brooklyn, Queens, Nassau, New Haven, Mercer, and Morris, to between 20 and 30 percent for Union, Bergen, Westchester, Middlesex, and Fairfield.

With a deliberate effort to concentrate suburban office growth in centers, as advocated by the Second Regional Plan, Newark could increase its office space from 14.2 million square feet in 1970 to 23.6 in 2000 (it would be somewhat smaller than the San Francisco CBD is at present); downtown Brooklyn would grow from 9.5 to 19.4 million; Jamaica–Rego Park from 3.4 to 14.7 (roughly the present size of Newark). In the inner suburbs, central Nassau County could conceivably increase from 4.2 to 14 million square feet (to be larger than Minneapolis in 1970); White Plains from 3 million to 14.5 million; central Bergen from 2.6 to 11; and Paterson–Clifton from 2.2 to 10 or more than that, if it is able to capture part of neighboring Bergen County's office growth. Farther out, New Haven and Trenton could grow from roughly 4 million square feet to about 12 each (roughly the present size of Cleveland's CBD), and New Brunswick, Bridgeport, and Morristown could conceivably expand to about 10 million square feet of office space each. The detailed office projections, by center, indicating also the rise in office employment, are presented in Table 5.22.

It should be borne in mind that, just like Manhattan, the subcenters presently contain a considerable amount of nonoffice employment and will continue to do so. However, whereas workers in office buildings in the Manhattan CBD represent close to 45 percent of total employment, their share in the subcenters is generally lower, in the 40 to 25 percent range. Thus, the multiplier to arrive at total CBD employment, given office employment, is higher in the subcenters than in Manhattan. To some extent, the subcenters will be subject to the same kind of forces as Manhattan; the out-migra-

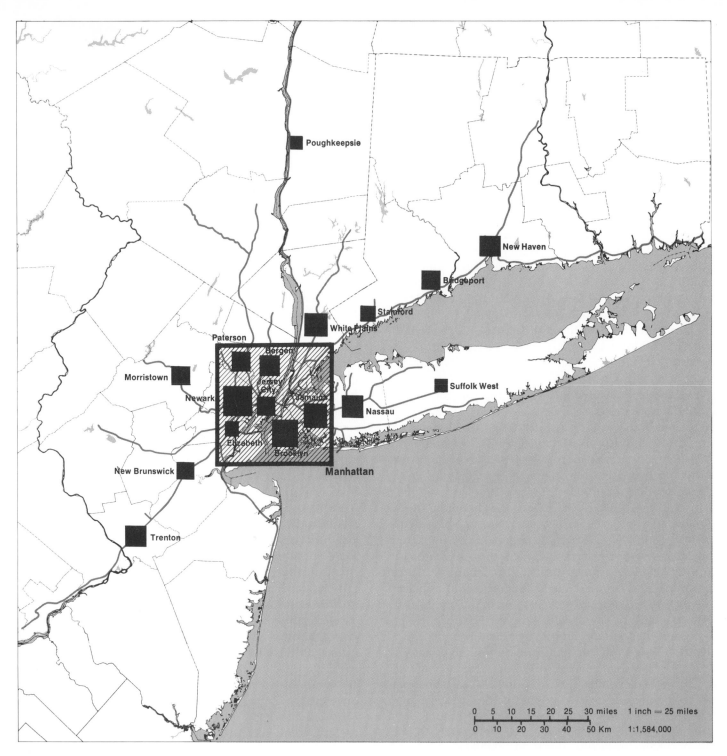

Potential 2000 floorspace in office buildings:

■ 5 million sq. ft.

■ 10 million sq. ft.

■ 20 million sq. ft.

▨ Manhattan CBD (400 million sq. ft.)

── Major Commuter Railroads

tion of production-oriented employment, especially from such industrially oriented cities as Paterson, Bridgeport, Trenton, and a general stability or mild increase in "other" types of employment, such as retail, services, and institutions. On the whole, office employment will increase as a share of total employment in the subcenters, but the net increment in total jobs may be, in contrast to Manhattan, in many cases greater than the increment in office jobs, especially if efforts to induce the location of universities, hospitals, and major retailing establishments in the subcenters prove successful.

The transportation requirements of the subcenters today are small compared to those of Manhattan. For example, while over 800,000 daily trips by mechanical modes are destined to the densest square mile of Manhattan, those to the densest square miles of downtown Brooklyn and Newark are 156,000 and 112,000, respectively, and those to the densest square miles of the other centers, such as Jamaica, White Plains, Paterson, New Haven, Bridgeport, Stamford, are on the order of 50,000. The four centers in the Region's core have a relatively low proportion of trips by automobile: about 20 percent to downtown Brooklyn, about 40 percent to Newark, and about 50 percent to Jamaica and Jersey City. However, the other centers are 75 percent to 95 percent automobile oriented.

The four centers in the Region's core have an excellent opportunity to use existing and programmed railroad and rapid transit capacity to bring in additional office workers; they can live, so to say, off the rail and rapid transit investment that is necessary because of Manhattan and contribute to its more efficient utilization. The other centers, though all located on rail lines, will remain more rubber-tire oriented. All of them will need additional expressway capacity; the higher densities of development implied by the office projections will make a higher proportion of trips by bus to all of them both more feasible and more necessary.

The Options of Concentration and Dispersal

The preceding discussion has assumed a fixed rate of growth for employment in office buildings in Manhattan, and has postulated two variants for the distribution of office building employment in the New York Region outside Manhattan: one that would reflect a strong policy for the clustering of office buildings in subcenters, both existing and new, and one that would continue the current trend toward greater dispersal of office buildings on campus-type sites throughout the inner, intermediate, and outer rings of development. These two variants are summarized as variants 1 and 2 in Table 5.23.

Map 5.4 Potential office centers in the New York Region, 2000

Table 5.23. Alternative Allocations of the 1970–2000 Increment of Office Space within the New York Region (in millions of gross square feet)

	Variant 1		Variant 2		Variant 3		Variant 4	
Manhattan CBD	153	33%	153	33%	200	43%	55	12%
15 major centers	118	25	49	10	98	21	118	25
Other centers	22	5	13	3	19	4	22	5
Dispersed	177	37	255	54	153	32	275	58
Region	470	100	470	100	470	100	470	100

Source: Regional Plan Association.
Note: Net increment to stock, without alterations or replacement, including increment from building completions 1970 through 1973.

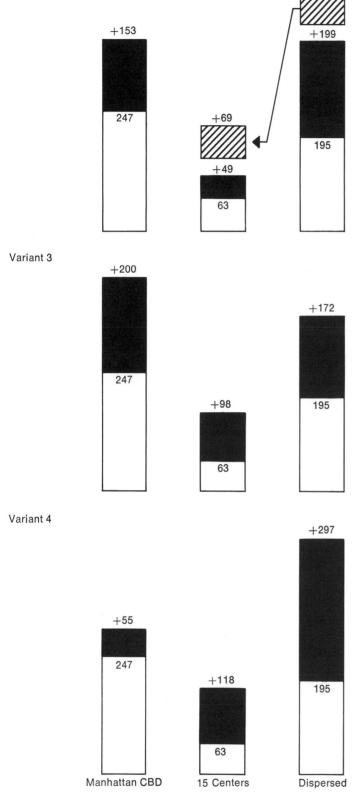

Variants 1 and 2

+153
247

+199
195

+69

+49
63

Variant 3

+200
247

+172
195

+98
63

Variant 4

+55
247

+297
195

+118
63

Manhattan CBD   15 Centers   Dispersed

Figure 5.8 Alternative locations of the New York Region's office space increment, 1970–2000

Table 5.23 and Figure 5.8 also indicate two other variants, one (variant 3) under which the 1963 to 1970 rate of building completions in Manhattan would be sustained over the remainder of the century, and the other (variant 4) under which net commuter flows to Manhattan from suburban areas would remain constant. Given the first assumption, Manhattan would capture 600,000, rather than the 400,000 office job increment between 1972 and 2000. Manhattan's growth in that hypothetical case would be increased largely at the expense of autonomous headquarter growth in subcenters and dispersed portions of the intermediate ring. Given the second assumption, which is based on Table 5.21, Manhattan's growth would be stinted and its requirement for space would be virtually met by the completion of new construction on the market, 1970–1975.

Thus, the difference between the "policy" variant 1 and the "trend" variant 2 is whether some 80 million square feet of office floor space are located in a dispersed manner on campus-type sites or in subcenters. The difference between variant 3 and the earlier two variants is whether Manhattan continues to expand at the 1963–1970 rate and, as a result, attracts 50 more million square feet of office space and 200,000 more office workers than were allocated to it under the previous two variants; the floor space and the workers come in roughly equal shares out of what was allocated to subcenters and to dispersed development in variant 1. Variant 3 emulates very closely the existing distribution in the Region and current locational behavior, with the exception that more emphasis is put on subcenters. Variant 1 assumes that current behavior cannot be sustained in the long run, in view of the long-term trends in the outward shift of the residential population, but that concentration in subcenters can succeed. Variant 2 assumes the greatest amount of dispersal, both from Manhattan and from the subcenters. Lastly, variant 4 ominously underscores the importance of social issues on the future of New York City's economy and illustrates the growing dependence of Manhattan's office function on the suburban residence of white-collar workers, unless the educational and housing facilities of the central city are vastly improved.

It is well known that at the present time we lack adequate means of evaluating large-scale alternatives of this sort. At best, some selected costs can be calculated, but the benefits associated with incurring these costs remain elusive. Still, a few selected cost figures are presented in Table 5.24. It should be stressed that, except for the net building construction costs, which are based on Table 5.10, the figures used are not necessarily representative averages but often fairly arbitrarily selected numbers, merely illustrating an approach. In broad dimensions, however, they suggest other, nonsocial burdens that will

Table 5.24. Some Illustrative Private and Public Costs of Office Building Construction in Manhattan, in a Subcenter, and on Open Land

Assumption: 1 million square feet, 4,000 office workers

1. Manhattan

Net construction cost	@ $41/sq ft (Table 5.10)	$41,000,000
Land requirement	@ FAR* 25 = 40,000 sq ft (1 acre)	
Land cost	@ say $300/sq ft	$12,000,000
Total private land and construction costs		$53,000,000
Major mode of travel	say 75% subway-rail	
Average trip length	say 9 miles	
Person-miles of capacity, bidirectional, needed in peak hour	4,000 × .75 × 9 × 2 = 54,000 person-miles or 1.35 track-miles	
Cost per 40,000 person-miles (1 track mile) of capacity	$10 million	
Cost of needed subway-rail capacity, bidirectional		$13,500,000
Directional imbalance	15–85	
Cost of subway-rail capacity, adjusting for imbalance (−15%)		$11,500,000

2. Subcenter

Net construction cost	@ $32/sq ft	$32,000,000
Land requirement	@ FAR 6 = 166,666 sq ft (4 acres)	
Land cost	@ say $40/sq ft	$6,600,000
Parking garage	say 1,000 spaces @ $2,000/space	$2,000,000
Total private land and construction cost		$40,600,000
Major mode of travel	say 38% private auto	
Assumed car occupancy	say 1.5	
Average trip length	say 5 miles	
Vehicle-miles of capacity, bidirectional, needed in peak hour	4,000 × (.38/1.5) × 5 × 2 = 10,000 vehicle-miles	
Cost per 1,600 vehicle-miles of expressway capacity	say $2 million	
Percentage of vehicle-miles on expressways	say 35%	
Lane-miles of expressway needed	(10,000/1,600) × .35 = 2.2	
Cost of needed expressway capacity, bidirectional		$4,400,000
Assumed directional imbalance	30–70	
Cost of expressway capacity, adjusting for imbalance (−30%)		$3,100,000

3. Open Land

Net construction cost	@ $25/sq ft (no elevators)	$25,000,000
Land requirement	@ FAR 0.3 = 3.3 million sq ft (76.5 acres)	
Land cost	@ say $2.00/sq ft or $87,000/acre	$6,600,000
Parking lot	say 3,000 spaces @ $400 pavement & landscaping	$1,200,000
Total private land and construction cost		$32,800,000
Major mode of travel	say 100% private auto	
Assumed car occupancy	say 1.3	
Average trip length	say 6 miles	
Vehicle-miles of capacity, bidirectional needed in peak hour	(4,000/1.3) × 6 × 2 = 36,000 vehicle-miles	
Cost per 1,600 vehicle-miles of expressway capacity	say $1 million	
Percentage of vehicle-miles on expressways	say 35%	
Lane-miles of expressway needed	(36,000/1,600) × .35 = 7.9	
Cost of needed expressway capacity, bidirectional		$7,900,000
Assumed directional imbalance	40–60	
Cost of expressway capacity, adjusting for imbalance (−40%)		$4,700,000

Source: Regional Plan Association.
Note: The costs are those of the late 1960s and do not reflect the very substantial escalation since that time.
* Floor/area ratio.

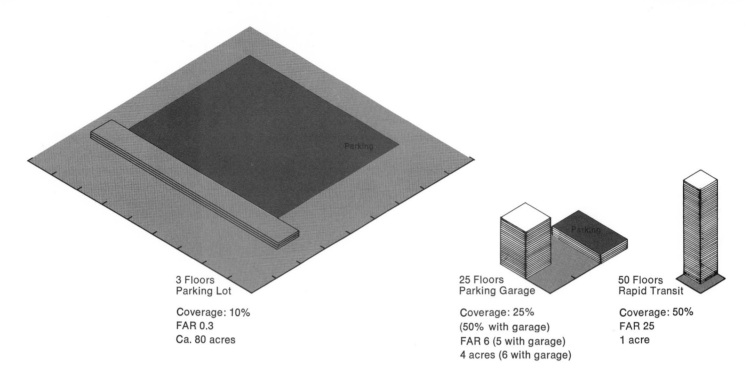

3 Floors
Parking Lot

Coverage: 10%
FAR 0.3
Ca. 80 acres

25 Floors
Parking Garage

Coverage: 25%
(50% with garage)
FAR 6 (5 with garage)
4 acres (6 with garage)

50 Floors
Rapid Transit

Coverage: 50%
FAR 25
1 acre

Figure 5.9 Illustrative densities and coverage for one million square feet of office space (FAR is floor/area ratio)

have to be borne if a large scale dispersal of office activity takes place.

Several basic relationships become apparent from studying Table 5.24. The first one pertains to land. While in Manhattan, with only a slight variance from present zoning regulations, 1 million square feet of office space can be accommodated on 1 acre of land, in a subcenter 1 million square feet would need about 4 acres, and in the outer suburbs, 76 acres (Figure 5.9).

The second interesting relationship pertains to the private development costs. Building construction costs quite obviously decline as one moves away from Manhattan, because simpler structures are required. The absence of elevators in a suburban campus-type, two-story building, assumed in case three, makes that building type particularly inexpensive. Though land costs drop precipitously with distance from Manhattan, over-all land cost per unit of building does not drop off too sharply because of drastically increased land requirements. The net effect is, nevertheless, a declining total private cost—from about $50 million per million square feet in Manhattan to about $40 million in a subcenter, to about $30 million on open land in the suburbs. These figures, as indicated in Table 5.24, include the cost of providing for automobile parking on the site.

The lesson to be learned is that cost figures in themselves are not very meaningful unless one has a notion of the benefits gained. Clearly, private enterprise would not be putting two-thirds of its money into office buildings in Manhattan, where costs are some two-thirds higher than on suburban land, if it did not derive a commensurate profit from the rent. And tenants would not pay the rent if they did not derive a benefit.

The third notable item in Table 5.24 is a rough indication of one aspect of public costs associated with private locational decisions—the major transportation investment in each case. Rail transit is assumed to cost $10 million per track-mile, which includes an allowance for low-cost construction on existing rights-of-way outside Manhattan, and expressways are assumed to cost $2 million per lane-mile in the denser areas near subcenters and $1 million per lane-mile farther into the suburbs. Given the assumptions on trip length, use of travel mode, and others shown in Table 5.24, the major transportation investment per 1 million square feet of office floor space comes to nearly $12 million for Manhattan, $3.1 million for a subcenter, and $4.7 million for a suburban location, in illustrative figures. In physical quantities, a 1 million square foot office building in Manhattan is assumed to require about 1.35 track-miles of rail transit; in a subcenter, about 2.2 lane-miles of expressway; and on suburban land, about 7.9 lane-miles of expressway. The reduced expressway requirements in a subcenter are

primarily a function of a high proportion of bus use—perhaps 40 percent—with some 20 percent of the non-auto commuters split perhaps evenly between walking and rail.

Given that the Region's prospective office space increment between 1970 and 2000 is nearly 500 million square feet (or the equivalent of 47 World Trade Centers), 70 million square feet are at issue as the major difference between variants 1 and 2: Are they located in 15 subcenters, or on campus-type sites throughout the suburbs? Locating them in subcenters would save some 5,000 acres of land, and perhaps some 400 lane-miles of expressways (100 miles of a four-lane expressway), among other things. Variant 3 would reduce the land requirement by another 2,000 acres or so, would further reduce expressway requirements, but would run up the Region's public transportations construction cost quite significantly, perhaps by $400 million. This is not to say that such an investment could not be worthwhile, or that the urban advantages of the Region would not be more effectively used in a tighter arrangement, provided that small-scale design offers adequate local openness and that internal transportation channels are well greased.

Lastly, the fourth variant assumes that no increase in net commutation to Manhattan would occur over the forecast period and that the CBD's prospect for office growth would reflect only the expansion of available white-collar skills among city residents, progressing at the same rate as during 1940 to 1960. This variant would place a modest 12 percent of the Region's floor space increment in Manhattan—a requirement that would virtually be met by building completions to 1975—and disperse more than 60 percent to scattered suburban sites and minor centers.

Aside from any design improvements of Manhattan, which are predicated on the growth of office space, this variant underscores the priority of urban social investments, an issue that was raised earlier. Clearly, the office sector cannot remain healthy in isolation from the rest of the city. And clearly, a much stronger commitment to manpower training, transportation, and housing investments is one that will benefit not merely the office industry but the Region's community at large.

Also at issue in this variant is whether a large-scale dispersal of the highly imageable and catalytic office activity should be tolerated. In so doing, the opportunity to cluster other regional activities that lend amenity to real downtowns will be forgone. If all the Region's expected increase in office stock were settled on open land at suburban densities, they would cut a swath nearly two-thirds of a mile wide from New York to Philadelphia when laid end-to-end. In contrast to the most concentrated variant 3, the dispersed office require-

New patterns of office location

Dispersal at highway interchange
Random dispersal at low density, shown here at the interchange of Interstates 287 and 684 in Harrison, Westchester County, results in total dependence on automobile travel, no opportunity for spontaneous linkages, no benefits to existing urban cores, and an excessive chopping up of the natural environment. The advantages of proximity to the interchange are less real than they appear, because of the difficulty of combining local on and off ramps with those designed for through movement.

Clustering at railroad station
A compact design at the suburban railroad station in Greenwich, Connecticut combines highway access with access by rail, capitalizes on nearby facilities in the town center, revitalizes the railroad station environment, and minimizes land-taking with garage parking under the buildings. The visual image of the buildings is memorable to both rail and highway travelers.

Dispersal in suburban quasi-center

Above, Central Nassau County appears as an office concentration on the map, but spread out over 5 square miles it does not function as a traditional downtown. Specifically, no pedestrian interaction with the county office building shown is possible because of the extent of surface parking around it. All internal, as well as external travel must be by automobile. The new building does not help an existing downtown, nor does it help create a new one.

Clustering in an existing downtown

Left, The high-rise Middlesex County office building in New Brunswick, New Jersey does help an old downtown, and can in turn capitalize on its advantages (note evidence of public transportation in the photo). The other buildings in view may lack glamour, but will not change unless private office buildings, with public assistance, follow the example set by the county.

Linear development

Facing page, Linear patterns formed by headquarters and middle market offices (*top*) along Route 9W in Englewood Cliffs, New Jersey, and by locally oriented offices (*bottom*) along Northern Boulevard in Nassau County. Though both provide some opportunity for access by bus, the overwhelming orientation is still to the automobile. From the viewpoint of linkages to other facilities as well, the somewhat denser and more structured pattern represents only a modest improvement on complete dispersal. Ideally, the roadside properties in both views could have remained a greenbelt, with the buildings clustered at higher density in a nearby center, such as Hackensack or Mineola.

Designed campus sites
American Can headquarters: 580,000 square feet of
office space for 2,200 employees on a 175-acre site (FAR 0.07) in
the rural northwestern corner of affluent Greenwich, Conn. To
reduce intrusion into the hilly landscape, parking for 1,700 cars
is provided in a 5-level underground garage (ramps seen in view).
To compensate for lack of external linkages, a cafeteria, general
store, bank, and health club for employees are provided on prem-
ises. Access is exclusively by auto, on local rural roads. The nearest moderate income housing—or the nearest railroad station—is
6 to 7 miles away. The Westchester County airport, used by corporate aircraft, is 2 miles away. Escape from the city epitomized.

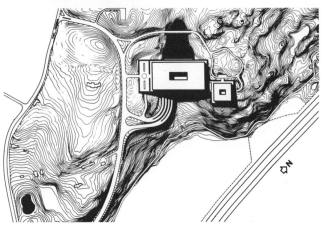

Blue Hill: 1 million square feet of office space in one 20-story and one 6-story building on a 240-acre site (FAR 0.1 in the initial phase), expandable to 3.8 million in 5 buildings in Rockland County, New York. About 3,000 parking spaces on the surface are provided initially. An effort to use large scale in order to overcome the lack of external linkages characteristic of campus sites. With 75,000 square feet of retail and service facilities and a covered pedestrian mall under the buildings, a piece of downtown is to be recreated in the open countryside. Access, however, is exclusively by automobile, over an arterial and several local roads: expressways are 3 to 4 miles away. Further expansion is constrained by the availability of clerical labor in the surrounding area and by traffic delivery to the site. The total transportation and social costs the public will have to bear because of the isolated location have not entered the site-selection process.

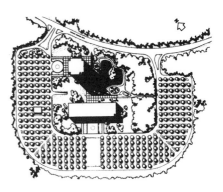

Redevelopment of existing centers
The New York Region's central business districts outside Manhattan have a poor "image" for the country-bound executive, but in fact possess numerous assets: an existing downtown infrastructure and linkages, a public transportation system that may be declining but does exist, expressway access in most cases, fairly compact labor markets with rapidly growing hinterlands, and often extensive urban redevelopment projects in progress, making available cleared land. With these assets, they could absorb a large share of the suburban office growth in the same general area where it occurs now, but in a much more compact manner, benefiting both the older cities and the suburban countryside. From the 15 centers listed in the text, 3 are illustrated here.

Above, White Plains has so far had the most success in attracting new office floor space; between 1963 and 1970 it increased its inventory from 1.4 to 3.0 million square feet, and captured 20 percent of Westchester County's growth. Much of the construction was private, without public aid. More ambitious publicly aided schemes are in progress. Stamford, in a similar geographic position, began its office space "takeoff" after 1970.

Left, New Haven has been well publicized for the amount of Federal urban renewal aid it received. The Church Street project, combining shopping, parking, a hotel, and the office building seen above, was one of the results. About 1 million square feet of new office floor space was built. However, overall demand for office space in the metropolitan area of New Haven has been sluggish, in part due to its remoteness from Manhattan. As a result, prime downtown sites reserved for office buildings have been given over to low-income housing, making large-scale future development much less likely.

Below, Paterson, the center of the third largest metropolitan area in the Region, has found the reorientation toward an office economy not easy, because of its manufacturing, blue-collar tradition. However, energetic urban renewal work has been going on. The first office project (relatively small, with 206,000 gross square feet of floor space, in addition to a garage and a motel) is ideally situated between the shopping area, the railroad station (*left*), and the county center (*right*).

ments of variant 4 would call for a total increase of more than 250 miles of four-lane expressway, nearly one-sixth of the Region's present expressway network.

Of course, transportation costs are not the only public costs affected by the locational decisions of offices. Sewerage and water supply costs, as well as the semipublic costs of providing power and telephone service are likewise affected. If the appropriate analytical work were done to quantify those depending on location, and if a taxation system were instituted that would apply equally throughout the Region, it would be possible to assess potential builders equitably for the public costs they are imposing on society. That would be an advance from the present arbitrary zoning regulations and from the present—locationally irrelevant or even counterproductive—system of taxation. In the context of the present study, such taxation policies would not favor variants 2 and 4 with their emphasis on dispersal. However, costs alone—whether private or public—are, as was previously shown, a very lopsided yardstick unless benefits are taken into account. The measurement of the public benefits of high accessibility, or of the economies of agglomeration—which is what office concentrations are all about—has progressed even less than the allocation of public costs. Clearly, this is the area in which future analytical work is most urgent. Its outcome, in the context of this study, could well have been to demonstrate the superiority of variant 3. While analysis has its limitations and the decisions that count are intuitive in the end, nobody has yet been hurt by an informed intuition.

New York, in contrast to London, seems to have made the intuitive decision that concentration of office workers in a large, high-density business district is good. Every year over the last few years, that decision has been backed by $500,000,000 invested in Manhattan office buildings by private investors. Of late, that decision has also been made an explicit matter of city policy.[3]

The issue of strengthening existing urban centers and discouraging office dispersal, illustrated here in the example of the New York Region, has strong national implications. Thus, large-scale federal investment in urban rapid transit and in new transit technology can make concentration feasible; analysis of the type presented here can establish the magnitude of potential downtown travel demand to be satisfied by these systems. Federal assumption of the financing of poverty services can free the strained resources of the central cities to create an environment hospitable to office concentration; analysis of the type presented here can establish the magnitude and direction of manpower training programs that match the prospective demand for white-collar jobs. On the other hand, national preoccupation with "decanting" population toward thinly settled parts of the country will retard progress in these directions, and national

indifference to questions of intrametropolitan location will encourage dispersal, because dispersal is easier in the short run. With questions about the desirable shape of our urban environment becoming ever more prominent in the public mind, it is hoped that this study will contribute a factual basis for rational discourse. In a field previously as neglected as this, it is, necessarily, only a beginning.

3. The reader is referred to New York City Planning Commission, *Plan for New York City: Part 1. Critical Issues* (Cambridge, Mass.: MIT Press, 1969).

Bibliography

British Institute of Management. *Office Relocation: A Series of Cost Studies.* Management survey report 3. London: British Institute of Management, 1971.

Carruth, Eleanore. "Manhattan's Office Building Binge." *Fortune,* October 1969, pp. 114–186.

Cowan, Peter (Dir.). *The Office—A Facet of Urban Growth.* New York: American Elsevier Publishing Company, Inc., 1969.

Croft, M. J. *Offices in a Regional Centre: Follow-up Studies on Infrastructure and Linkages.* Research Paper No. 3. London: The Location of Offices Bureau, 1969.

Daniels, P. W. "Office Decentralization from London: Policy and Practice." *Regional Studies,* Volume 3 (1969), 171–178.

Economic Consultants Ltd. *Demand and Supply for Office Workers and the Impact of Office Development.* London: The Location of Offices Bureau, 1971.

The Economist Intelligence Unit. *A Survey of Factors Governing the Location of Offices in the London Area.* London: The Location of Offices Bureau, 1964.

Fisher, R. M. *The Boom in Office Buildings.* Technical Bulletin No. 58. Washington, D.C.: Urban Land Institute, 1967.

Foley, Donald L. "Factors in the Location of Administrative Offices, with Particular Reference to the San Francisco Bay Area." *Papers and Proceedings of The Regional Science Association,* Volume II (1956), 318–326.

Foley, Donald L. *The Suburbanization of Administrative Offices in the San Francisco Bay Area.* Real Estate Research Program Research Report 10. Berkeley, Calif.: University of California, 1957.

Goddard, John. "Changing Office Location Patterns within Central London." *Urban Studies,* Volume 4, No. 3 (November 1967), 276–285.

Goddard, John. "Multivariate Analysis of Office Location Patterns in the City Centre: A London Example." *Regional Studies,* Volume 2, No. 1 (September 1968), 69–85.

Goodwin, William. "The Management Centers in the U.S." *Geographical Review,* Volume 55, No. 1 (January 1965), 1–16.

Gottmann, Jean. "Urban Centrality and the Interweaving of Quaternary Activities." *Ekistics,* Volume 29, No. 174 (May 1970), 322–331.

Gottmann, Jean. "Why the Skyscraper." *Geographical Review,* Volume 56 (April 1966), 190–212.

Greater London Council. *Greater London Development Plan: Industrial and Office Floorspace Targets.* Background papers B390 and B452. London: Greater London Council, 1970, 1971.

Greater London Council. *Greater London Development Plan: Tomorrow's London.* London: Greater London Council, 1969.

Haig, Robert Murray (Dir.). *Regional Plan of New York and Its Environs. Economic and Industrial Survey: The Retail Shopping and Financial Districts.* Regional Survey Volume 1B. New York: Committee on Regional Plan of New York and Its Environs, 1927.

Haig, Robert Murray. *Regional Plan of New York and Its Environs. Major Economic Factors in Metropolitan Growth and Arrangement.* Regional Survey Volume I. New York: Committee on Regional Plan of New York and Its Environs, 1927.

Hammond, E. "Dispersal of Government Offices: A Survey." *Urban Studies,* Volume 4, No. 3 (November 1967), 258–275.

Herrera, Philip. "That Manhattan Exodus." *Fortune,* June 1967, pp. 106–147.

Hoover, Edgar M., and Vernon, Raymond. *New York Metropolitan Region Study. Anatomy of a Metropolis: The Changing Distribution of People and Jobs within the New York Metropolitan Region.* Cambridge, Mass.: Harvard University Press, 1959.

Jensen, Robert. "Tall Office Buildings: The Process of Development." *Architectural Record,* April 1969, pp. 181–196.

Krooss, Herman. "America's Front Office." Unpublished report of the *New York Metropolitan Region Study,* New York, 1959.

Location of Offices Bureau. *Annual Report, 1963–64, 1964–65, 1965–66, 1966–67, 1967–68, 1968–69, 1969–70.* London: The Location of Offices Bureau, 1964, 1965, 1966, 1967, 1968, 1969, 1970.

Meier, Richard L. *A Communications Theory of Urban Growth.* Cambridge, Mass.: MIT Press, 1962.

New York City Planning Commission. "The Demand for Office Space in Manhattan." Unpublished technical report. New York: New York City Planning Commission, 1971.

New York City Planning Commission. "Relocation of Corporate Headquarters." Unpublished technical report. New York: New York City Planning Commission, 1971.

The 1969 Frank Report. 100 "International Cities": Office Space Study of 60 Countries. New York: E. René Frank Associates, Ltd., 1970.

Regional Plan Association. *The Region's Growth. A Report of the Second Regional Plan.* New York: Regional Plan Association, 1967.

Regional Plan Association. *The Second Regional Plan: A Draft for Discussion.* New York: Regional Plan Association, 1968.

Robbins, Sidney M., and Terleckyj, Nestor E. *New York Metropolitan Region Study. Money Metropolis: A Locational Study of Financial Activities in the New York Region.* Cambridge, Mass.: Harvard University Press, 1960.

Schwartz, Lawrence. "An Econometric Study of the Relocation of the Central Office and Its Workers." Unpublished Ph.D. dissertation, Harvard University, 1963.

Stern, John. "The Manhattan CBD. Part I: There's Nothing Else Like It." Unpublished Interim Technical Report 4124–9311. New York: Tri-State Transportation (Regional Planning) Commission, 1969.

Taylor, S. "A Study of Post-War Office Developments." *Journal of Town Planning Institute,* Volume 52, No. 2 (February 1966), 54–56.

Townroe, P. M. "Locational Choice and the Individual Firm." *Regional Studies,* Volume 3, No. 1 (April 1969), 15–24.

Tri-State Transportation (Regional Planning) Commission. *Manhattan Business District Floor Space Trends.* Regional Profile Volume I, No. 6. New York: Tri-State Transportation (Regional Planning) Commission, 1967.

Walker, Mabel. *Business Enterprise and The City.* Princeton, N.J.: Tax Institute, Inc., 1958.

Wright, Maurice. "Provincial Office Development." *Urban Studies,* Volume 4, No. 3 (November 1967), 218–257.

List of Sources

ADAPSO 1967 Directory of Data Processing Service Centers. Abington, Pa.: The Association of Data Processing Service Organizations, Inc., 1967.

Advertising Age. Chicago: Advertising Publications, Inc., 1967.

American Banker. New York: The American Banker, 1967.

Directory of Industrial Research Laboratories in New York State. Albany, N.Y.: New York Department of Commerce, 1964.

F. W. Dodge Division, McGraw-Hill Information Systems Company. "Dodge Construction Statistics, 1963 through 1969." (Individualized Marketing Control Service Specifications for Regional Plan Association.) New York: McGraw-Hill Co., 1970.

Dun & Bradstreet Middle Market Directory, 1965, 1967. New York: Dun & Bradstreet, Inc., 1964, 1966.

Dun & Bradstreet Million Dollar Directory, 1965, 1967. New York: Dun & Bradstreet, Inc., 1964, 1966.

James Felt & Co., Inc. "Downtown Manhattan Postwar Office Buildings: Chambers Street–Battery." Unpublished mapped inventory. New York: James Felt & Co., Inc., 1967.

James Felt & Co., Inc. "Manhattan Postwar Office Buildings: 31st–66th Streets." Unpublished mapped inventory. New York: James Felt & Co., Inc., 1969.

Fortune. Annual Supplement: The Fortune Directory, 1958, 1963, 1964, 1965, 1969. New York: Time, Inc., 1959, 1964, 1965, 1966, 1970.

Industrial Research Laboratories in New Jersey. Trenton, N.J.: New Jersey Department of Conservation and Economic Development, 1966.

Moody's Bank and Finance Manual, 1967. New York: Moody's Investor Service, Inc., 1967.

National Planning Association, Center for Economic Projections. *Economic and Demographic Projections for Two Hundred and Twenty-Four Metropolitan Areas. Industry Employment in 224 Metropolitan Areas.* Volume I. Regional Economic Projections Series Report No. 67–R–1. Washington, D.C.: National Planning Association, 1967.

New Jersey State Industrial Directory, 1963, 1968. New York: New Jersey State Industrial Directory, Inc., 1963, 1968.

New York State Industrial Directory, 1963, 1968. New York: New York State Industrial Directory, Inc., 1963, 1968.

The New York Times. "Manhattan Office Building Construction," January 2–18, 1964, 1965, 1966, 1967, 1968, 1969, 1970.

News Front. New York: News Front, Inc., 1967.

Office Building Experience Exchange Report. Chicago: Building Owners and Managers Association International, 1969.

Polk's Bank Directory, 1964. Nashville, Tenn.: R. L. Polk & Co., 1964.

Poor's Register of Corporations, Directors and Executives, United States and Canada, 1966, 1967. New York: Standard & Poor's Corporation, 1966, 1967.

The Real Estate Board of New York, Inc. *Office Building Construction—Manhattan, 1901–1953.* New York: The Real Estate Board of New York, Inc., 1952.

The Real Estate Board of New York, Inc. *Office Building Construction—Manhattan, 1947–1967.* New York: The Real Estate Board of New York, Inc., 1967.

Tri-State Transportation (Regional Planning) Commission. "Home-Interview Survey." Unpublished survey. New York: Tri-State Transportation (Regional Planning) Commission, 1963.

Tri-State Transportation (Regional Planning) Commission. "Land Use Inventory." Unpublished inventory. New York: Tri-State Transportation (Regional Planning) Commission, 1963.

U.S. Bureau of the Census. *County Business Patterns: Middle Atlantic States, 1959.* Part 3A. Washington, D.C.: U.S. Government Printing Office, 1961.

U.S. Bureau of the Census. *County Business Patterns: New England States, 1959.* Part 2. Washington, D.C.: U.S. Government Printing Office, 1961.

U.S. Bureau of the Census. *County Business Patterns: Connecticut, 1965, 1967.* Reports CBP–65–8, and CBP–67–8. Washington, D.C.: U.S. Government Printing Office, 1966, 1968.

U.S. Bureau of the Census. *County Business Patterns: New Jersey, 1965, 1967.* Reports CBP–65–32, and CBP–67–32. Washington, D.C.: U.S. Government Printing Office, 1966, 1968.

U.S. Bureau of the Census. *County Business Patterns: New York, 1965, 1967.* Reports CBP–65–34, and CBP–67–34. Washington, D.C.: U.S. Government Printing Office, 1966, 1968.

U.S. Bureau of the Census. *Enterprise Statistics: 1963. Part 2, Central Administrative Offices and Auxiliaries.* Final Report ES3(63). Washington, D.C.: U.S. Government Printing Office, 1968.

U.S. Bureau of the Census. *Enterprise Statistics: 1967. Central Administrative Offices and Auxiliaries.* Preliminary Report ES67(P)-1. Washington, D.C.: U.S. Government Printing Office, 1970.

U.S. Bureau of the Census. *Historical Statistics of the United States, Colonial Times to 1957.* Washington, D.C.: U.S. Government Printing Office, 1960.

U.S. Bureau of the Census. *U.S. Census of Business: 1958, 1963. Selected Services, United States Summary.* Final Reports BC58-SA1, BC63-SA1. Washington, D.C.: U.S. Government Printing Office, 1960, 1965.

U.S. Bureau of the Census. *U.S. Census of Manufactures: 1963. Summary Statistics: General Summary.* Final Report MC63(1)-1. Washington, D.C.: U.S. Government Printing Office, 1966.

U.S. Bureau of the Census. *U.S. Census of Population: 1940. Comparative Occupational Statistics for the United States, 1870–1940.* By Dr. Alba M. Edwards. Washington, D.C.: U.S. Government Printing Office, 1943.

U.S. Bureau of the Census. *U.S. Census of Population: 1960. Detailed Characteristics, Connecticut.* Final Report PC(1)-8D. Washington, D.C.: U.S. Government Printing Office, 1962.

U.S. Bureau of the Census. *U.S. Census of Population: 1960: Detailed Characteristics, New Jersey.* Final Report PC(1)-32D. Washington, D.C.: U.S. Government Printing Office, 1962.

U.S. Bureau of the Census. *U.S. Census of Population: 1960. Detailed Characteristics, New York.* Final Report PC(1)-34D. Washington, D.C.: U.S. Government Printing Office, 1962.

U.S. Bureau of the Census. *U.S. Census of Population: 1960. Detailed Characteristics, United States Summary.* Final Report PC(1)-1D. Washington, D.C.: U.S. Government Printing Office, 1963.

U.S. Bureau of the Census. *U.S. Census of Population: 1960. General Social and Economic Characteristics, United States Summary.* Final Report PC(1)-1C. Washington, D.C.: U.S. Government Printing Office, 1962.

U.S. Bureau of the Census. *U.S. Census of Population: 1960. Subject Reports. Journey to Work.* Final Report PC(2)-6B. Washington, D.C.: U.S. Government Printing Office, 1963.

U.S. Bureau of Labor Statistics. *Employment and Earnings Statistics for States and Areas, 1939–67.* Bulletin No. 1370–5. Washington, D.C.: U.S. Government Printing Office, 1968.

U.S. Department of Commerce. *Construction Review.* Volumes 12, 13, 14, 15. Washington, D.C.: U.S. Government Printing Office, 1966, 1967, 1968, 1969.

U.S. Department of Commerce. *Construction Statistics, 1915–1964. A Supplement to Construction Review.* Washington, D.C.: U.S. Government Printing Office, 1966.

List of Illustrations

List of Maps

List of Tables

Photograph Credits

Page 4
Top, British Information Services; *bottom,* Jean Biaugeaud

Page 5
Top, I. Korolev and A. Malkin; *bottom,* Swedish Information Service

Page 12
Aerial Explorations, Inc.

Page 13
Port of New York Authority

Pages 64–65
Jerry Spearman

Page 105
Top, Gil Amiaga

Page 162
Ezra Stoller

Page 163
Uris Blue Hill Corporation

Page 165
John C. Warnecke, architect

Pages x, 7, 22, 54, 90, 104, 113
William F. Armstrong

Pages 66, 67, 105 (*bottom*), 111, 158, 159, 160, 161, 164
Regional Plan Association

Index